VOL. XCV
NO. 3

The Catholic Historical Review

NELSON H. MINNICH
Editor

ROBERT TRISCO
Associate Editor

ELIZABETH FOXWELL
Staff Editor

Advisory Editors:

LIAM M. BROCKEY
Princeton University

MAUREEN C. MILLER
University of California, Berkeley

SIMON DITCHFIELD
University of York

JOSEPH WHITE
The Catholic University of America

THOMAS KSELMAN
University of Notre Dame

Table of Contents

JULY, 2009

THE CATHOLIC HISTORICAL REVIEW

Official Organ of the American Catholic Historical Association

All communications concerning direct subscriptions and advertising should be addressed to the Business Manager. Communications concerning editorial matters should be sent to the Editor, 320 Mullen Library, The Catholic University of America, Washington, D.C. 20064; telephone and fax number: 202-319-5079; electronic mail address: CHR@CUA.EDU. Manuscripts of articles must not exceed thirty pages, must be typewritten or computer-printed with double spacing (including the footnotes), and must be accompanied by a self-addressed, stamped manila envelope if the return of the manuscript is desired in case of rejection.

Subscription price: Institutional: United States and Canada $60.00; foreign $55.00; single issue $15.00.

A missing issue will be replaced without charge only if a claim is made within thirty days after the following issue is received.

Published Quarterly by

The Catholic University of America Press
The Catholic University of America, Washington, D.C. 20064

Periodicals postage paid at Washington, D.C., and at additional mailing offices.

The Catholic Historical Review is indexed in the *Catholic Periodical Index* and in *Religion Index One: Periodicals, Index to Book Reviews in Religion, Religion Indexes: RIO/RIT/IBRR 1975- on CD-ROM* and *ATLA* [American Theological Library Association] *Religion Database on CD-ROM* (http://www.atla.com). The articles are analyzed and indexed in the *Bulletin Signalétique Sciences Humaines* and in *IBZ* (International Bibliography of Periodical Literature). The medieval articles are indexed in the *International Medieval Bibliography* and in the *Bulletin of Medieval Canon Law*. The modern European articles are abstracted in *Historical Abstracts*, and the American articles in *America: History and Life*. The book reviews are indexed in *Book Review Index*, and *An Index to Book Reviews in the Humanities*, and in *IBR* (International Bibliography of Book Reviews).

International Standard Serial Number (ISSN) 0008-8080

Postmaster: Send address changes to Business Office, The Catholic University of America Press, *The Catholic Historical Review*, 620 Michigan Ave., N.E., Leahy Hall, Room 240, Washington, D.C. 20064.

Cover illustration credit: Clockwise from upper left: Foundresses Marie-Égide-d'Assise, Marie-Frédéric, Marie-Dominique, and Marie-Anne-de-Jésus, who arrived in Baie-Saint-Paul on November 13, 1891, to staff Sainte-Anne's Home. Archives de la Maison-Mère, Baie-Saint-Paul, Quebec. Reproduced by permission of Les Petites Franciscaines de Marie.

BOOK REVIEWS

General and Miscellaneous

Ancient Church

Medieval

The Catholic Historical Review

| VOL. XCV | JULY, 2009 | No. 3 |

PETER OF LEICESTER, BISHOP GODFREY GIFFARD OF WORCESTER, AND THE PROBLEM OF BENEFICES IN THIRTEENTH-CENTURY ENGLAND

BY

MICHAEL BURGER*

In 1287, Bishop Godfrey Giffard of Worcester fell out with his clerk, Peter of Leicester, denouncing him for ingratitude. Yet the bishop faced a problem: Peter's ecclesiastical benefices. For lords, benefices had distinct advantages in allowing them to support bureaucrats without directly affecting their own finances, but for someone of Giffard's position, the situation was far more disagreeable—the law and the courts made benefices largely irrevocable. Giffard's maneuvers regarding Peter's benefices indicate that benefices were a poor instrument of accountability, a characteristic that deserves some attention.

Keywords: benefice; Giffard, Godfrey, Bishop; ecclesiastical courts; medieval administration; Peter of Leicester

*Dr. Burger is professor of history in the Department of History, Political Science, and Geography at Mississippi University for Women in Columbus; in August, he will become associate professor of history and dean of the School of Liberal Arts at Auburn University at Montgomery. The author thanks David Smith, Nicholas Vincent, and *The Catholic Historical Review*'s anonymous referees for their comments on earlier versions of this article, as well as Robert Berkhofer III for his remarks on the occasion of its presentation at a session of the Annual International Congress of Medieval Studies. Thomas C. Richardson and Gail Gunter afforded access to important scholarly resources. He is also indebted for material support from Mississippi University for Women's Faculty Research Committee and a summer stipend from the National Endowment for the Humanities. He alone is responsible for all errors.

On receiving a parish, a clerk in thirteenth-century England entered upon (at least) two relationships. First, the new rector or vicar became his new flock's pastor. This relationship has earned the bulk of the attention from both medieval and modern commentators concerned with how well or badly parish priests served their cures.[1] That bright light of complaint has, however, left in relative shadow another relationship shaped by the reception of an ecclesiastical benefice: that between the recipient of the benefice and the holder of the advowson—that is, the person who, by right, presented the clerk to the bishop for institution to receive legal title to the benefice from the bishop. That relationship pertained whether the benefice came with cure of souls or not. Patrons presented clergy to benefices for many reasons, first and foremost to reward hangers-on.

This practice furnished the material backbone of administration in the high and late Middle Ages. Bureaucrats had to be rewarded and, as most were clerks, they could be rewarded with a parish or a prebend endowed with an income. This use of benefices is often—indeed usually—explained in terms of lords' attempts to cut costs. Why pay administrators out of pocket when one can pay them out of church revenues instead?[2] Some historians have also equated the practice of giving benefices to administrators with the provision of salary. Thus one reads that "the benefice might make up the clerk's entire salary or only be supplementary to it"[3] or that "royal proctors were paid

[1]See, recently, Jeffrey H. Denton, "The Competence of the Parish Clergy in Thirteenth-Century England," in *The Church and Learning in Later Medieval Society: Essays in Honour of R. B. Dobson, Proceedings of the 1999 Harlaxton Symposium*, ed. Caroline Barron and Jenny Stratford (Donington, UK, 2002), pp. 273-85; Nicholas Bennet, "Patrons and Masters: The Beneficed Clergy of North-East Lincolnshire, 1290-1340," in *The Foundations of English Ecclesiastical History: Studies Presented to David M. Smith*, ed. Philippa Hoskin, Christopher Brooke, and Barrie Dobson (Woodbridge, UK, 2005), pp. 40-62 (for positive assessments) and C. H. Lawrence, "The English Parish and Its Clergy in the Thirteenth Century," in *The Medieval World*, ed. Peter Linehan and Janet L. Nelson (London, 2003), pp. 648-70 (a more negative appraisal).

[2]For example, R. N. Swanson, "Learning and Livings: University Study and Clerical Careers in Later Medieval England," *History of Universities*, 6 (1987), 81-103, here 88 (a discussion that in some other respects is very sensitive to the position of those seeking benefices); Frederic Cheyette, "Kings, Courts, Cures, and Sinecures: The Statute of Provisors and the Common Law," *Traditio*, 19 (1963), 295-349, here 297; W. A. Pantin, *The English Church in the Fourteenth Century* (Cambridge, UK, 1955), pp. 41-42; C. R. Cheney, *English Bishops' Chanceries 1100-1250* (Manchester, UK, 1950), p. 9.

[3]E. Gemmill, "Ecclesiastical Patronage of the Earls during the Reign of Edward I," in *Thirteenth Century England III: Proceedings of the Newcastle Upon Tyne Conference*, ed. P. R. Coss and S. D. Lloyd (Woodbridge, UK, 1991), pp. 65-74, here p. 68.

salaries mainly by the provision of benefices."[4] Examples can be multiplied.[5] It should be noted that none of these scholars who refers to benefices as salary makes a point of saying so. Their remarks were made in passing; they were concerned primarily with other matters.

There are, however, some points worth making here. To equate salary and benefices can mislead, for a salary is, and was, an important tool in the discipline of the receiver. If one fails to do one's job, one loses it—no work, no pay. That threat is perhaps the biggest one in an employer's armory. But an aspect of medieval ecclesiastical governance that could use more stress is that benefices did not offer that essential element of discipline. In other words, they were poor tools of accountability.[6] Salaries could have worked much better. Moreover, an appreciation of that fact highlights the value of benefices not from the giver's point of view, but from the recipient's. That perspective deserves more consideration by historians than it has perhaps received. The concern of recipients for security, not just the requirements of cost-cutting patrons, needs fuller consideration.

These points are evident through a case study of a relationship between a bishop and his clerk. The bishop was Godfrey Giffard, bishop of Worcester from 1268 to 1301. The clerk was Peter of Leicester. Unusually, the two men had a falling out that ruptured their

[4]Jane E. Sayers, "Proctors Representing British Interests at the Papal Court, 1198-1415," in *Proceedings of the Third International Congress of Medieval Canon Law, Strasbourg, 3-6 September 1968*, ed. Stephan Kuttner (Vatican City, 1971), pp. 143-63, here p. 159.

[5]For example, R. V. Turner, *The English Judiciary in the Age of Glanville and Bracton, c. 1176-1239* (New York, 1985), p. 186; Cheyette, "Kings," p. 297; Rose Graham, "The Metropolitical Visitation of the Diocese of Worcester by Archbishop Winchelsey in 1301," in her *English Ecclesiastical Studies* (London, 1929), pp. 330-59, here p. 333; Charles Fonge, "Patriarchy and Patrimony: Investing in Medieval Colleges," in *The Foundations of Medieval English Ecclesiastical History*, pp. 77-93, here p. 83; M. J. Franklin, "The Bishops of Winchester and the Monastic Revolution," in *Anglo-Norman Studies*, ed. Marjorie Chibnall, 12 (1990), pp. 47-75, here pp. 56-57. For the unqualified notion of benefices as "payment," which also strikes me as a bit anachronistic given the argument here: R. W. Dunning, "Patronage and Promotion in the Late-Medieval Church," in *Patronage, the Crown, and the Provinces in Later Medieval England*, ed. R. A. Griffiths (Gloucester, UK, 1981), pp. 167-80, here p. 167; J. R. Strayer, *The Reign of Philip the Fair* (Princeton, 1980), pp. 62-63; Robert E. Rodes, *Ecclesiastical Administration in Medieval England* (Notre Dame, 1977), pp. 157-58.

[6]This is a modern term usefully introduced into studies of medieval administration by Robert Berkhofer III, *Day of Reckoning: Power and Accountability in Medieval France* (Philadelphia, 2004).

relations; Peter ceased to serve Giffard.[7] That rupture led Giffard to attempt to expel Peter from benefices he had received from other patrons, as well as a valuable one Giffard himself had given to Peter. In legal terms, Giffard's efforts involved manipulation by claiming that Peter violated restrictions on pluralism and asserting that Peter's legal mode of possession was other than what the evidence suggests it had been. The fact that such manipulation was necessary indicates the limits imposed on even a bishop in using benefices as a tool to make his clerks accountable. So does the fact that Giffard ultimately failed, even after years of effort. Peter, it is true, had influential friends to help him, but he also could—and did—make use of ecclesiastical courts of appeal. Giffard was ultimately constrained by those courts.

It deserves stress that Giffard's conflict with Peter was atypical. Most bishops got along better with their clerks than did Giffard with Peter, and so such problems did not arise.[8] Rather, Giffard's vigorous attack and Peter's resistance reveal the contours of bureaucratic service in a way that the smoother relations between more ordinary bishops and bureaucrats do not.

Peter evidently first entered Giffard's service in 1283, when the bishop appointed him as his proctor in the court of Canterbury to

---

[7]So far as I can tell, Peter's relations with Giffard have attracted the attention of four historians. Three are concerned largely with the story as it illuminates Giffard's relations with his metropolitan or the archbishop's own policy: Graham, "The Metropolitical Visitation," pp. 355-57; Decima L. Douie, *Archbishop Pecham* (Oxford, 1952), p. 222; and Jeffrey H. Denton, *Robert Winchelsey and the Crown, 1294-1313, a Study in the Defence of Ecclesiastical Liberty* (Cambridge, UK, 1980), pp. 281-82. The fourth and most extensive discussion primarily concerns Giffard's relationship with Peter for its own sake and, indeed, points out the aggravation Giffard must have felt when unable to expel a clerk who had received a benefice from him: Susan Jane Davies, "Studies in the Administration of the Diocese of Worcester in the Thirteenth Century," PhD thesis, University of Wales (1971), pp. 345-57. My account is less sympathetic to Giffard. I am very grateful to the author for allowing me to obtain a photocopy of this illuminating thesis.

[8]Excluding archdeacons, I have found only a few instances: Bishop Pontoise of Winchester's change of heart regarding William Segin del Gotto and Bishop Pandulph of Norwich's regarding James his clerk; see, respectively, *Registrum Johannis de Pontissara Episcopi Wyntoniensis A.D. MCCXXXII–MCCCIV*, ed. C. Deedes (London, 1915-24), pp. 86-67, 792, 801-02, and *English Episcopal Acta 21: Norwich 1215-1243*, ed. Christopher Harper-Bill (Oxford, 2000), no. 8 and n. I plan to explore these cases as part of a larger project. See also Giffard's dealings with Nicholas de Chilbauton below, n. 59. Archdeacons—who held a benefice that was also an administrative office—may have been a special case.

carry on a suit against Robert de Plessetis, dean of the collegiate church of Warwick.[9] The next year, Giffard appointed Peter steward of his lands, and Peter was still serving in that capacity in 1286.[10]

Nothing in the sources prepares one for the storm that broke in March 1287. On March 14 Giffard issued three letters to his subordinates, none that survives to Peter himself. One letter orders that Peter be peremptorily cited to answer before the bishop for one of his benefices.[11] The next is hotter: in his pride, Peter is guilty of the "vice of ingratitude"; he is no longer Giffard's *familiaris*, and action is to be taken regarding two of Peter's other benefices.[12] The third informs another of the bishop's men, William Pikeril, that Pikeril is to avoid counsel with Peter, "our former *familiaris*," so as to avoid also the vice of ingratitude, and is indeed to write back on the matter without delay.[13]

[9]*Episcopal Registers of the Diocese of Worcester: Register of Bishop Godfrey Giffard, September 23rd, 1268, to August 15th, 1301,* ed. J. W. Willis Bund (Oxford, 1898-1902) (henceforth "Reg. Giffard of Worcester"), p. 199 (Worcester Record Office—County Hall Branch [henceforth "WRO"] Rf.x716.093 BA 2648/1[i] fol. 180, p. 351). This edition is, in fact, a rather haphazard calendar. Where further evidence or correction is needed, I have cited, as here, the MS—WRO Rf.x716.093 BA 2648/1(i)—following the edition. The MS in turn presents a difficulty in citation. Its foliation is marked in Roman numbers and by a later hand in Arabic numbers. Unfortunately, these numerations are not always consistent. Moreover, some of the folios are out of order, which probably explains why a third hand consecutively paginated the MS throughout in its current order. Where the MS is cited, I have given the Arabic folio number followed by the page number.

[10]Reg. Giffard of Worcester, pp. 229, 303. The latter document bears no date, but a date of 1286 fits its place in the register, which is generally ordered chronologically.

[11]*Ibid.*, p. 306 (fol. 265v, p. 522).

[12]*Ibid.* (both calendar and MS).

[13]*Ibid.*, p. 306 (fols. 265v-266r, pp. 522-23). Pikeril had been Giffard's official, but had ceased to hold that office by 1284 (Davies, "Administration," pp. 273-74). He and Peter already had some connections in common. In 1279 he had granted Hanlegh to Hugh Burnel, knight, a grant that John Kirkby (apparently Peter's friend—see below, at n. 56) attested; see *Calendar of the Close Rolls Preserved in the Public Record Office, Edward I* (London, 1900-08), 1: p. 579. Hugh was the brother of Robert Burnel (*Oxford Dictionary of National Biography,* ed. H. C. G. Matthew and Brian Harrison [Oxford, 2004], sub "Robert Burnel"), who on one occasion wrote on Peter of Leicester's behalf (see below, n. 55). The abbey of Tewksbury was another connection. On Pikeril's death, Tewksbury would present Peter to Pikeril's benefice of Thornbury (see below at nn. 67-68) and on Peter's own death Peter would leave Tewksbury property in London; see *Calendar of the Wills Proved and Enrolled in the Court of Husting, London, A.D. 1258-A.D. 1688,* ed. Reginald A. Sharpe (London, 1889-90), 1: p. 168.

What caused the break is unrecoverable.[14] It is conceivable that the conflict was over Bishop's Cleeve, which by late 1293 Giffard was campaigning to appropriate to his own mensa, a move that would have required Peter's resignation.[15] Perhaps Peter refused to cooper-

[14]Could a change of affiliation or multiple affiliation lie behind Peter's conflict with Giffard? Graham *seems* to imply that a transfer to royal service was at issue (Graham, "The Metropolitical Visitation," p. 356). But if that is Graham's point, it is undermined by the fact that Peter's royal service long antedated the break with Giffard (see below, at n. 20). While Peter as a royal clerk can have been expected to call on royal support in his conflict with Giffard, he seems to have relied principally on ecclesiastical courts for his defense (see below, at nn. 46-57), although Peter may have at one point also relied on the influence of men high in royal administration (below, at n. 55). Certainly it was not unusual for a thirteenth-century clerk to move from one master to another, taking his benefices, like a snail with its shell, with him. So, too, some clerks remained in one lord's service while serving another; for a study of one such, see Nicholas Vincent, "Master Elias of Dereham (d. 1245): A Reassessment" in *The Church and Learning in Later Medieval Society: Essays in Honour of R. B. Dobson, Proceedings of the 1999 Harlaxton Symposium* (Donington, UK, 2002), pp. 128-59. I hope to examine such phenomena in a longer study. Could serving king and bishop at the same time have ruptured Peter's relations with Giffard? Conceivably, but I have found no evidence that this was the explanation. Indeed, it has been argued, for a later period, that clerks who served more than one master reduced conflicts between their lords; see R. A. Griffiths, "Public and Private Bureaucracies in England and Wales in the Fifteenth Century," *Transactions of the Royal Historical Society*, 5th ser., 30 (1980), pp. 109-30, here pp. 128-29. If, however, Peter continued his connection with the earl of Warwick after entering the bishop's service, it does not seem to have ameliorated the earl's conflicts with the bishop (for which see Reg. Giffard of Worcester, p. xxxiii). It is reasonable to think that multiple affiliations could divide clerks' loyalties. Interestingly, Peter the king's clerk served on the tribunal that dealt with proceedings against his patron Ralph Hengham and his friend Thomas de Weyland, but only after those men had fallen on accusations of corruption or worse. Perhaps their fall had opened a door for the king to appoint Peter. For the proceedings and Peter, see *State Trials of the Reign of Edward the First, 1289-1293*, ed. T. F. Tout and Hilda Johnstone, [3rd ser. 9], (London, 1906), pp. xiii-xiv and the corrections of Paul A. Brand, "Edward I and the Judges: The 'State Trials' of 1289-93," in *Thirteenth Century England I*, ed. P. R. Coss and S. D. Lloyd (Woodbridge, UK, 1986), pp. 31-40, here p. 35. The reasons Tout and Johnstone offer for Peter's appointment are not mutually exclusive with the suggestion here. For a hint that Peter may have acted against Giffard in his capacity as proctor, which, if true, does suggest a problem with dual affiliation; see below at nn. 41-43.

[15]Reg. Giffard of Worcester, p. 222 and see pp. 223-24. Most such arrangements took place while a benefice was vacant. Another bishop who desired similarly to appropriate a church while it was full asked the incumbent, "his friend . . . dearest," himself to advocate the appropriation of his church to the bishop's estate, offering as compensation an appropriate pension, whatever the rector would fitly ordain ("amico suo . . . karissime": *The Register of John de Halton, Bishop of Carlisle A.D. 1292-3124*, ed. W. N. Thompson [London, 1913], p. 240). If Giffard had offered such an inducement, it seems that Peter had rejected it. It was possible to arrange an appropriation to take effect in the future but still only on the incumbent's death or resignation at that future point (e.g., *Registrum Johannis de Pontissara*, p. 137).

ate. If so, then the heart of the dispute was the very security of tenure that, as will become evident, Giffard attempted to overcome. All that is clear is an angry bishop who accused Peter of ingratitude, after he had received what Giffard regarded as "many benefits."[16] But a break it certainly was. Peter never reentered Giffard's service.

In his campaign against Peter, Giffard chose to attack him through his benefices. To fully examine Giffard's tactics, it is necessary first to outline the benefices Peter had collected. By 1287 Peter had acquired the assortment of benefices that suited an important clerk.[17] He was the rector of Preston Bagot, received in 1275 on the presentation of Peter de Montfort, lord of Beaudesert.[18] He had next acquired Budbrooke on the presentation of Ralph Hengham in 1282.[19] Hengham provides a link to two sides of Peter's career. On the one hand, this Ralph Hengham was indeed the distinguished royal justice. Peter had already entered the exchequer on the nomination of William Beauchamp IV, the earl of Warwick,[20] and perhaps it was through royal service that Peter came to Hengham's notice. On the other hand, Hengham was a friend to Giffard,[21] himself chancellor of the exchequer before his elevation some twenty years before. Perhaps it was through Hengham that Peter gained Giffard's attention. Peter also, at some unknown date, had gained a prebend in the collegiate church of St. Mary's, Warwick, Hengham's college. Although his institution to that prebend is unrecorded, the college's patrons were the earls of Warwick, so the hand that had started him in the exchequer was at work here as well. Peter is first found in the prebend in 1286, when Giffard did his clerk the favor of uniting Peter's church of Budbrooke with the prebend, and so, Giffard said, freed Peter from the obligation to reside at Budbrooke; a priest was to be maintained there to ensure the cure of souls. The union was to last only as long as Peter's tenure

[16] Reg. Giffard of Worcester, p. 306 (WRO Rf.x716.093 BA 2648/1[i] fol. 265v, p. 522).

[17] I have not included in this survey Haselor, which Peter gained in 1281 and resigned in 1282 (*ibid.*, pp. 134, 168), since it does not figure in the benefices through which Giffard could attack in 1287. For benefices that eventually fell into Peter's hands, see below, n. 25.

[18] *Ibid.*, p. 67.

[19] *Ibid.*, p. 169. Hengham presented by right of his prebend in St. Mary's, Warwick.

[20] Graham, "The Metropolitical Visitation," p. 356. Peter served Giffard while he served the king, *pace* the implication of Christopher Dyer, *Lords and Peasants in a Changing Society: The Estates of the Bishopric of Worcester, 680–1540* (Cambridge, UK, 1980), p. 66 and Davies, "Studies," p. 345.

[21] Reg. Giffard of Worcester, p. lxi. The bishop would collate the Archdeaconry of Worcester to Hengham in 1289 (*ibid.*, p. 334).

in one of these benefices, thus leaving patronal rights unaffected.[22] (So far as the cure of souls was concerned, the move may not have even been very necessary. Budbrooke was only about three miles from Peter's prebend at Warwick. Indeed, perhaps their closeness as well as their union is expressed by a drawing of two churches cheek by jowl in the margin by the entry in Giffard's register recording the annexation.) Peter's fourth benefice in 1287 was Bishop's Cleeve, which had been collated to him by Giffard in 1286, less than a year before the break.[23] Bishop's Cleeve had its own vicarage, thus freeing Peter from pastoral duties for that church.[24] It should be stressed that Peter received all these benefices but Bishop's Cleeve from patrons other than Giffard. That fact will help explain why Giffard pressured Peter over Bishop's Cleeve with special determination. I have not traced other benefices in Peter's possession up to this point.[25]

[22]*Ibid.*, p. 286 (fol. 252v, p. 496).

[23]*Ibid.*, p. 290.

[24]*Ibid.*, p. 117 and the online *Taxatio* of Nicholas IV: <http://www.hrionline.ac.uk/db/taxatio/printbc.jsp?benkey=WO.GL.WI.18>.

[25]Later evidence indicates that Peter held other benefices, but he cannot be shown to have been in them in 1284, when he and Giffard entered hostilities, and he probably was not. Peter would die in possession of the prebend of Bishopshull in Lichfield Cathedral (John Le Neve, *Fasti Ecclesiae Anglicanae 1300-1541 X: Coventry and Lichfield Diocese*, comp. B. Jones (London, 1964), p. 20). And he can be shown to have held an unnamed prebend in that chapter only as early as 1299. (I am grateful to Jeffrey Denton for this information from the notes assembled by Diana Greenway for the volume of Le Neve's *Fasti* for the diocese for the period 1066-1300 [now in preparation by Denton], citing *Registrum Roberti Winchelsey Cantuariensis Archiepicopi*, ed. Rose Graham [Oxford, 1952-56], pp. 365-66). This puts his first appearance as prebendary in the episcopate of the royal treasurer Walter Langton, a natural patron for Peter given his connections. Langton became bishop in 1296, which would put Peter's tenure in Bishopshull after the start of his conflict with Giffard. In 1297 Giffard would assert that Peter held several other benefices: Rokeby in the Archdiocese of York, Hendon in the Diocese of London, and Wolfehamcote and Wappenbury in the Diocese of Coventry and Lichfield (Reg. Giffard of Worcester (WRO Rf.x716.093 BA 2648/1[i] fol. 422v, p. 870). Rokeby cannot be confirmed. Hendon can be, through a papal dispensation to Peter to hold it in 1303; see *Calendar of Entries in the Papal Registers Relating to Great Britain and Ireland*, ed. W. H. Bliss et al. (London, 1893-), 1:603. Peter is attested as incumbent in Wolfhamcote, but again only in 1303 (*ibid.*). But Bishop Langton granted him the custody of the sequestration of Wolfhamcote in 1300, which at least also confirms Peter's favor with that bishop and increases the likelihood of collation of a prebend by him to Peter; see *The Register of Walter Langton, Bishop of Coventry and Lichfield, 1296-1321*, ed. J. B. Hughes (Woodbridge, UK, 2001-07), no. 405. It should also be noted that one Edmund de Langley appears as parson of a Wolfhamcote in 1299 in the patent rolls; see *Calendar of the Patent Rolls Preserved in the Public Record Office: Edward I* (London, 1893-1901), 3: p. 261. If this is the same Wolfhamcote as in the Diocese of Coventry and Lichfield, then one can conclude that

Regarding Giffard's intentions about Peter's benefices outside of Bishop's Cleeve: his orders of March 14, 1287, are somewhat confusing. When Giffard cited Peter to appear before him, Peter was to come before the bishop to be *instituted* to Preston Bagot, with Giffard stating that the *commendation* of Peter to Preston Bagot was revoked. The bishop also expressed concern that Preston Bagot should have a resident priest.[26] For a clerk to be *instituted* to a benefice meant that he received full title to it; however, a clerk receiving a benefice *in commendam* received only the right to hold the benefice temporarily, at the bishop's pleasure.[27] The confusion here is that Giffard's register states that Giffard had, in fact, instituted Peter to Preston Bagot.[28] If Peter had subsequently resigned Preston Bagot and received it back *in commendam*, there is no trace of those maneuvers in the register. Moreover, in the end Peter kept Preston Bagot,[29] which the bishop could have taken at any time had it been a commend, especially after Giffard's efforts regarding Peter's other benefices were exhausted. Thus it is logical to think that Giffard must simply have been wrong, and probably deliberately wrong, in his assertion that Peter did not enjoy the full title of *institution* to Preston Bagot. Perhaps the point had been simply to summon Peter to appear personally before Giffard. (To be harangued? To be offered a reconciliation? No evidence addresses the question.)

On March 14 Giffard also revoked the annexation of Budbrooke to Peter's prebend in St. Mary's, Warwick.[30] He, at the same time, declared

---

Peter received it only after 1299, which fits his reception of custody of the sequestration in 1300, presumably during a vacancy. The patent rolls' editor, however, assigns this church to Middlesex (index, sub verb.), although I have not found a church of this name in the online *Taxatio* of Nicholas IV (<http://www.hrionline.ac.uk/taxatio>); perhaps the editor is in error? I have not been able to confirm Wappenbury. Bracketing the specific evidence pertaining to these benefices, it is likely that, given Giffard's charge of pluralism against Peter in 1284, Giffard would have mentioned these other benefices had Peter had them at that point.

[26]Reg. Giffard of Worcester, p. 306 (WRO Rf.x716.093 BA 2648/1[i] fol. 265v, p. 522).

[27]Thus, the holder lacked any permanent legal title to the benefice and enjoyed the income only temporarily. In an attempt to prevent the abuse of commendation, the Second Council of Lyons limited the duration of commends to six months; see *Decrees of the Ecumenical Councils*, ed. Norman P. Tanner (Washington, DC, 1990), 1:322; Rodes, *Ecclesiastical Administration*, p. 160; J. R. H. Moorman, *Church Life in England in the Thirteenth Century* (Cambridge, UK, 1955), pp. 32–33.

[28]Reg. Giffard of Worcester, p. 67, confirmed by WRO Rf.x716.093 BA 2648/1(i) fol. 49.

[29]He gave it up only in 1302, after Giffard's death (Graham, "The Metropolitical Visitation," p. 355).

[30]Reg. Giffard of Worcester, p. 306.

Budbrooke, which Peter claimed by right of presentation (and so presumably institution), to be vacant, despite Peter's "crafty devices"—unfortunately unspecified.[31] On the same day, he declared the revocation of his collation of Bishop's Cleeve to Peter, finding Peter to have been notoriously ungrateful.[32]

Thus Giffard undid a favor (the union of the prebend in St. Mary's with Budbrooke) and declared two benefices vacant. But why these benefices rather than the others? An answer may be provided by a consideration, first, of the canon law regarding pluralism, and second, of the values of the benefices. Pluralism regulations are significant here. By the late-thirteenth century, all clergy were, in theory, restricted to institution to one benefice with cure of souls.[33] Of course, papal dispensations could allow for more. But even without a dispensation, a clerk could hold alongside his one and only benefice with cure of souls any number of "compatible" benefices—that is, benefices like prebends to which no cure of souls was annexed. The law permitted pluralism of that kind, and, in practice, people got away with more.

It may be that Giffard's moves of March 1287 were an attempt to manipulate pluralism regulations. Peter is not known to have enjoyed a dispensation for pluralism. If Giffard's moves had succeeded where pluralism concerns had been raised, what would have been the result? Peter would have been left with Preston Bagot, a rectory with cure of souls, holding by institution; he would have lost one benefice (Budbrooke); retained Bishop's Cleeve, which had an ordained vicarage[34]; and retained the prebend in St. Mary's, Warwick. In other words, he would have held one benefice with cure of souls and two compatible benefices. Thus Giffard's move is consistent with forcing Peter to live up to restrictions on pluralism. But Giffard's sudden concern regarding Peter's pluralism appears to be a blind. That conclusion is confirmed by Giffard's accusation of ingratitude. Indeed, in 1279 Giffard had suggested that papal strictures on pluralism were unsuitable for the English church.[35] His sudden worry that Peter was not resident in Preston Bagot also looks convenient. In addition, neither

---

[31]"callidis machinacionibus": *ibid.*, p. 306 (fol. 265v, p. 522).

[32]*Ibid.*, p. 327 (fol. 288v, p. 568).

[33]A classic statement was that of the Fourth Lateran Council, cap. 29.

[34]Reg. Giffard of Worcester, p. 117 and the online *Taxatio* of Nicholas IV, <http://www.hrionline.ac.uk/taxatio/index.html>, sub "Bishop's Cleeve."

[35]Reg. Giffard of Worcester, p. 116.

pluralism nor residency regulations account for the move against Peter's possession of Bishop's Cleeve, with its ordained vicarage.

As to the value of these benefices, the best evidence is the *Taxatio* of Pope Nicholas IV. Dating to 1291, this survey sought to assess the value of most English benefices. Tax assessments are always only approximate, and it is likely that some under assessment went into the returns.[36] Such under assessments were not of equal degree; some benefice holders were no doubt more lucky or more influential than others. One can hope, however, that the *Taxatio* allows a rough and ready comparison of the incomes produced by benefices.

The two benefices that Giffard would allow Peter to keep were valued by the *Taxatio* as follows: Preston Bagot, £4 6s 8d, and the prebend in St. Mary's, Warwick, £2 13s 4d.[37] As to the value of Peter's benefices that Giffard planned to remove, the first, Budbrooke, was worth £10 13s 4d. Therefore, keeping Preston Bagot (£4 6s 8d) over Budbrooke (more than £10) meant relinquishing a richer benefice and retaining the poorer one. Moreover, through the loss of Bishop's Cleeve, Peter's income would decline by a significant £40 a year, according to the *Taxatio*.[38]

A third factor shaping these moves was probably the matter of advowsons. Only in one case did Giffard actually revoke title to one of Peter's benefices without a clearly expressed canonical pretext: the lucrative Bishop's Cleeve, which was in the bishop's own gift. Preston Bagot was, Giffard asserted, a commend, but one in which Peter would have to accept institution. Giffard implied that he was ejecting Peter from Budbrooke on grounds of nonresidence. An outright revocation of institution to Preston Bagot or Budbrooke would have injured the patrons to those benefices, bringing trouble no bishop wanted. Peter's patrons were men of substantial local or national influence. Common-law actions over the right to advowson might

---

[36]J. H. Denton, "The Valuation of the Ecclesiastical Benefices of England and Wales in 1291–2," *Historical Research*, 66 (1993), 221–50, here 240; W. E. Lunt, *The Valuation of Norwich* (Oxford, 1926), pp. 147–52; Rose Graham, "The Taxation of Pope Nicholas IV," in her *English Ecclesiastical Studies*, pp. 271–301, here pp. 286–96.

[37]For all values from the *Taxatio* used here, see <http://www.hrionline.ac.uk/taxatio/index.html>, sub the name of the benefice.

[38]The vicarage pertaining to Bishop's Cleeve was worth £10. The £40 value listed in the *Taxatio* would have been after the value of the vicarage has been deducted. The *Taxatio* lists values of churches after vicarages worth more than £4 have been deducted, despite papal instructions (Denton, "The Valuation," p. 238).

have provided such men with tools with which to harass Giffard, although in the end the king's courts recognized episcopal control over admission and deprivation.[39] Indeed, the death of Peter de Montfort, who had originally presented Peter to Preston Bagot, may have emboldened Giffard in proceeding against Peter regarding that benefice. De Montfort had died by early March 1287, leaving a minor as heir when Giffard's quarrel with his clerk appears in the sources.[40]

But with Giffard as patron, no danger arose from unhappy patrons regarding Bishop's Cleeve. Or did Giffard have a canonical pretext to expel Peter from Bishop's Cleeve? The canon law was largely silent regarding the rights of patrons to revoke benefices for failure to serve the patron. There were two exceptions. First, the canon law permitted deprivation of those who had violated their oaths of homage to their prelate as their lord. Indeed, the case that had prompted Honorius III's rescript that formed the basis of this principle was that of a clerk (an archdeacon) who had sued his bishop in a secular court over spiritual matters.[41] This oath of homage was glossed as being the more ecclesiastical *fidelitas et obedientia* the archdeacon had sworn the bishop by reason of his archdeaconry.[42] But Giffard never seems to have invoked an oath in making his case against Peter. Perhaps such oaths of fidelity and obedience were understood in ways sufficiently circumscribed (fidelity and obedience in regard to what, precisely?) that their usefulness in Giffard's case was limited. Perhaps, in practice, courts preferred to set the bar for deprivation higher. Second, the law offered the limited case where a proctor or advocate had received a benefice but then represented an opponent of his patron. In such cases, Pope Gregory IX had ruled, such a lawyer, an "ingrate," could be deprived of his benefice received from the betrayed patron.[43] Peter had indeed

---

[39] W. R. Jones, "Relations of the Two Jurisdictions: Conflict and Cooperation in England during the Fourteenth and Fifteenth Centuries," *Studies in Medieval and Renaissance History*, 7 (1970), 79–210, here 102–32; R. H. Helmholz, *The Oxford History of the Laws of England I: The Canon Law and the Ecclesiastical Courts from 597 to the 1640s* (Oxford, 2004), pp. 477–80, 482.

[40] G. E. C., *The Complete Peerage*, rev. H. A. Doubleday and Lord Howard de Walden (London, 1936), 9:127–28.

[41] X.5.31.15.

[42] Commentary on X.5.31.15 in *Corpus juris canonici emendatum et notis illustratu,* Gregorii xiii. pont. max. iussu editum (Rome, 1582), col. 1784, <http://digital.library.ucla.edu/canonlaw>.

[43] X.1.37.3. The point was picked up by the glossators (James A. Brundage, "The Ethics of Advocacy: Confidentiality and Conflict of Interest in Medieval Canon Law," in

served as Giffard's proctor, Giffard had given Bishop's Cleeve to Peter via his own collation, and Giffard did accuse Peter of ingratitude in relation to Bishop's Cleeve. Perhaps Peter had acted as proctor against Giffard? If so, I have found no trace of it.

There is a problem, however: the commend that, according to Giffard, Peter asserted he had in Preston Bagot, but that Giffard said he had revoked—a commend that, as previously explained, Giffard appears to have invented when, in fact, Peter had been instituted. For reasons explained above, however, it also makes no sense for Giffard to have done so if the idea was to force Peter to relinquish his other benefices in favor of puny Preston Bagot. Peter would have been better off had he successfully asserted the commendation Giffard says he asserted, losing Preston Bagot and keeping one of the others. Again, perhaps Giffard's goal had been simply to force Peter into a face-to-face meeting.[44]

Whatever Giffard's plans, the results could not have pleased him. Further maneuvers regarding Preston Bagot, Budbrooke, and the prebend in St. Mary's are untraceable, but Peter never lost his grip on them.[45] Bishop's Cleeve was another matter. And it is to Bishop's Cleeve that the problem of a patron disciplining a clerk most properly pertains. Giffard's difficulties with Peter over Preston Bagot and Budbrooke illustrate the problems that any bishop could face when proceeding against a determined, well-connected incumbent. The fact that Giffard's rupture with his clerk sparked the bishop's move against these benefices, which Peter successfully resisted, illuminates the security incumbents enjoyed in general.

Grundlagen als Rechts: Festschrift für Peter Landau zum 65. Gerburtstag, ed. Richard H. Helmholz, Paul Mikrat, and Michael Stolleis [Paderborn, 2000], pp. 453–66, here p. 460).

[44]There is another mystery. Giffard could also have attacked Peter on the grounds that Peter had held benefices with cure of souls without being ordained a priest within a year of institution. Years later Archbishop Winchelsey would try to deprive Peter of Budbooke on just this ground and succeed (Graham, "The Metropolitical Visitation," p. 356). Yet Giffard seems to have made no such attempt.

[45]Indeed, once Giffard died, Peter asked the prior and convent of Worcester to confirm the annexation of Budbrooke to his prebend in St. Mary's; see *The Liber Albus of the Priory of Worcester,* ed. James Maurice Wilson (London, 1919), pt. 1, no. 27 and *The Register of the Diocese of Worcester during the Vacancy of the See,* ed. J.W. Willis Bund (Oxford, 1897), p. 21. Archbishop Winchelsey, however, would make trouble over Peter's holding these and other benefices in undispensed plurality, prompting Peter to procure the usual papal indulgence; see Graham, "The Metropolitical Visitation," pp. 356–57 and *Les registres de Boniface VIII,* ed. Antoine Thomas *et al.* (Paris, 1884–1934), 3: no. 477.

Since Peter kept Budbrooke, presumably Peter appealed Giffard's attempt to declare it vacant. Regarding Bishop's Cleeve, however, Giffard's register preserves some of the process of Peter's appeal for tuition to the court of Canterbury over that benefice, implying Peter had appealed to the papal curia. In 1287 the dean of Arches warned Giffard to cite a number of men for having, in an armed multitude, occupied Bishop's Cleeve and to inhibit them from doing so.[46] Indeed, these men were acting on behalf of Robert de Wyse, another of Giffard's clerks,[47] to whom the bishop had given what he regarded as a vacant Bishop's Cleeve.[48] It appears as if Giffard was behind this vigorous opposition to Peter, or at least deeply implicated in it. Several circumstances excite suspicion that Giffard was at work here: Robert's connection with Giffard and Giffard's ignoring the order of the dean of Arches to restore Peter and protect his church of Cleeve are two.[49] Another is Giffard's request to the sheriff of Gloucestershire, in which Bishop's Cleeve lay, that "our men of Cleeve" unjustly imprisoned (for unnamed crimes) be released.[50] As the name suggests, the bishops of Worcester had a manor at Bishop's Cleeve.[51] Giffard would not have found it difficult to mobilize men to occupy the church.

The case continued[52] until in October 1287, when it seemed Giffard grasped victory, or at least partial victory. It is not clear that he was winning in court; indeed, the official of the court of Canterbury was advising Giffard to end a problematic case.[53] But in October Peter resigned Bishop's Cleeve. Some sort of deal seems to have been struck, for on the same day Giffard conferred on Peter a prebend in the church of Westbury.[54] Giffard may have said that he gave that

---

[46]Reg. Giffard of Worcester, p. 311 (WRO Rf.x716.093 BA 2648/1[i] fols. 269v–70v, pp. 530–32). There is a very general "X" drawn over the names of these men; the names recur in subsequent entries on the same matter, sometimes also with an "X." It is not clear how seriously to take this as a cancellation.

[47]*Ibid.*, p. 315 (fol. 277, p. 545).

[48]*Ibid.*, p. 327.

[49]Douie, *Archbishop Pecham*, p. 222.

[50]Reg. Giffard of Worcester, p. 312 (WRO Rf.x716.093 BA 2648/1[i] fol. 273r, p. 537). The letter is vague and undated, but follows immediately one of the entries detailing the complaint about the occupation of Bishop's Cleeve.

[51]*The Cartulary of Worcester Cathedral Priory (Register I)*, ed. R. R. Darlington (London, 1968), no. 433.

[52]Reg. Giffard of Worcester, pp. 315–16.

[53]WRO Rf.x716.093 BA 2648/1(i) fol. 277, p. 545. The calendar is particularly unhelpful here.

[54]Reg. Giffard of Worcester, pp. 334, 422–23.

prebend in "the intuition of charity," but the whole transaction took place at Westminster, and the bishop also was said to have given the prebend at the petition of certain royal councilors.[55] One of these was John Kirkby, bishop of Ely and Edward I's treasurer, and another was one Th. de Weyland, presumably Thomas de Weyland, chief justice of the King's Bench.[56] In other words, Peter had powerful friends in the king's government; ecclesiastical courts of appeal were not the only force that impelled Giffard to compromise.

That compromise, however, fell apart, for in 1293 Peter was claiming Bishop's Cleeve, appealing to Canterbury for help and, it seems, winning. The official of the court of Canterbury announced that Bishop's Cleeve had been restored to Peter; Giffard and his men were contumacious and excommunicate; Bishop's Cleeve itself, under occupation by the enemy, was under interdict.[57] The dispute was settled by another compromise later in 1293. Peter gave up Bishop's Cleeve, but received in return a pension of £24 a year from Bishop's Cleeve, with a bond guaranteeing a penalty for nonpayment of £60. The pension could be extinguished by Peter's reception of a benefice worth £60.[58]

This agreement probably illuminates the first compromise, the one that had collapsed. There may well have been elements to the earlier arrangements that are lost to the record—perhaps a nice pension like

[55]*Ibid.* (WRO Rf.x716.093 BA 2648/1[i] fols. 291, 363v-64, pp. 573, 718-19). Such friends had intervened on Peter's behalf on previous occasions. Robert Burnel, bishop of Bath and Wells and chancellor of the exchequer, had written *c.* February 1283 to an unknown person excusing Peter, as chamberlain of the exchequer, from being present during a visitation of the diocese (National Archives: PRO, SC1/29/5). This probably relates to the visitation of the Diocese of Worcester conducted by the archbishop of Canterbury in spring 1283 (on which, see Douie, *Archbishop Pecham*, p. 162).

[56]Reg. Giffard of Worcester, p. 334; see WRO Rf.x716.093 BA 2648/1(i) fol. 291, p. 573. For Thomas de Weyland, see Paul Brand, "Chief Justice and Felon: The Career of Thomas Weyland," in *The Political Context of Law*, ed. Richard Eales and David Sullivan (London, 1987), pp. 26-46, rpt. in Paul Brand, *The Making of the Common Law* (Rio Grande, OH, 1992), pp. 113-33.

[57]Reg. Giffard of Worcester, pp. 429-30. The excommunication of Peter by the bishop had, moreover, been maliciously carried out by one of Giffard's clerks, although this entry is cancelled in the register: *ibid.*, p. 437 (fol. 373, p. 737). There is no evidence that Giffard asked for a caption against Peter as an obdurate excommunicate (National Archives: PRO, C85/159-163). Perhaps Peter did not qualify, or perhaps he did but Giffard could not expect royal cooperation against Peter.

[58]For these arrangements, see Reg. Giffard of Worcester, p. 441; see WRO Rf.x716.093 BA 2648/1(i) fol. 377v, p. 746. The calendar can mislead on some of this.

the one Peter received in the second compromise. It should be noted that the prebend in Westbury was worth only £6 13s 4d, according to the *Taxatio*—a good sum, but hardly comparable to Bishop's Cleeve. A pension like the one Peter received in 1293 would explain his willingness to accept the earlier deal.

On the whole, the security of tenure Peter enjoyed in his benefices while in conflict with his very angry bishop is impressive. Despite his control of his see's administration and use of armed force, Giffard still failed to expel his former steward from Budbrooke, and it took seven years to remove Peter definitively from Bishop's Cleeve and only then with major concessions. Bishops could make life unpleasant for those beneficed in their diocese. But given Peter's case, benefices do not look like a very usable tool with which to discipline administrators.

Indeed, Giffard's and Peter's relations were, in one sense, unusual. Their story is the story of a relationship gone very bad.[59] The conditions that shape a relationship sometimes stand out only when the relationship fails. Personality was probably part of this particular failure; Giffard was bad tempered.[60] He was often sick and gouty.[61] By the

[59]Although Giffard, evidently true to form, had had a falling out with another of his clerks, Nicholas de Chilbauton. The evidence for this is a letter from Giffard to Nicholas, "suo quondam obsequali," admitting him to Giffard's grace in 1284 (*ibid.*, p. 229; fol. 204, p. 400). In the previous year, Giffard had been pursuing Nicholas on charges of pluralism, complaining that Nicholas had left his benefices for Rome without Giffard's permission (*ibid.*, p. 273). In addition, in 1282, Giffard had been trying to oust Nicholas from the church of Mickleton (*ibid.*, p. 152). Presumably the odd "revocation" by the bishop of the collation of any church ("cuiuscunque ecclesie") if the bishop had made one ("si quam fecerit") to Nicholas (*ibid.*, p. 151; fol. 141, p. 274) pertains to Mickleton. This case—with the attempt to undo a collation, the citation for pluralism as a means to that end, and Nicholas's presence at the curia suggesting an appeal to a higher jurisdiction—resonates with Peter of Leicester's conflict with Giffard. How far matters went is unclear. Giffard's relationship with Nicholas, whether still a source of trouble or pacified, was cut short by Nicholas's death in 1284 (*ibid.*, p. 273).

[60]On his irritability, see the *Oxford Dictionary of National Biography*, sub nom. and Davies, "Studies," p. 6. The Worcester annalist, admittedly not a friendly source, noted that after Giffard failed to get the priory and convent's cooperation regarding Westbury, he left *iratus*; see *Annales Monastici*, ed. H. R. Luard (London, 1864–69), 4:504. If an allegation by a proctor opposed to Giffard is to be believed, Giffard's belligerence antedated his ascension to the episcopate. The proctor accused him of spurning an offer to talk over a dispute over a benefice to which Giffard and another clerk had rival claims. Giffard preferred to fight in court (Hereford Dean and Chapter Archives, no. 2921; I am grateful to the archives for supplying a digital photograph of this document to me.) For an account more sympathetic to the bishop, see Reg.

time of the contretemps with Peter, he had been bishop of Worcester for twenty years, a time by which many bishops were dead. His actions may reflect a bishop who had himself grown too secure.[62] Indeed, Giffard could not quite stop harassing Peter even after the bargain over Bishop's Cleeve of 1293. In 1297, Giffard cited five men for pluralism on his visitation of the diocese. Peter was one of them[63]; but nothing ever came of it, and Peter lost nothing.[64] Another of the men cited was William Pikeril, Giffard's man whom the bishop had warned to cut off contact with Peter the ingrate. Giffard seems to have failed in that attempt too, for Pikeril disappeared from Giffard's service at the same time Peter did.[65] If Pikeril was on the list of people to harass in 1297, the attempt went nowhere, and Pikeril soon died.[66] When, also in 1297, the abbot and convent of Tewksbury presented Peter to Thornbury—to which the abbot and convent had years earlier presented Pikeril[67]—Giffard refused to institute Peter and put in his own choice.[68] Once again, a superior jurisdiction came to Peter's rescue, and Peter obtained Thornbury on appeal to the court of Canterbury.[69]

Giffard of Worcester, p. xxii. For Giffard's troubled relationship with another clerk, see previous note.

[61]See the *Oxford Dictionary of National Biography*, sub nom. and Davies, "Studies," pp. 68-69. The year before the rupture with Peter, Giffard was excusing himself from attending Convocation on grounds of gout (Reg. Giffard of Worcester, p. 295).

[62]Although there are signs of the attitude starting early. From his first year as bishop Giffard's personal estate was being conflated with that of the bishopric (Dyer, *Lords and Peasants*, p. 58).

[63]Reg. Giffard of Worcester, p. 487.

[64]He would, however, eventually get caught on pluralism charges by Archbishop Winchelsey (Graham, "Metropolitical Visitation," pp. 356-57). But he pretty well landed on his feet, passing one of his benefices to his clerk and keeping the rest (*ibid.*).

[65]Following Peter's (and his own) break with Giffard, Pikeril appears as chancellor of Oxford; see A. B. Emden, *A Biographical Register of the University of Oxford to A.D. 1500* (Oxford, 1957), sub nom. Pikeril evidently kept some connection in the diocese, however. He was engaged there in a lawsuit for debt in 1286 against Clement, parson of Chaddesly. Giffard was attached as ordinary to get Clement to court; it is tempting to suspect that Giffard was less than cooperative with the court because of his bad relations with Pikeril; see National Archives: PRO, CP 40/69, m 101d, available online in *The Anglo-American Legal Tradition,* the digital archive assembled by Robert C. Palmer and Elspeth K. Palmer, CP 40/69 AALT 5013: <http://aalt.law.uh.edu/E1/CP40no69/bCP40no69dorses/IMG_5013.htm>. But such episcopal failures were not unusual. I have found no evidence of a special connection between Clement and Giffard.

[66]Emden, *A Biographical Register*, sub nom.

[67]Reg. Giffard of Worcester, p. 171.

[68]*Ibid.*, p. 489.

[69]*Ibid.*, p. 493 (fols. 422-23, pp. 869-71). For good measure, he leveled a complaint that Giffard had been illicitly consuming Thornbury's fruits in the meantime (*ibid.*, MS).

Indeed, Peter had the last laugh: a royal writ ordered Giffard's successor to distrain the benefices of Giffard's executors so as to force them to answer to the exchequer for Giffard's debts to the king. It was issued "teste P. de Leycestre."[70]

To these personality problems of bad temper and tenacity one might also add indications of a suspicious-minded bishop. Thirteenth-century bishops do not seem often to have wanted their own clerks to issue them bonds guaranteeing their good behavior.[71] So it is worth noting that Giffard took a bond from Peter to guarantee that Peter would aid the bishop should Peter's institution to Budbrooke be challenged.[72] Giffard also received another bond from Robert de Wyse—to whom he would eventually try to give Bishop's Cleeve after seizing it from Peter—when the bishop instituted Robert to Twining, in case Twining turned out not to be vacant. Robert committed himself to resigning Twining if there was trouble, thus shielding Giffard.[73] Indeed, even after the conflict over Bishop's Cleeve was over, the bishop did not collate a new benefice (Alvechurch) to Robert until Robert had surrendered the letter of institution to Bishop's Cleeve.[74] Giffard evidently suspected Robert might want to claim too much.

Trust, however, must have been a necessary component of the relations between thirteenth-century bishops and their men. Bishops, like any superior, would have found it hard to monitor their subordinates; trust could help fill the gap. But clerks had to trust their bishop as well. One example is the many times a bishop's clerk resigned one benefice to receive collation of another. Such moments required that a clerk be confident that that collation would come—that the bishop would really confer what must have been promised before the clerk resigned the first benefice. Such a leap of faith was short, but it was over a deep chasm.

---

[70]*The Register of William de Geynsburgh, Bishop of Worcester, 1302–1307*, 2nd ed., ed. J. W. Willis Bund (London, 1929), p. 67.

[71]I have found very few examples: one at Exeter (*The Register of Walter Bronescombe, Bishop of Exeter 1258–1280*, ed. O. F. Robinson [Woodbridge, UK, 1995–2003], no. 1033)—the archdeacon making the bond had received collation of the archdeaconry from this bishop (*ibid.*, no. 1033); one at Hereford (*Registrum Ricardi de Swinfield, Episcopi Herefordensis, A.D. MCCLXXXIII–MCCCXVIII*, ed. W. W. Capes [London, 1909], p. 85). Bishops used bonds more frequently as a disciplinary tool for clergy in a pastoral context, a use I hope to explore elsewhere.

[72]Reg. Giffard of Worcester, p. 169 (WRO Rf.x716.093 BA 2648/1[i] fol. 151, p. 295).

[73]*Ibid.*, p. 171 (fol. 153v, p. 298).

[74]*Ibid.*, p. 517.

Although historians rightly stress the importance of large social, cultural, and institutional structures in understanding the past, the contingencies of personality also mattered. In this case, Giffard's peculiarities, by leading him to push against the expectations and institutions of his world, illuminate them for the historian working centuries later. Indeed, if it is the case that medieval bishops generally lived up to medieval theorists' expectations that rewards were for service already rendered, not for continued or future service, then Giffard in his wrath violated that expectation.[75]

Most bishops and bureaucrats had better relationships than Giffard and Peter, which explains the lack of examples of thirteenth-century bishops trying to expel erstwhile servants from their benefices.[76] Indeed, patrons, lay as well as episcopal, probably did not expect to use benefices to exact continued service or good behavior—that is, as tools of accountability.[77] But Giffard's experience could have served as a warning to any inclined to try. It also suggests where any such bishop might look: to pluralism and residency regulations. If the law's protection of security of tenure in benefices was the problem,[78] the law's strictures on pluralism and nonresidence could, in theory, have provided part of the solution.

It does not, however, appear that they were frequently resorted to by bishops (or, for that matter, by other patrons) for this purpose.[79]

[75]On this point regarding medieval theory about service and gifts, see Andrew M. Spencer, "Royal Patronage and the Earls in the Reign of Edward I," *History*, 93 (2008), 20–46, here 44 and his comments regarding the gifts given by Edward I and Edward III at 42. Spencer, it should be noted, is talking about secular gifts among secular people. It is, moreover, possible that benefices and clerks were simply different. For bishops collating benefices and stating that they expect or hope for future service from the recipients, see *Registrum Roberti Winchelsey*, pp. 292–93; *Registrum Johannis de Pontissara, episcopi Wintoniensis, A.D. MCCLXXXII–MCCCIV*, ed. C. Deedes (London, 1915–24), p. 792.

[76]See above, n. 8.

[77]This is a matter I plan to explore further, at least regarding clerks, in a longer study.

[78]From a bishop's point of view, the legal revolution of the twelfth century was not an entirely good thing. Charles Duggan stressed the way in which the canon law came to constrain bishops; see Duggan, "Papal Judges Delegate and the Making of the 'New Law,'" in *Cultures of Power: Lordship, Status, and Process in Twelfth-Century Europe*, ed. Thomas N. Bisson (Philadelphia, 1995), pp. 172–99, here pp. 194–95.

[79]Although a consideration of patronage can shed new light on Bishop Cantilupe of Hereford's mildly notorious campaign against pluralism in his diocese. Various motives—a sincere hostility to pluralism when it was unlicensed, a dislike of the aliens who held multiple benefices, personal rivalries, and larger political conflicts—have

Again, Peter's experience with Giffard looks exceptional. If benefices were not tools of accountability, what was? There is a modern analogy—imperfect, certainly, but useful. A teacher once noted that it was all very well to argue that security of tenure made benefices poor tools of accountability, but that modern university faculty obtain tenure and still keep working. She was right. But why do tenured professors keep working so hard? It is not, by and large, the money, and certainly not the danger of losing it. The tenured labor endlessly because they occupy a certain (academic) culture with certain expectations. So did thirteenth-century diocesan bureaucrats. Benefices were irrevocable gifts rather than salary, pointing to the gift-giving

---

been adduced to explain why Cantilupe, a pluralist of note before his elevation to the episcopate, embarked on this campaign: David M. Smith, "Thomas Cantilupe's Register: The Administration of the Diocese of Hereford 1275-1282," in *St. Thomas Cantilupe, Bishop of Hereford, Essays in His Honour*, ed. Meryl Jancey (Leominster, UK, 1982), pp. 83-101, here p. 91; W. Nigel Yates, "Bishop Peter de Aquablanca (1240-1268): A Reconsideration," *Journal of Ecclesiastical History*, 22 (1971), 303-17, here 312-17; *The Register of Thomas de Cantilupe, Bishop of Hereford (A.D. 1275-1282)*, ed. R. G. Griffiths and W. W. Capes (London, 1906-07), p. xxxvi; although see also David Carpenter's objections to xenophobia as a motive, "St. Thomas: His Political Career," in Jancey, *St. Thomas Cantilupe*, pp. 57-72, here p. 71n66. What should also be noted is that, had Cantilupe's efforts succeeded, more than half of the benefices thus vacated would have been in his gift. It should likewise be noted that, unlike Giffard, Cantilupe was trying to undo his predecessors' collations, not his own. In Cantilupe's gift: the precentorship of the cathedral (*Register of Thomas de Cantilupe*, p. 111; *Acta Sanctorum Quotquot Toto Urbe Coluntur vel a Catholicis Scriptoribus Celebrantur*, ed. J. Stiltingo *et al.* [Paris and Rome, 1866], October 1, col. 562b); the prebend held by Hervey de Boreham (*Register of Thomas de Cantilupe*, p. 121); the archdeaconry of Shropshire (*ibid.*, p. 150; *Acta Sanctorum*, October 1, col. 562b); the prebend of Ledbury (*ibid.*; *Register of Thomas de Cantilupe*, p. 63); the prebend of Preston (*Register of Thomas de Cantilupe*, p. 187); two portions of Bromyard (*ibid.*, p. 141); (*Registrum Ricardi de Swinfield*, p. 527 for the bishop's right); Whitbourne (Smith, "Thomas Cantilupe's Register," p. 91, and *Register of Thomas de Cantilupe*, p. 251 for the bishop's right); Ullingswick (*ibid.*, pp. 126, 136, 138, 142, 241 for the bishop's right); Ross (*Acta Sanctorum*, October 1, col. 562b; *Registrum Ricardi de Swinfield*, pp. 527-28 for bishop's right); Morton (*Register of Thomas de Cantilupe*, pp. 141, 186, 225 for bishop's right). Not in Cantilupe's gift: Tretire (*Register of Thomas de Cantilupe*, pp. 127, 131; *Registrum Ricardi de Swinfield*, p. 542 for advowson); portion of Castle Holgate (*Register of Thomas de Cantilupe*, pp. 136-37, 141-42; *Registrum Ricardi de Swinfield*, pp. 524-25 for advowson); Hope Mansel (*Register of Thomas de Cantilupe*, pp. 142, 188; *Registrum Ricardi de Swinfield*, pp. 530, 532 for advowson); Worthen (*Register of Thomas de Cantilupe*, pp. 145, 150; *Registrum Ricardi de Swinfield*, p. 542 for advowson); Westbury (*Register of Thomas de Cantilupe*, pp. 145, 628 for advowson); two (or three?) portions of Pontesbury (*Register of Thomas de Cantilupe*, pp. 145, 150, 152-53, 159-60, 189-91, 193; *Registrum Ricardi de Swinfield*, p. 532 for advowson).

that established and maintained social relationships in a gift-giving culture. Bishops gave legally protected benefices just as lords in the secular sphere gave legally protected grants in fee.[80] If Peter of Leicester and Godfrey Giffard point the administrative historian in search of thirteenth-century accountability anywhere, they point in that direction too.

The comparison with academic tenure also redirects attention to the junior partner in these relationships. Historians hold that bishops and other lords gave their clerks benefices because it was cheap; the costs of administration were thus transferred from the lord's pocket to the Church, or at least to a church.[81] Indeed, for lords that surely was one of the attractions of holding an advowson and using it. But such a lord-centered account is not complete.[82] As modern professors find tenure part of the allure of the academic life, so medieval clerks found the benefices to which their lords presented them. Peter of Leicester illustrates why. Benefices offered not just income but also secure income. In giving benefices, bishops and other lords gave their people what they wanted: independence.

[80]I hope to discuss this analogy further in the study alluded to above.
[81]See above, n. 2.
[82]Nor, of course, is this one. For example, benefices conferred status as well as income, a topic I plan to explore elsewhere.

ST. PAUL AND THE POLEMICISTS: THE ROBERT PARSONS–THOMAS MORTON EXCHANGES, 1606–10

BY

Michael L. Carrafiello*

The author examines St. Paul's prominent place in the polemical exchanges between the English Jesuit Robert Parsons and the Protestant cleric Thomas Morton during the controversy over the Jacobean Oath of Allegiance that followed the Gunpowder Plot's failure in 1605. The most important topics were the relative supremacy of kingly and papal authority and the use of equivocation in the taking of oaths. While Parsons and Morton could each find some basis of claiming St. Paul as an authority, Parsons proved to be much more successful in this regard, thereby depriving English Protestants like Morton of an important source of support for the Jacobean establishment.

Keywords: Gunpowder Plot; Morton; Parsons; St. Paul

Given that the 2008–09 year has been proclaimed as the Year of St. Paul,[1] the saint's theological and political importance deserves further exploration. Protestants as well as Catholics have claimed him for their own. A case in point is St. Paul's prominent place in the polemical exchanges between the early-modern English Jesuit Robert Parsons and the Protestant cleric Thomas Morton immediately following the failure of the Gunpowder Plot in 1605. These exchanges, which captured the flavor and state of religious and political affairs between English Catholics and Protestants at that time, offer a unique glimpse into how both sides used St. Paul in defending their respective positions and in articulating a compelling vision

*Dr. Carrafiello is director of the Colligan History Project at Miami University in Hamilton, Ohio.

[1]The Year of St. Paul (June 2008–June 2009) was proclaimed by Pope Benedict XVI on June 28, 2007.

to their partisans. Appropriately enough, the exchanges took place during the reign of another Paul—the Borghese Pope Paul V.[2]

English Catholics faced intense pressure from the new Jacobean Oath of Allegiance devised in the wake of the Gunpowder Plot. The plot to blow up king and Parliament, it may be recalled, was hatched by a group of conspirators—including Robert Catesby, Thomas Wintour, Thomas Percy, Sir Everard Digby, and Guy Fawkes—who had initially expected gaining some measure of toleration from King James I. Spain's conclusion of a peace treaty with James in 1604 without provision for toleration, however, convinced these plotters that persecution by the English establishment would only grow worse, and so they devised their far-fetched scheme. But the government thwarted the plot—dramatically apprehending the enigmatic Fawkes as he dug his mine under Parliament—and the case for toleration of English Catholics, such as it was, was dealt a mortal blow.[3]

The English government subsequently increased persecution and instituted a series of strict anti-Catholic laws. The penalty for recusancy skyrocketed to £60 per year, and Catholics could not own property through marriage, become lawyers or physicians, or live in certain localities. At the heart of the government's program, however, was the Oath of Allegiance. It required Catholics to swear "that the Pope, neither of himself, nor by any authority of the Church or see of Rome . . . has any power to depose the King . . . or to discharge any of his subjects of their allegiance and obedience to His Majesty." A fierce controversy erupted on the nature and relative importance of papal and kingly authority between the great cardinal, St. Robert Bellarmine, S.J., on the one hand, and King James I, on the other.[4]

[2]Pope Paul V (Camillo Borghese) reigned 1605–21.

[3]There are, of course, countless works on the Gunpowder Plot and its spectacular failure in November 1605. Among these, two differing views can be found in Mark Nicholls, *Investigating Gunpowder Plot* (Manchester, UK, 1991) and Francis Edwards, *Guy Fawkes: The Real Story of the Gunpowder Plot?* (London, 1969). For a very lucid account of the exchanges between Cardinal Robert Bellarmine and King James I on papal and kingly power, see J. P. Sommerville, *Politics and Ideology in England, 1603–1640* (London, 1986), pp. 196–98.

[4]The controversy surrounding the Jacobean Oath of Allegiance has received much attention. Notable considerations include Sommerville, *Politics and Ideology*, which in turn takes much of its analysis on the oath from his "Jacobean Political Thought and the Controversy over the Oath of Allegiance" (PhD diss., University of Cambridge, 1981). Sommerville's "Papalist Thought and the Controversy over the Jacobean Oath of Allegiance," in *Catholics and the "Protestant Nation": Religious Politics and Identity in*

With this international controversy over the oath brewing, English Catholics were both harried and divided as to the appropriate course of action. Some Catholics, like the Appellants, had for over a decade sought a rapprochement with the English establishment in the hopes of achieving some kind of toleration. They concluded that the oath was benign and justified given the course of events since the accession of James.[5] Other Catholics, most notably exiled Jesuits like Robert Parsons, had spent the better part of their adult lives working for the restoration of the Catholic faith and Catholic rule in England. Parsons's *Memorial for the Reformation of England* (1596) provided a blueprint for such a revival. He came to believe that the oath was sacrilegious and inimical to the long-term survival of English Catholicism.[6]

At the same time, English Protestants eagerly exploited this Catholic schism as both proof of Catholics' inconstancy and further justification for the extreme measures planned to extract the oath from every Catholic in the country. Arguably the most effective proponent of the English establishment's position was the well-known cleric and accomplished political theorist Thomas Morton. Morton combined a staunch Calvinist view of the Jacobean church with complete devotion to James's form of *jure divino* kingship. One historian, in fact, has described him as the very model of "a zealous defender of royal sovereignty against Catholics."[7] As a result, Morton would be rewarded with

---

Early Modern England, ed. Ethan H. Shagan (Manchester, UK, 2005), pp. 162–84, is similarly enlightening.

[5]The Appellants were secular priests who opposed the institution of an English archpriest in the 1590s. The best account of what would become the Appellant-Jesuit struggle remains Arnold Pritchard, *Catholic Loyalism in Elizabethan England* (Chapel Hill, 1979).

[6]Parsons spent the last three decades of his life in exile after accompanying Edmund Campion on the heroic, if ill-fated, English mission of 1580–81. A recent assessment of Parsons's career is found in Victor Houliston, *Catholic Resistance in Elizabethan England: Robert Persons's Jesuit Polemic, 1580–1610* (Rome, 2007), which both complements and differs somewhat from the view expressed in my earlier *Robert Parsons and English Catholicism, 1580–1610* (Selinsgrove, PA, 1998). The *Memorial for the Reformation of England,* meanwhile, was circulated in manuscript form in the 1590s; excerpts include those found in the Stonyhurst, Petyt, and Westminster Cathedral Archives. It was printed a century later by the Protestant Edward Gee: *The Jesuit's Memorial for the Intended Reformation of England* (London, 1690).

[7]Sommerville, *Politics and Ideology,* pp. 45, 224. Two excellent scholarly treatments of the career of Morton, meanwhile, are found in Nicholas Tyacke, *Anti-Calvinists: The Rise of English Arminianism, c. 1590–1640* (Oxford, 1987) and Anthony Milton, *Catholic and Reformed: The Roman and Protestant Churches in English Protestant Thought, 1600–1640* (Cambridge, UK, 1995). Morton was the quintessence of a moderate Calvinist cleric and as such a bulwark of the Jacobean establishment.

a series of important ecclesiastical offices within the Church of England. He held in succession the deaneries of Gloucester and Winchester, and served as a canon in York. In 1616, he became bishop of Chester and then acceded to the see of Lichfield and Coventry, and eventually to that of Durham (1632). Most impressively, he managed to survive the upheavals of the Civil War decades. Morton died at the ripe old age of ninety-five shortly before the Restoration, having attained the rare achievement of an undisturbed retirement.

Parsons and Morton were among the most prolific, skilled, and widely read polemicists of the early-seventeenth century.[8] At the same time he confronted Morton, Parsons responded to attacks penned by the Protestant Dean of Exeter, Matthew Sutcliffe, including Sutcliffe's strident *Subversion of Robert Parsons His confused and worthless worke* (1606). Perhaps even more famously, Parsons throughout the decade would offer up his counterpoints to Sir Edward Coke on the nature of the English constitution and the course of English history, most notably in his celebrated *Answere to the Fifth Part of Reportes Lately set Forth by Syr Edward Cooke* (1606). Morton, for his part, would author or coauthor a number of books delineating the Calvinist nature of the English Church and seeking to distinguish its moderate tendencies from those of the emerging puritan faction. Most noteworthy of these works was the *Catholic Appeale to Protestants* (1609), which gained favor at the English court and a wide readership throughout Europe. But only in their exchanges with each other did the two clerics rely so heavily on St. Paul. Parsons and Morton's repeated and extensive use of the Apostle is unmatched in the polemical literature of the period.

The Parsons-Morton exchanges involving St. Paul, then, emerged as the direct outcome of the disputes surrounding the Oath of Allegiance and English Catholics' obligations to the Jacobean state. In 1606, Morton published the little book *An Exacte Discoverie of Romish*

---

[8]Milton and Houliston agree that Morton was renowned for and unequalled in his polemical ability to employ Catholic authorities against Parsons and other Catholic writers. According to Milton, Morton both pioneered and perfected the device whereby "Romanist writers were manipulated in order to act as testimonies of Protestant doctrine and to attack each other" (*Catholic and Reformed,* p. 233). Houliston (*Catholic Resistance,* chap. 8) is critical of Morton's (and subsequent Protestants') skill in this regard as indicative of a kind of cynicism and abasement of intellectual discourse. Houliston and I concur that Parsons's responses prove that he was easily a match for such tactics, however.

Doctrine in the Case of Conspiracie and Rebellion, followed by three additional books: *A Full Satisfaction Concerning a Double Romish Iniquitie* (1606), *A Preamble unto an Incounter with P. R. Concerning the Romish Doctrine of Rebellion and Equivocation* (1608), and *The Encounter against M. Parsons by a Review of His Last Sober Reckoning* (1610). Parsons, for his part, offered the most direct responses to these texts in his *Treatise Tending to Mitigation towardes Catholicke-subjects in England* (1607) and *A Quiet and Sober Reckoning with M. Thomas Morton* (1609). The exchanges ceased with Parsons's death in 1610. While a variety of topics were considered and contested, the two most prominently featuring St. Paul were questions regarding the relative supremacy of kingly and papal authority and, not surprisingly, equivocation—especially in the case of the administration and taking of oaths. Morton and Parsons found that they could not make their respective arguments without generous references to St. Paul's epistles.[9]

Morton provided his defense of kingly power primarily in his *Preamble* and his *Full Satisfaction.* He looked to the classic Pauline exposition on the subject, Romans 13, "Let everyone obey the authorities that are over him, for there is no authority except from God, and all authority that exists is established by God. As a consequence, the man who opposes authority rebels against the ordinance of God; those who resist thus shall draw condemnation down upon themselves."[10] Morton directly cited this passage no fewer than seven times in his books against Parsons and what he considered the specter of Catholic rebellion. The Protestant cleric also looked to a number of Catholic authorities to substantiate this Pauline point: "Though all means whereby kings come to the crowns be not commanded of God, yet

[9]The most comprehensive and synthetic treatment of the centrality of St. Paul and the other apostles in the shaping of both Catholic and Protestant political theory remains Quentin Skinner, *The Foundations of Modern Political Thought* (Cambridge, UK, 1978), especially vol. 2. The first part of this second volume largely concerns Martin Luther's use of St. Paul in promulgating the basic religious and political doctrines of Lutheranism.

[10]For clarity, all scriptural passages cited by Parsons and Morton are here excerpted from *The New American Bible,* St. Joseph ed. (1970). It is important to keep in mind that Parsons and Morton in this context were making polemical use of the scriptural passages to which they referred. Morton's reference to Romans 13, meanwhile, is found in *A Full Satisfaction Concerning a Double Romish Iniquitie,* [Early English Books Online Series, hereafter EEBO], (n.p., 1606), 1:30-31, 98; 3:25, 35, 37-38, 45, as well as *A Preamble unto an Incounter with P. R. Concerning the Romish Doctrine of Rebellion and Equivocation* (n.p., 1608), EEBO, p. 35.

whatsoever means they use, whether by election, succession, or invasion, wheresoever they are by consent of the kingdom so established, this is the ordinance of God; and henceforth he, as sent from God, is to rule, and the people to obey."[11]

Morton also referred to another important Pauline pronouncement on obedience, 1 Timothy 6, "All under the yoke of slavery must regard their masters as worthy of full respect; otherwise the name of God and the church's teachings suffer abuse."[12] In other words, obedience to temporal masters had to be unconditional and absolute, even as those rulers, in turn, had an absolute mandate from the Almighty. Morton declared, "in the prince a Christian man does not behold only man, but the hand of God."[13] He made this point repeatedly for emphasis: "Wherein [St. Paul] prescribed not a *may* but a *must*; and thereby enjoined not a *possibility*, but a *necessity* of loyal subjection."[14] Morton contrasted his view with what he presumed was that of the theorist William Reynolds. The latter had supposedly compared the pronouncements of Ss. Peter and Paul on the subject: "The governor whom S. Peter calls a creature of man, S. Paul calls the ordinance of God."[15] For Morton, kingly power had both a divine and natural basis: "it is placed in certain men (from the beginning) by suffrages of the people, yet the election of princes does flow from the law of nature, which God created; and from the use of reason, which God poured into man, and which is a little beam of divine light drawn from that infinite brightness in Almighty God."[16] English Protestants would settle for no less than an unequivocal assurance of absolute and unconditional obedience from English Catholics.

Morton made use of St. Paul's letters to the Romans and the Corinthians to uphold unconditional nonresistance to tyrannical rulers as well. He noted several times that St. Paul had allowed himself to be subjected to Caesar as a competent authority even though the latter could never have been regarded as a benign ruler. Morton alluded to other scriptural examples on this topic: "Jacob did covenant with Laban an idolater; and the maid to whom St. Peter swore, was compe-

---

[11]Morton, *Full Satisfaction*, 1:30. I have modernized spelling, capitalization, and punctuation.

[12]*Ibid.*, 1:100.

[13]*Ibid.*, 3:38.

[14]Morton, *Preamble*, p. 35. Emphasis in original.

[15]*Ibid.*, p. 119.

[16]*Ibid.*, p. 100.

tent enough to hear a true oath."[17] Morton touted the pronouncement of St. Paul in 2 Timothy 4 that they who gladly and meekly suffer tyrants would receive a divine reward. St. Paul had said, "From now on a merited crown awaits me; on that Day the Lord, just judge that he is, will award it to me—and not only to me, but to all who have looked for his appearing with eager longing." Morton proclaimed that "the patient suffering of the tyranny of kings, be the more excellent Christian power, than acting and working the death of kings, and that therefore that power was practiced of our Lord Christ, and bestowed on the Apostles for the confirmation of the glorious faith."[18]

On the other hand, Morton said that those Catholics who had fomented the Gunpowder Plot were like those whom St. Paul characterized in Romans 3. Rebellious Catholics "swiftly run their feet to shed blood; ruin and misery strew their course. The path of peace is unknown to them; the fear of God is not before their eyes." At the same time, the Protestant cleric emphatically rejected any similarity between the suffering of Catholic priests and the heroic death of New Testament martyrs. The blood spilled by English Catholics bore no resemblance to "the blood of the martyr Stephen, and of the Prophets by the Jews, of the blood of the saints by the heathen."[19] Morton thereby provided the classic Pauline statements on nonresistance to buttress his argument that all kings required "an inviolable subjection."[20]

Notwithstanding, by the time Morton came to write the *Encounter* in 1610, most of his references to St. Paul's teachings on the subject of obedience had been dropped. One reason for Morton's omissions is that Parsons made even more generous use of St. Paul in his counterarguments. Of course, Parsons would not and could not contradict the Pauline instructions on obedience and injunctions against resistance to temporal authorities. Instead, the English Jesuit looked to the Apostle as a way of suggesting that while temporal power indeed came from God and therefore was deserving of all due subjection, divine power held an even more exalted status that commanded an even greater degree of reverence and adherence.

Parsons used that same classic passage from Romans 13 to suggest that Catholic priests should not be resisted since they, too, drew their

---

[17]Morton, *Full Satisfaction*, 3:86.
[18]*Ibid.*, 3:20.
[19]Morton, *Preamble*, p. 108.
[20]*Ibid.*, p. 100.

authority immediately from God.[21] In fact, he said that the claim to priestly authority was much stronger and more immediate given that priests are "mediators between God and man." Parsons celebrated the supremacy of "spiritual power, dignity, authority and function thereof."[22] The Jesuit noted out of Philippians that Christ himself had been a priest first and an earthly king second: "He did not think it was usurpation to be equal to God his Father according to his divinity."[23] There was, in fact, more than enough "proof of Christ's divinity" and the "high dignity of Christ's priesthood."[24] Parsons believed that such proof is found in Hebrews 5. Christ had received the priestly office "from the One who said to him, 'You are my son; today I have begotten you'; just as he says in another place, 'You are a priest forever, according to the order of Melchizedek.'"[25] Parsons pointed to another example out of Hebrews 7, as well: "Under the old covenant there were many priests because they were prevented by death from remaining in office; but Jesus, because he remains forever, has a priesthood which does not pass away."[26] In addition, Parsons referred to the implication out of Philippians 2 that Christ had thereby been granted divinity equal to that of the Almighty: "God highly exalted him and bestowed on him the name above every other name, So that at Jesus' name every knee must bend, in the heavens, on the earth, and under the earth, and every tongue proclaim to the glory of God the Father: Jesus Christ is Lord!"[27] The early-modern English descendants of the ancient priesthood of Melchizedek, therefore, were granted through Christ a permanent and exalted status. Indeed, according to Parsons, "St. Paul does immediately infer this conclusion about the supreme dignity of Christ his priesthood."[28]

Parsons believed that the implications of Christ's preeminent priesthood for seventeenth-century Europe were obvious. The Jesuit found them succinctly stated by St. Paul in 1 Corinthians 9 and 10. Here the Apostle suggested that the spiritual state always held primacy over the temporal realm. St. Paul's teaching is based upon the

---

[21]Robert Parsons, *A Treatise Tending to Mitigation towardes Catholicke-subjects in England* (St. Omer, 1607), EEBO, p. 69.

[22]*Ibid.*, p. 154.

[23]*Ibid.*, p. 151.

[24]*Ibid.*, pp. 252, 151.

[25]*Ibid.*, pp. 154, 251–52.

[26]*Ibid.*, pp. 151–52.

[27]*Ibid.*, p. 151.

[28]*Ibid.*, p. 153.

supremacy of the Eucharist over pagan sacrifices, which Parsons here cited as absolute: "You cannot drink the cup of the Lord and also the cup of demons. You cannot partake of the table of the Lord and likewise the table of demons."[29] In the same way, the historic kingdom of the Jews presaged the far superior state of the heavenly kingdom of Christ, just as the temporal state at best can only foretell the excellence of the spiritual state.

Parsons examined the ideas and actions of St. Paul himself in this regard. The Jesuit believed that the Apostle had taken pains to protect the special status of the spiritual commonwealth. According to Parsons, St. Paul rightly claimed spiritual authority even though he had not been ordained by Christ himself. The celebrated passage from Acts 13 substantiated this point: "I have made you a light to the nations, a means of salvation to the ends of the earth."[30]

Additionally, Parsons noted out of 1 Corinthians 15 that Paul had expressly eschewed temporal profit (and ultimately the temporal life) so as the accentuate his spiritual mission: "I swear to you, brothers, by the very pride you take in me, which I cherish in Christ Jesus our Lord, that I face death every day. If I fought those beasts at Ephesus for purely human motives, what profit was there for me?"[31] In other words, St. Paul gave up everything for his evangelization on behalf of Christ. In Parsons's estimation "this was perfection in that glorious Apostle."[32]

So while Parsons would not—indeed could not—detract from biblical injunctions enjoining obedience to temporal authority, he employed many of the same Pauline passages used by Morton to present a vigorous case for obedience to spiritual authority. Parsons also countered Morton's repeated attempts to set up what the Jesuit called "absolute kings."[33] While Parsons never directly mentioned the authority of the papacy in this context, the implications of his arguments were quite clear. Papal authority came immediately from God and therefore in no way could be discounted or set aside. Parsons offered more direct support for papal primacy in some of his other

---

[29]Robert Parsons, *A Quiet and Sober Reckoning with M. Thomas Morton* (St. Omer, 1609), EEBO, p. 421.

[30]*Ibid.*, p. 193.

[31]Parsons, *Treatise*, p. 461.

[32]*Ibid.*

[33]*Ibid.*, p. 186.

works, but in these exchanges with Morton he demonstrated conclusively that St. Paul could be used by Catholic theorists to defend the historic authority of Catholic princes, priests, and popes.[34] The fact that Morton did not return to St. Paul in reiterating these points in the *Encounter* shows that Parsons had been entirely successful in claiming St. Paul as his own in delineating the limitations of obedience to temporal authority.

The condemnation of the Jesuit Superior Henry Garnet for his presumed equivocation in connection with the Gunpowder Plot gave special impetus to Morton's denunciation of the practice.[35] The Protestant cleric looked to the teachings of St. Paul to contend that equivocation could never be legitimated or countenanced. For Morton and other members of the English Protestant establishment, equivocation and lying were synonymous, meaning that apparent inconsistencies in the Apostle's writings had to be addressed. As an example, Morton explained that St. Paul did not equivocate when he failed to visit the Corinthians after promising to do so. For Morton, "he is only a liar, who thinks contrary to that which he says," and that obviously had not been the case with St. Paul.[36] In fact, the Apostle offered a direct condemnation of lying and in 1 Corinthians 10 and forewarned of annihilation from the "Destroyer" for those who indulged in such sinfulness. Referring to the Israelites under Moses, St. Paul instructed, "These things that happened to them serve as an example. They have been written as a warning to us, upon whom the end of the ages has come."[37] Morton believed he had found an even stronger condemnation of prevarication in 1 Timothy 1. Here the Apostle taught that God's law itself is designed to punish "the lawless and the unruly, the irreligious and the sinful, the wicked and the godless, men who kill their fathers or mothers, murderers, fornicators, sexual perverts, kidnappers, liars, [and] perjurers."[38] At the same time, Morton took pains again in this context to state that St. Paul had recognized

[34]For example, Parsons very effectively related the historic role of the papacy in England in his *Treatise of Three Conversions of England* (1603-04).

[35]Garnet had been in contact with some of the conspirators before November 1605. He was executed by the state after being judged complicit in the Gunpowder Plot, but my own view is that he was a "man who knew too much" and one who was in no way convinced of the merits or efficacy of the scheme. See *Robert Parsons and English Catholicism*, p. 105. Other accounts of Garnet's predicament can be found in Edwards, *Guy Fawkes* and Nicholls, *Investigating Gunpowder Plot.*

[36]Morton, *Full Satisfaction*, 3:51.

[37]*Ibid.*, 3:71.

[38]*Ibid.*, 3:84.

Caesar as a competent judge and so would not resort to lying. Morton reminded his readers that "St. Paul in his cause appeared to Caesar's tribunal seat, who was a pagan."[39]

St. Paul was not the only high authority who shunned lying. According to Morton, many specific references out of Hebrews and Ephesians made clear that God under no circumstances could be seen to have equivocated, even when revealing his truth in the fullness of time. Morton believed that the beginning of the letter to the Hebrews substantiates this point: "In times past, God spoke in fragmentary and varied ways to our fathers through the prophets; in this the final age, he has spoken to us through his Son, whom he has made heir of all things and through whom he first created the universe."[40] In the same way, Christ could never have been said to have dissembled but, rather, was the very oracle of truth. To the contrary, Morton declared, "there is as little affinity between Christ's sentences and M. Parsons his reservation, as between light and darkness, truth and a lie."[41]

At the other extreme, Morton charged that Catholics had been worse than the heathen in their repeated equivocation—that is, lying. In 1 Corinthians 5, Morton found what he believed was an apt injunction as to how to deal with this kind of Catholic treachery. St. Paul had written that some of the Corinthians had been worse than the unbelievers in their personal conduct, pronouncing that "it is blasphemy against God for a Christian to be more vile in life than a pagan." Additionally, Morton asserted that St. Paul had provided strictures against associating with such persons: "What I really wrote about was your not associating with anyone who bears the title 'brother' if he is immoral, covetous, and idolater, an abusive person, a drunkard, or a thief. It is clear that you must not associate with such a man. . . . 'Expel the wicked man from your midst.'"[42] In other words, there could be no social intercourse with or tolerance of Catholics so long as the practice of equivocation endured. In fact, Catholics were in Morton's estimation worse than infidels or the heathen:

[W]hat can this work in the Turks and all pagans at this day, but obstinacy in their infidelity, and blasphemy of that faith, which is the only life of souls,

---

[39]*Ibid.*, 3:86.

[40]Morton, *Preamble*, p. 139.

[41]Thomas Morton, *The Encounter against M. Parsons by a Review of His Last Sober Reckoning* (n.p., 1610), EEBO, 2:137.

[42]Morton, *Full Satisfaction*, 3:89–90, 101.

especially seeing I may as justly say concerning the equivocation of your contagious Romanists as the blessed Apostle wrote of the incestuous among the Corinthians, "I hear that there is such fornication among you, as is not found among the heathen."[43]

As a counterpoint, Morton sought to remind Parsons and other English Catholics that oaths such as the one being exacted of them were to be taken without hesitation or reservation. Morton proclaimed that oaths are "the most sacred bond that God has allowed unto men."[44] Here once again St. Paul was said to be the preeminent authority. Looking to Hebrews 6, Morton sought to prove that "oaths are the end of all contention."[45] St. Paul affirmed this very point when he wrote in the context of God's promise to Abraham:

> Men swear by someone greater than themselves; an oath gives firmness to a promise and puts an end to all argument. God, wishing to give the heirs of his promise even clearer evidence that his purpose would not change, guaranteed it by oath, so that, by two things that are unchangeable, in which he could not lie, we who have taken refuge in him might be strongly encouraged to seize the hope which is placed before us.[46]

Those who violate or cheapen such oaths, according to Morton, are "persons perfidious and treacherous." They leave the hearer "in a perpetual suspense and doubt" and prove themselves to be "as deceitful as was Judas."[47] As such, nations "have provided punishments for all such as willfully transgressed therein."[48] Morton thereby used St. Paul to give an unequivocal condemnation of equivocation.

In response, Parsons employed St. Paul with great frequency and skill to establish the efficacy, if not necessity, of equivocal speech.[49] The Jesuit referred in his works to no fewer than five occasions when St. Paul himself had equivocated or concealed some portion of the truth. Among these instances, the Apostle in Hebrews 7 "equivocated" in

---

[43]*Ibid.*, 3:101.

[44]*Ibid.*, 1:82.

[45]This line stated at least three times by Morton: *Full Satisfaction*, 1:82, 3:98; *Encounter*, 2:172.

[46]Morton, *Preamble*, p. 139.

[47]Morton, *Full Satisfaction*, 1:82.

[48]*Ibid.*, 3:98.

[49]See Michael L. Carrafiello, "Robert Parsons and Equivocation, 1606-1610," *The Catholic Historical Review*, 79 (1993), 671-80. I made the point in that article that Parsons in these exchanges with Morton defended the practice of equivocation while simultaneously recommending its infrequent use.

describing the lineage of Melchizedek out of his meeting with Abraham in that he seemed to imply that Melchizedek had neither a father nor mother.[50] A further instance of equivocation Parsons purported to find out of 1 Corinthians 4 wherein St. Paul seemed to discount the role of the Apostles in favor of the Corinthians so as to reproach and teach the latter:"We are fools on Christ's account. Ah, but in Christ you are wise! We are the weak ones, you the strong! They honor you, while they sneer at us! Up to this very hour we go hungry and thirsty, poorly clad, roughly treated, wandering about homeless."[51] St. Paul thereby shaded and disguised the truth to make a larger point regarding the significance of salvation. Ultimately, Parsons concluded that St. Paul often "was accounted to swear, that is to say, to call God to witness, that he spoke the truth, and yet he cannot be presumed to think as he spoke, or as the words literally do import."[52]

Parsons went even further and stated directly that St. Paul had resorted to equivocal speech to convey the larger and truer meaning of the final Resurrection. Here the example is from 1 Corinthians 15: "Perhaps someone will say 'How are the dead to be raised up? What kind of body will they have?' A nonsensical question! The seed you sow does not germinate unless it dies. . . . What is sown is ignoble, what rises is glorious. Weakness is sown, strength rises up. A natural body is put down and a spiritual body comes up."[53] Similarly, Parsons asserted that St. Paul had "concealed" the truth to effect the socialization of Timothy in that the Apostle "did feign himself to be an observer of the Jewish law." Ultimately, however, St. Paul did not lie, Parsons said, even though he concealed the truth on this and many other occasions. "Yet he deceived them not, for that he did not observe those ceremonies in the law, to the end to deceive them, but rather that by concealing his own opinion for a time, he might gain them, or at least not alienate them from Christ."[54] For Parsons, a godly end justified the use of equivocal means.

More pointedly, Parsons related the instance out of Acts 23 when Paul used "equivocal speech" to escape the Sanhedrin: "My brothers, I did not know that he was the high priest. Indeed Scripture has it, 'You shall not curse a prince of your people.'" In addition, the Apostle used

---

[50]Parsons, *Treatise*, pp. 293-94.
[51]*Ibid.*, p. 318.
[52]*Ibid.*
[53]*Ibid.*, p. 333.
[54]*Ibid.*, p. 397.

his speech to try to foment dissension among the Pharisees and Sadducees: "Brothers, I am a Pharisee and was born a Pharisee. I find myself on trial now because of my hope in the resurrection of the dead." This tactic, Parsons said, had proven particularly effective in that it provoked a "loud uproar" between the Pharisees and Sadducees, the latter of whom did not believe in the Resurrection.[55] He very nearly taunted Morton on this point: "and what will Thomas Morton now answer to this? Did St. Paul lie in this equivocation? Or was his dissimulation impious, for that one that was deceived? Or had he committed profanation if he had sworn it?"[56] On the contrary, Parsons said that St. Paul apparently received commendation from on high for taking this action. Christ appeared to St. Paul and said: "Keep up your courage! Just as you have given testimony to me here in Jerusalem, so must you do in Rome."[57] In other words, St. Paul had done whatever necessary to stay alive so as to carry out his godly mission. The parallel to the divine charge Parsons believed had been given to seventeenth-century English Catholic priests, he hoped, would not be missed.

Parsons asserted a higher authority still for substantiating that equivocation had been sanctioned throughout the history of the church. Christ himself, Parsons said, used "mental reservation" when he proclaimed that all who believed in him would be saved. Given the sinful nature of man, this could not have been meant to be literally true, the Jesuit believed. "The words of Christ cannot absolutely be true, without mental reservation or restriction in his understanding, for that all eaters of his flesh, and drinkers of his blood have not life everlasting thereby, but some rather damnation."[58] Therefore, according to Parsons, "the proposition of Christ had some reservation of mind in it, for that otherwise it had been false."[59] In fact, Parsons in his exchanges with Morton offered two blanket statements that the New Testament was replete with examples of numerous witnesses to Christ's equivocation, and the Jesuit was sure that there were many examples of "secret meanings" in Christ's speeches and exhortations to his disciples. Parsons also contended that St. Paul could have been taken to mean that Christ used mental reservation when declaring that only the Father knew the hour of final judgment. According to Parsons, Christ could not have spoken literally given St. Paul's description of the

[55]*Ibid.*, pp. 469, 550.
[56]*Ibid.*, p. 469.
[57]*Ibid.*
[58]*Ibid.*, p. 367.
[59]*Ibid.*, p. 378.

Savior's role in Colossians 1:"It pleased God to make absolute fullness reside in him and, by means of him, to reconcile everything in his person, both on earth and in the heavens, making peace through the blood of his cross."[60] Even the Savior's identity was concealed from the Jews this way, according to Parsons:"He said to the Jews *non cognovistis eum*:you do not know him; which seems untrue in itself, for that the Jews did profess to know him. . . . so as here also an equivocation of speech was used by our Savior."[61]

The Almighty was said to have used equivocal speech, as well, at least according to St. Paul. The Apostle famously wrote in Romans 1 that God permitted humans to be deceived and punished so as to advance his own divine purposes:

> God delivered them up in their lusts to unclean practices; they engaged in the mutual degradation of their bodies, these men who exchanged the truth of God for a lie and worshiped and served the creature rather than the Creator. . . . God therefore delivered them up to disgraceful passions. . . . They did not see fit to acknowledge God, so God delivered them up to their own depraved sense to do what is unseemly.[62]

According to Parsons, "all which places, according to the interpretations of Holy Fathers, and Doctors of the Catholic Church are to be understood that God does permit men to be deceived."[63]

Likewise, God also concealed the truth, according to Parsons. Again, the Jesuit found scriptural evidence from St. Paul, this time in Romans 8:"Indeed the whole created world eagerly awaits the revelation of the sons of God."[64] The Almighty also concealed according to his own purposes and the edification of humanity. St. Paul in Hebrews 6 and 7 documented this phenomenon in his discussion of God's fulfillment of the promise to Abraham: "And so, after patient waiting, Abraham obtained what God had promised." Likewise, St. Paul related that God had chosen a different course with Melchizedek from the one promised in his own law:"The law provides that the priests of the tribe of Levi should receive tithes from the people, their brother Israelites, even though all of them are descendants of Abraham; but

---

[60]*Ibid.*

[61]Parsons, *Quiet and Sober Reckoning*, p. 685.

[62]Parsons, *Treatise*, p. 401.

[63]*Ibid.*

[64]*Ibid.*, p. 453.

Melchizedek, who was not of their ancestry, received tithes of Abraham and blessed him who had received God's promises."[65] For Parsons, St. Paul was an important authority in showing that God countenanced concealment to attain his divine ends. Additionally, there was the case of St. Paul himself. According to Parsons, St. Paul had resorted to equivocation and never recognized Caesar as a competent judge: "There was no oath at all of the Apostle, whereby Caesar might be constituted his competent judge."[66]

The culmination of Parsons's lively defense of equivocation was firmly grounded in St. Paul's epistles as well. First, Parsons cited St. Paul in 1 Corinthians 9 and 15 to contend that priests in no way had to confess to their clerical state since their mission transcended any earthly authority: "when preaching I offer the gospel free of charge and do not make full use of the authority the gospel gives me. . . . I have made myself all things to all men in order to save at least some of them."[67] Parsons thought this statement by St. Paul implied that English priests were not duty bound to swear directly, even if some had already done so. Catholic clerics could look to the Apostle's words notwithstanding that some had already "upon their apprehension confessed themselves to be priests, [since that action] infers no law, that all men are bound to do the like."[68] For Parsons, St. Paul had never accepted Caesar as a competent authority and, consequently, priests preaching the gospel did not have to subject themselves to the oath of the English Protestant establishment.

What, then, are the conclusions to be drawn from the Parsons-Morton polemical exchanges? First, both Parsons and Morton looked to St. Paul as an important authority on obedience and equivocation, meaning that the Apostle's writings remain crucial to our understanding of the religious and political thought of both Reformation churches. Second, Parsons and Morton could each find some basis for claiming St. Paul as their own since both used the Apostle's letters to make their respective points. But, third, Parsons ultimately proved to be more successful in this regard. He made greater and more skillful use of St. Paul and returned to the Apostle with greater frequency in his later works than Morton did in his later treatises. Consequently, Parsons's effectiveness forced Morton to turn from St. Paul to other

[65]*Ibid.*
[66]Parsons, *Quiet and Sober Reckoning*, p. 104.
[67]Parsons, *Treatise*, p. 461.
[68]*Ibid.*

scriptural and secular authorities, a significant and perhaps unexpected departure for a Protestant cleric in the Reformation era. Fourth, Morton's inability to return to St. Paul on a consistent basis as an authority for absolutism reveals that members of the Jacobean establishment were deprived by Catholic polemicists like Parsons of an important source for the support of *jure divino* kingship. A weakened basis for absolutism would have major implications for the Stuart monarchy in the decades that followed. Fifth, Parsons's consistent and efficacious use of St. Paul may well have strengthened Catholic resistance to the Oath of Allegiance and served to buttress recusancy throughout the country. Finally, the polemical exchanges incorporating St. Paul between these two important English clerics provide a vivid example of why there was not—and could never be—peace between Catholics and Protestants in early-modern England.

The controversy over the oath eventually subsided, but fears of popery and popish plots continued in England, as did disagreements over the meaning of St. Paul's epistles. While Parsons and Morton each sought godly ends, the polemical means dictated to them by the strife of the seventeenth century served to deprive them and their respective flocks of stability and concord. Nevertheless, Parsons's adept use of St. Paul in his exchanges with Morton must be regarded as a significant intellectual milestone in English Catholics' long journey toward toleration and freedom.

ON CHURCH GROUNDS: POLITICAL FUNERALS AND THE CONTEST TO LEAD CATHOLIC IRELAND

BY

THOMAS J. BROPHY*

Political funerals organized by Irish nationalists, who intended to use the heady mixture of sacred ceremony and political imperative to create a secular sainthood, bedeviled much of Cardinal Paul Cullen's Dublin episcopate (1852-78). Cullen, who did not share the principles or aspirations of the men who sought his acquiescence in their funereal ventures, would not countenance the use of church resources or rituals as means to what he perceived as irreligious republican ends. In the competition for the political allegiance of Ireland's Catholics these demonstrations came to epitomize the divide between the cardinal and nationalists from parliamentary and militant groups.

Keywords: Cullen, Cardinal Paul; funeral rites; Irish independence movement; political protests

For much of the nineteenth and the early-twentieth centuries, dead patriots proved effective instruments for European nationalists. Irish political funeral planners had much in common with counterparts in Poland who resisted Russian rule and in Hungary who chafed under Viennese domination. Because of their attachment to and commonality with the whole of the population—life's great leveler is death—funerals constituted valuable conduits for aggrieved organizations to connect with the oppressed populations they aspired to lead. In Ireland where mourning practices were quite intricate and involved communities, not just families, nationalist obsequies' organizers played upon the people's emotions and customs as much or more than their political inclinations. They gained easy access to the public consciousness and lodged their message into the collective memory.

*Dr. Brophy is an instructor in the Department of History at the Chinese University of Hong Kong.

Irish nationalists intended to use the heady mixture of sacred ceremony and political imperative to create a secular sainthood. A cleri-
cally officiated performance of the complete Christian burial service
would stamp the funeral organizers' immediate and long-term designs
with a liturgical seal of approval. Dublin's Ultramontane Cardinal Paul
Cullen (1803–78, see figure 1) resisted such obvious manipulation. As
the Catholic liturgy reflects not only ceremonies but also values,
Cullen, who did not concur with the goals of the men who sought his
cooperation with their obsequial ventures, would not countenance the
use of church resources or rituals as tools to accomplish their ends. In
the competition for the political allegiance of Ireland's Catholics these
demonstrations came to epitomize the divide between the cardinal
and nationalists from both parliamentary and militant camps. The
thrust and parry between Cullen and the Irish Republican
Brotherhood (IRB, aka the Fenians) led funeral committees derived
from his stances when Terence Bellew McManus (1861), the
Manchester Martyrs (1867), John O'Mahony (1877), and Charles
McCarthy (1878) all died in the embrace of what the cardinal considered irreligious republicanism.

Making use of a life lived and transforming it into an institutional
device made for interesting contests between nationalists of different
stripes who battled for control of the departed's corpse. What the
funeral planners sought was leadership of nationalist (largely Catholic)
Ireland and authority to advance a political agenda on its behalf, two
things that they sought to wrest, at least in part, from the Church.
Public obsequies allowed their planners to skirt the on-again, off-again
Party Processions Acts that prohibited partisan demonstrations in
Ireland that would arouse sectarian distemper. British authorities rarely
interfered with Irish nationalist funerals because more often than not
they heightened tensions among the varying groups seeking hegemony. The mild British reaction differed substantially from what the
Poles encountered with Russian authorities. The occasion of the
funeral of Warsaw Archbishop Antoni Melchior Fijalkowski on October
10, 1861 (almost a month before Cullen endured the first such Fenian
display) spurred a large nationalist demonstration and incited a tsarist
crackdown that included Cossacks breaking into Catholic churches to
disperse worshippers and ban patriotic songs.[1] Just seven months
before his own death, Archbishop Fijalkowski, although described by

---

[1] Norman Davies, *God's Playground, A History of Poland*, vol 2: *1795 to the Present*
(Oxford, 1981), p. 351.

FIGURE 1. Cardinal Paul Cullen of Dublin (1803–78). Image courtesy of the
Multitext Project in Irish History, University College Cork. Reproduced by
permission.

Brian Porter as among the most reactionary and supportive of state
authority among his Polish peers,[2] had led, along with two other bishops, the funeral procession of five nationalist demonstrators shot dead
by Russian troops in Warsaw.

Many historians have echoed Emmet Larkin's description of Cullen
as first and foremost a Roman. In 1820 he was seventeen years old
when his family dispatched him from County Kildare to the Urban
College of Propaganda Fide in Rome. Cullen returned to Ireland thirty
years later, fully immersed in the ways of the Vatican and in its relationship with the Church in Ireland, as well as bearing an uncompro-
mising loyalty to the pope. Of the experiences that forged Cullen's per-
sona, near the top of the list must surely be his witnessing of Pius IX's

[2]Brian Porter, "Thy Kingdom Come: Patriotism, Prophecy, and the Catholic Hierarchy
in Nineteenth Century Poland," *The Catholic Historical Review,* 89 (2003), 213–39, here
224.

escape in disguise from the Eternal City on November 24, 1848, followed by a Roman republic that was declared less than three months later. From his post as rector of the Irish College, Cullen provided sanctuary for several clerics sought by the new government. Out of the wave of revolutions that swept through Europe at the midpoint of the nineteenth century, Cullen came away with the perception that a Giuseppe Mazzini lurked behind every tree. The revolutions by Parisians, Danes, Rumanians, Poles, Germans, Hungarians, and Young Italy was replicated, to a poor end, by Young Ireland and its leaders William Smith O'Brien, Patrick O'Donoghue, Thomas Meagher, and the Liverpool native Terence Bellew McManus.

After escaping exile in Tasmania, McManus led a largely nonpolitical life in California, but he did stir the nationalist pot in February 1860 when he publicly refused efforts by Ireland's amnesty movement on his behalf: "If the land that gave me birth, if the land sanctified to me by the graves of my forefathers . . . cannot welcome me back without the consent of a foreign ruler, then my foot shall never press her soil."[3] In this rejection he sowed the seeds that germinated into his elaborate obsequies. Less than a year later, the 1848 rebel died alone at San Francisco's St. Mary's Hospital and was buried the next day. After McManus's first funeral on January 16, 1861, the Ancient Order of Hibernians (AOH) formed a fund committee and solicited Irishmen across America to show sympathy for Ireland's cause and to display their hostility to the oppressive British government by contributing to a monument fund to decorate McManus's grave.[4] Composed largely of middle-class merchants and some professional men, the Hibernians raised $1000.[5] The more working-class Fenian Brotherhood[6] wanted to make a grandiose statement, and returning McManus's remains to Ireland fit that bill. On July 17, the turf fight within San Francisco's Irish community over McManus's remains came to a grudging resolution when the Fenians bested the AOH.

On August 20, when McManus's coffin arrived at the altar of St. Mary's Cathedral, San Francisco Archbishop Joseph Alemany entered

[3]Terence Bellew McManus to John Maguire, February 1, 1860; qtd. in Thomas G. McAllister, *Terence Bellew McManus* (Maynooth, Ireland, 1972), p. 41.

[4]*Irish-American*, March 16, 1861, p. 4.

[5]*San Francisco Monitor*, July 1861, repr. the *Irish-American*, August 17, 1861, p. 2.

[6]In conjunction with Michael Doheny and James Stephens, John O'Mahony founded the Fenian Brotherhood in New York in 1858 and dedicated it to the overthrow of British rule in Ireland.

Britain is watching!

the sanctuary, attended by a priest, a deacon, and a subdeacon, to cel-
ebrate the requiem Mass. One Father Cotter reprised his role from the
previous January as McManus's eulogizer:"His defence was not simply
for political rights, but also for that sanctuary consecrated by Ireland's
saints and crimsoned by the blood of Ireland's martyrs."[7] As he sat
nearby during Cotter's eulogy, Alemany gave his implicit approval of
the tone, tenor, and import of the priest's words. The Fenians must have
been overjoyed. Alemany concluded the ceremony, and six priests led
the McManus procession from the cathedral to the wharf, where the
coffin was loaded onto a ship, the *Uncle Sam*.[8] The *Uncle Sam*
embarked for Panama where the coffin traveled via rail and then was
loaded onto the New York-bound steamship *Champion*.

For more than two months New York's Fenian Brotherhood had
anticipated its role in revitalizing Irish separatism by means of the
McManus reburial. Thomas Meagher—former Young Irelander, friend of
McManus, chairman of the McManus Obsequies Committee, and a
colonel in the U.S. Army—led a delegation to visit New York's archbishop, John Hughes, to secure church approval and participation in
their planned ceremonies. The archbishop promised that every respect
that the Church could pay to the deceased would be paid in St.
Patrick's Cathedral and would include a few nonpolitical words of his
own on the occasion. In return, he exacted pledges from New York's
McManus Committee that club members would not come to the cathedral in costume and that no oration would be made subsequent to the
requiem Mass.

On September 13, twenty-four days after leaving San Francisco,
McManus's remains reached New York City. Forty-eight hours later
(after Sunday Masses), a procession along Broadway brought his coffin
to the cathedral. The next day, the Young Irelander had his solemn high-
requiem Mass; at its conclusion, Hughes addressed the congregation.
He spoke at length regarding St. Thomas Aquinas's conditions for rebellion against a government—the people's grievances must be genuine,
the resistance must be broadly based, and a reasonable chance of success must exist—and declared McManus and his fellow rebels of 1848
to have met those standards: "(O)ne who because he loved his country, did not cease on that account to love his God."[9] From a New York

[7]*Irish-American,* September 14, 1861, p. 2

[8]*San Francisco Monitor,* August 24, 1861, repr. *Evening Freeman,* September 24,
1861, p.2.

[9]*Irish-American,* September 21, 1861, p. 3.

vantage point Hughes had reconciled rebellion and religion in Ireland. After the ceremonies at St. Patrick's, a parade took the coffin to the East River, and a ferry conveyed it to Queens County's Calvary Cemetery where it remained for a month. On October 18, the committee returned McManus's remains to Manhattan and accompanied them to the North River's Pier 44. Twelve days later the *City of Washington* reached Queenstown (now Cobh) in County Cork, and the American representatives surrendered control of McManus's obsequies to their Irish colleagues. Proving Irish hierarchical hostility to nationalist funerals not to be monolithic, Archbishop William Keane of Cloyne allowed McManus's coffin to rest in his church and people to pay their respects. The next morning the parish's curate sang a High Mass for McManus. Afterward the coffin was put aboard the steamer *Lee* and taken to Cork City.

On the strength of the honors paid to McManus in the United States and Queenstown, the Cork and Dublin McManus Committees hoped the same or similar would occur in their locales. Cork's archbishop, William Delany, would not permit McManus's remains to enter any of the city's Catholic churches. Initially, Cullen did not preclude any Catholic service for McManus in Dublin. If the committee had announced that the service would not be a political demonstration— that is, staging no oration—some agreement might have been reached.[10] This proved organizationally unacceptable to the Fenians who had seized control of Dublin's McManus Committee and considered the panegyric to be critical to their long-term prospects. These graveyard machinations proved to be the conclusive undoing of any compact between the cardinal and the funeral organizers.[11] Cullen could and would not sanction any partisan secular element that interfered with the sacred aspect of the Catholic burial service, and he prohibited his diocese's priests to participate in the departed nationalist's burial services (see figure 2 for an illustration of Cullen's influence).

In San Francisco, New York, and Queenstown, Archbishops Alemany, Hughes, and Keane all had received assurances that there would be no partisan displays—that is, no uniforms would be worn inside of churches nor speeches would be made over the coffin while it was in their jurisdictions. Cullen reasonably expected the planners of the

---

[10]A. M. Sullivan to William Smith O'Brien, October 13, 1861, William Smith O'Brien Papers, National Library of Ireland (NLI) MS 447/3250.

[11]After McManus's panegyric, the Catholic Cemeteries Committee banned such pronouncements from Glasnevin.

THE FIERY CROSS!

FIGURE 2. This cartoon from the British magazine *Punch* (August 31, 1851) paints an all-encompassing picture of Cardinal Paul Cullen's influence. Image courtesy of the Multitext Project in Irish History, University College Cork. Reproduced by permission.

Dublin funeral to show him the same deference. When the McManus Committee wrote to Cullen in early October "[t]hat your Grace will be pleased to order a solemn funeral in the Cathedral for the soul of Terence Bellew McManus,"[12] he balked. To the committee's inquiry a miffed Cullen replied, "[P]ublic funeral service is not ordered in this church."[13] The archbishop also requested the committee to explain why McManus merited such honors.[14] Among the Young Irelanders

[12]E. J. Ryan to Paul Cullen, October [n.d.] 1861, Paul Cullen Papers, DDA Section 240/2, no. 122.

[13]James Murray to E. J. Ryan, October 18, 1861, Paul Cullen Papers, DDA Section 334/1 Secretaries, no. 6.

[14]*Ibid*.

McManus had not achieved any special prominence—he was simply one of many Irishmen to die in exile. When no answer to his query arrived, Cullen wrote to the planners that in such a circumstance he was not in a position to act on the matter.[15] The McManus Committee's high-handed approach and obvious political intent made support from Cullen impossible. Bishop Thomas Furlong of Ferns contended, "It's a piece of American Mountebankism which will leave for a nine days wonder and be forgotten."[16]

Isabella McManus pleaded her brother's case to Dublin's archbishop. Her first letter to Cullen broached the sound argument that the sacred services freely given to every Catholic should not be denied her sibling: "It seems to me sufficient that my brother lived and died a true Catholic to entitle his remains the same respect at least in his own country which was so freely given at the hands of strangers in a foreign land."[17] She reminded the archbishop of the many churchmen in her family. Six days after her first letter, Isabella wrote asking for the courtesy of a reply. Cullen wrote instead to Tobias Kirby, the rector of the Irish College in Rome: "I answered that such things were not ordered unless for persons who had rendered gt [great] services to religion or country, and I asked them to tell me what public services had been performed by McM." Cullen said he would incur any odium rather than show any approval for Smith O'Brien and the uprising in 1848.[18]

Before McManus's remains reached Dublin, A. M. Sullivan, editor of the *Nation* and a supporter of the more moderate forces on the McManus Committee, tried to mend fences with Cullen and to secure Church validation in the committee's effort to lead nationalist Ireland. Sullivan agreed that McManus was not of elevated public stature, and the services should not be regarded as equivalent to those of the lay Irish Catholic leader Daniel O'Connell fourteen years earlier. He wrote that Cullen, like many others, was ill informed as to the nature of the

[15]James Murray to E. J. Ryan, October 26, 1861, Paul Cullen Papers, DDA Section 334/1 Secretaries, no. 7.

[16]Thomas Furlong to Paul Cullen, November 7, 1861, Paul Cullen Papers, DDA Section 334/1, no. 102.

[17]Isabella McManus to Cullen, October 15, 1861, Paul Cullen Papers, DDA Section 340/2, no. 122.

[18]Paul Cullen to Tobias Kirby, October 31, 1865; qtd. in Emmet Larkin, *The Consolidation of the Roman Catholic Church in Ireland, 1860-1870* (Dublin, 1987), p. 65.

McManus demonstration and criticized the committee for its failure to publish a funeral program:"It ought not to surprise anyone if his Grace before taking part in them should desire to be made acquainted with the whole of the arrangements."[19] Sullivan had complained of this to Smith O'Brien two weeks earlier:"If they mean a political demonstration . . . let them say it honestly by a published statement."[20] Sullivan knew if the committee made a declaration of an intended political demonstration it would fall foul of the Party Processions Act and be open to censure.

On the morning of November 8, poster-sized copies were plastered around Dublin of a letter by Father Patrick Lavelle,[21] originally published by the *Freeman's Journal*. In it, Lavelle pointed to the action of the bishops in New York and Cloyne and declared that the laws of the Church did not differ from diocese to diocese. He cast Cullen as the agent of the empire, authoritarianism, and exploitation:"He [McManus] is denied the honours accorded to every Castle-slave, time-serving hypocrite, and whigling sycophants, whose creed is to sell his creed and his country to the first buyer for prompt payment!"[22] Lavelle's rhetoric grew hotter as the letter reached its conclusion: "And in Poland, there the strong hand of the Czar closes the Church against the patriotic priest and people alive; here the Church closes herself against the Patriotic Dead."[23] Thus a Catholic priest laid the blame for the lack of religious respect to McManus's remains squarely at the door of Dublin's archbishop, and the committee had cover.

In his commentary on the incident, Fenian leader Thomas Clarke Luby described Lavelle's letter as "well timed" and "doing yeoman's service."[24] IRB leader (aka head-centre) James Stephens proved more circumspect:"Success would be independent of Lavelle's letter which merely did something towards saving the character of the clergy" (see figure 3).[25] In response Cullen asked Lavelle's archbishop, John MacHale of Tuam, to take appropriate action. MacHale answered that

[19]*Nation*, October 26, 1861, pp 136–37.

[20]A. M. Sullivan to William Smith O'Brien, October 13, 1861, William Smith O'Brien Papers, NLI MS 447/3250.

[21]Lavelle had risen to prominence in nationalist circles through his agitation in Mayo on the land question; the priest also served as a vice president of the Brotherhood of St. Patrick, the instigators of the McManus reburial in Ireland.

[22]*Freeman's Journal,* November 8, 1861, p. 5.

[23]*Ibid.*

[24]Thomas Clarke Luby Papers.

[25]Stephens to O'Mahony, December 16, 1861, Margaret McKim Maloney Collection.

FIGURE 3. James Stephens (1823–1901), leader of the Irish Republican Brotherhood (IRB), *c.* 1866. Image courtesy of the Multitext Project in Irish History, University College Cork. Reproduced by permission.

he would send Lavelle a copy of Cullen's letter and let the priest respond to it himself. Cullen sent copies of all the correspondence and the original offensive document to the Vatican.[26] Cullen's secretary, James Murray, described Lavelle's letter as a "wicked and mischievous production."[27] Commenting on the McManus funeral, Murray wrote, "The whole thing was got up for the purpose of sowing a political demonstration and making us their servants in upholding their wicked principles."[28]

While much sound and fury resulted from Cullen's disavowal of the McManus obsequies, it did not occupy much of the IRB's leadership's time. Had Cullen given the same endorsement to their efforts as that

[26]Larkin, *The Consolidation of the Roman Catholic Church in Ireland,* pp. 68–69.
[27]James Murray to Tobias Kirby, November 8, 1861, qtd. in Larkin, *The Consolidation of the Roman Catholic Church in Ireland,* p. 68.
[28]*Ibid.*

of his American counterparts, the Fenians would have been thrice blessed; as it was, twice was enough. In a letter to John O'Mahony,[29] Stephens complained at length of the opposition of the "Trusted Leaders" (old-line Irish nationalists), but he said little about the clergy's. The Fenians kept the remnants of Young Ireland squarely in their sights. The cleric who most concerned them was not Dublin's archbishop but a mischief-making Young Irelander, Father John Kenyon. A last-minute attempt by Kenyon and his cohort John Martin to commandeer McManus's corpse failed. At its final meeting, the funeral committee settled that the oration would not be provided by an aggrieved Kenyon, and word came that Cullen might allow McManus's remains to enter the Pro-Cathedral for a Mass before the procession to Glasnevin.[30] The IRB-controlled assembly yelled "too late!"[31]—their respect for McManus's Catholicism coming a distant second to their political ambitions. The effort begun when San Francisco's Fenians disinterred McManus from the foot of Lone Mountain ended with Californian Captain Michael Smith speaking by torchlight in Glasnevin Cemetery. The longest wake in Irish history had secured the most tangible success for the Fenians. The recurring allusions to McManus's funeral in Cullen's correspondence demonstrated that it was a thorn he never quite removed from his side. In September 1865, when police arrested the IRB leadership, Cullen bragged, "Almost all the gentlemen who took part in McManus' funeral four years ago are now in prison. I was denounced on all sides for opposing that funeral. The proceedings of the last month prove I was quite right."[32]

In his examination of Fenianism, R. Vincent Comerford criticized lionizers of the McManus funeral and questioned the demonstration's importance to the development of Fenianism and the advance of Irish nationalism. He rightly challenged its milestone status as bequeathed by enthusiastic historians or nationalist propagandists who claimed it to be a "turning point" in Irish history;[33] still, Comerford's tone is overly dismissive. His comparison between attendance figures for

---

[29]John O'Mahony participated in the 1848 Uprising, helped to found the Irish Republican Brotherhood, and served as its locus in the United States.

[30]T. N. Underwood to William Smith O'Brien, January 1, 1862, William Smith O'Brien Papers, NLI MS 447/3257; Thomas Clarke Luby Papers.

[31]Thomas Clarke Luby Papers.

[32]Cullen to Kirby, October 8, 1865, qtd. in Larkin, *The Consolidation of the Roman Catholic Church in Ireland*, p. 404.

[33]R. V. Comerford, *The Fenians in Context: Irish Politics and Society, 1848-82* (Dublin, 1985), p. 78.

McManus's funeral attendance versus Queen Victoria's August 1861 visit to Ireland and attributing them to a bored populace looking for something to do shortchanges the Fenian demonstration. A large summer turnout for arguably the most famous person in the world, the monarch of the British Empire, is unsurprising; in contrast, 100,000 onlookers and a mile-long procession on a snowy morning for an indigent exile shocked the planners of McManus's procession. Police and newspaper accounts for these nineteenth-century political funerals that took place between November and February—dire weather months in Ireland—reported all as profound spectacles. Measuring the value of the obsequies with a turnstile count demeans both their immediate and long-term impacts. Notwithstanding the incalculable tote of raised public consciousness and insertion into the collective memory, the McManus funeral demonstrations raised the profile of Irish America's involvement in home affairs, helped to rein-vigorate a rebel ethos among Irishmen, sharpened the debate between nationalist factions, and deepened the divide between the majority of the Irish hierarchy and supporters of a secular Irish state. These are all weighty accomplishments for the send-off of a man that even the dyed-in-the-wool Fenian John O'Leary in his *Recollections* admitted was of low profile.

The IRB was hardly a secret organization. Few cell-assembled revolutionary groups were as frequently and effectively infiltrated by informants, had branches in another country (the United States) that regularly publicized the organization's interests and plans at conventions, or published their own newspaper. Founded by Fenian leader Stephens in November 1863, *Irish People* published a city block from Dublin Castle (the seat of British authority in Ireland). Never a moneymaker, it did raise awareness among young Catholic men who found toeing the Church's political line philosophically insufficient. Oliver Rafferty detailed how practicing Fenians remained practicing Catholics and saw their secular proclivities undermine the Church's position as social arbiter and political leader. Rank-and-file IRB members, who mirrored much of Mass-going Ireland, were dissatisfied with the Church's O'Connellite bit-by-bit reform inclinations and doubted its ability to assert itself as the guardian of Catholic Ireland's interests.[34] Fenianism had come to provide an ideological way-station for young men dissatisfied with life under British rule, and the

[34]Oliver Rafferty, *The Church, the State and the Fenian Threat 1861-75* (Basingstoke, UK, 1999), pp. 95–96.

Church had come to serve as a brake on their hostile intentions. John Francis Maguire, the MP from Cork, acknowledged this in May 1867, when he said in the House of Commons that the Irish Roman Catholic clergy served as a buffer between the people and the influence of violent men.[35]

In the Jubilee year of 1865, Cullen issued a pastoral letter that members of secret, oath-based organizations, long opposed by the Church, could only receive spiritual redress for their deviation in the confessional where they had to assure they had severed such ties. This same year Cullen crowed when he witnessed the arrest, conviction, and incarceration of much of the Fenian leadership. Despite this opposition, Fenianism continued to percolate among the Irish Catholic community, boiled over in early 1867 into its crushing failure of an attempt at armed insurrection, and revealed its true power in the countrywide reaction to executions in the uprising's wake. Even though they had backed into it, the IRB leadership had brought about a revolutionary change within Ireland, if not a successful revolution.

Throughout the Fenian funeral phenomenon that bedeviled Cullen's episcopate, his consistency stood in stark contrast to the oscillations within Irish nationalism. During the seventeen-year span under consideration the splits within nationalist Ireland proved philosophical, tactical, and generational. Whether identified as Trusted Leaders versus young men of the IRB, aspirationist versus republican, Home Rulers versus men who advocated physical force, or, as Emmet Larkin put it, ultras versus opportunists, from McManus's first funeral, when eight Hibernians served as pallbearers and Fenians sat in the pews, Irish nationalists competed among themselves for the seat at the head of the table, or more exactly, the spot at the head of the cortege. The dividing line among them was pursuit of a distinct Irish identity within the United Kingdom's political processes or a commitment to rupturing that link by whatever means proved necessary, which included revolution. To the misfortune of everyone involved, Cullen painted almost every nationalist from organizations resistant to his influence with the same condemnatory brush. He was not alone.

In the wake of the futile Fenian uprising in winter 1867, Bishop David Moriarty of Kerry declared in his sermon on the night of February 19 that eternity was not long enough nor hell hot enough to

[35]Norman, *The Catholic Church in Ireland in the Age of Rebellion*, p. 119.

punish such miscreants";[36] even Cullen found the sentiments extreme. When he read a response to Moriarty's condemnation by his nemesis Father Lavelle in the *Connaught Ranger*, Cullen conceded:"The worst of the letter is that it tells a good deal of truth."[37] In November 1867, when the British hangman William Calcraft supervised the executions of the Fenians William Allen, Michael Larkin, and William O'Brien[38] (aka the Manchester Martyrs), Cullen viewed the demonstrations sparked by the death sentences as retribution for England's support of Giuseppe Garibaldi's campaign against the pope. Using some of his kindest words regarding the IRB he wrote, "Three Fenians hanged yesterday. They were not half as bad as the Garibaldians."[39] The groundswell of support and sympathy for the Manchester Martyrs from the Catholic laity and lower clergy disquieted Dublin's cardinal. Cullen told his priests it was fine to pray for Allen, Larkin, and O'Brien as well as say private Masses for them, but they could not engage in public events that supported their politics.[40] Whereas Britain saw three murderers hanged, Catholic Ireland witnessed something quite different. Three days after the executions the veteran repealer William J. O'Neill Daunt wrote:"This is foul judicial murder."[41] With sympathies crossing class lines most of Ireland's local clergy responded to the will of their parishioners and held requiem Masses across the country. Some bishops grew discomforted at the sight of their priests embracing Fenianism. In Navan, Bishop Thomas Nulty reassigned an otherwise exemplary priest:"I removed F[ather] Mullen . . . to Kilbeg because it seems to me to be the only place in the Diocese his Fenian propensities could not do any harm."[42]

On December 1, in Cork, Youghal, and Bandon, the first set of laity-driven mock funerals in Ireland occurred. In Youghal, the *Cork Examiner* reported that almost the entire population for miles around flocked to the town's church where a large number of clergymen held

[36]*Freeman's Journal,* February 20, 1867, p. 6.

[37]Cullen to Kirby, March 18, 1867; qtd. in Edward R. Norman, *The Catholic Church in Ireland in the Age of Rebellion* (London, 1965), p. 118.

[38]Allen, Larkin, and O'Brien were arrested and convicted for their role in the escape of two Fenian leaders that resulted in the killing of a police sergeant.

[39]Cullen to Kirby, November 24, 1867; qtd. in Desmond Bowen, *Paul Cullen and the Shaping of Modern Irish Catholicism* (Dublin, 1983), p. 270.

[40]Cullen to Alessandro Barnabo, December 16, 1867; qtd. in Larkin, *The Consolidation of the Roman Catholic Church in Ireland,* p. 430.

[41]William J. O'Neill Daunt Papers.

[42]Thomas Nulty to Cullen, November 25, 1867, Paul Cullen Papers, DDA Section 334/4, no. 88.

a requiem Mass. At the service's conclusion the officiating priests went to the center aisle where an empty coffin draped in mourning rested: "Standing around this honorary shrine, the clergy chaunted (sic) in a most impressive manner that most pathetic and beautiful of Christian prayers, the burial service of the Catholic Church, the thousands of pious faithful kneeling round, joining with hearty and unaffected devoutedness."[43] A chagrined hierarchy and uncertain Dublin Castle did not know how to publicly react to such emotive and potent grass-roots displays. These bottom-up demonstrations proved so effective and had such wide-ranging actual and potential manifestations that they moved Cullen to press for the Vatican's formal censure of Fenianism lest priests be tempted to join the movement.[44] While Cullen saw the political bogeyman marching in these public funeral processions, he turned a blind eye to the personal exertions of the people who composed the Church. In Dublin, Cullen's orders to his diocese's clergy were followed, and accounts of the metropolis' immense mock funeral do not mention any priests participating.

Edward R. Norman claimed: "To Cullen it must have seemed like the McManus affair all over again."[45] From its beginning he dissented from the martyrs' phenomenon: "It appears to me to be a great mistake to canonise such men."[46] At the ongoing displays of reverence Cullen wailed: "They were not honoured or prayed for because they were good men or died penitent but because they were Fenians. The great processions were not got up for prayers but to make a display in favour of Fenianism."[47] The only thing left to Cullen and to the majority of his colleagues was to weather the surge in pro-Fenian sentiment, until, as Norman and Larkin agreed, it waned with time. To deflect some of the public's attention from the martyrs' Masses, the Dublin Archdiocese took out a page-1 advertisement in the *Freeman's Journal* announcing a solemn pontifical Mass on the feast of the Immaculate Conception (December 17) with the cardinal providing a funeral sermon on the

---

[43] *Freeman's Journal,* December 4, 1867, p. 5.

[44] Donal Kerr, "Priests, Pikes and Patriots: The Irish Catholic Church and Political Violence from the Whiteboys to the Fenians," in *Piety and Power in Ireland, 1760-1960: Essays in Honor of Emmet Larkin,* ed. Stewart J. Brown and David W. Miller (Notre Dame, 2000), pp. 16–42, here p. 37.

[45] Norman, *The Catholic Church in Ireland in the Age of Rebellion,* p. 182.

[46] Cullen to Kirby, December 20, 1867; qtd. in Larkin, *The Consolidation of the Roman Catholic Church in Ireland,* p. 431.

[47] Cullen to Kirby, February 7, 1868; qtd. in Peadar MacSuibhne, *Paul Cullen and His Contemporaries* (Naas, Ireland, 1972), 4:226.

Irish soldiers who gave their lives in defense of the Holy See.[48] In Rome, pontifical authorities told British envoys they blocked an effort by forty Fenians in the Papal Army to arrange a Mass for Allen, Larkin, and O'Brien.[49]

Whereas Cullen sought to keep the Manchester Martyrs' controversy at arm's length, Tuam's MacHale embraced it. The latter donated £5 to the national penny subscription for the martyrs and presided at a requiem Mass in their honor. Many of MacHale's fellow bishops bemoaned his action: "It is very much to be regretted that Dr. MacHale should have given such an apparent sanction to the Fenian movement. In the present excited state of the English mind it must necessarily make a very unfavourable impression,"[50] wrote Bishop John MacEvilly of Galway. MacEvilly also complained that both the Augustinian and Franciscan orders had offered Masses for the Manchester Martyrs without consulting him: "Putting religion altogether out of the question, this public display in favour of the poor Manchester men is most foolish thing imaginable."[51] With parliamentary action on large legislative issues affecting Catholic Ireland on the horizon, the general preoccupation with the Manchester executions proved an unwanted diversion for much of the Irish hierarchy.

The most significant aspect that emerged from the martyrs' mock funerals was evidence of what Comerford described as the socializing force of Fenianism. "Autonomous fraternisation"[52] filled the void in many young Irishmen's lives whose economic opportunities were limited and who would marry late if at all. The mock funerals came together by local initiatives and touched entire communities. Women and children often led the processions, and police reports detailed how "respectable persons" (members of Catholic Ireland's expanding middle class) participated. Fenianism, bereft of its veteran national leadership, dug deep into the nation's common clay and took a form that was as potent as it was ordinary in appearance. The ersatz political obsequies for Allen, Larkin, and O'Brien epitomized the threat Fenian sympathies posed to church leadership of Catholic Ireland's

---

[48]*Freeman's Journal,* December 9, 1867, p. 1.

[49]Norman, *The Catholic Church in Ireland in the Age of Rebellion,* p. 122.

[50]John MacEvilly to Cullen, December 26, 1867, Paul Cullen Papers, DDA Section 334/4, no. 96.

[51]MacEvilly to Cullen, December 27, 1867, Paul Cullen Papers, DDA Section 334/4, no. 98.

[52]Comerford, *The Fenians in Context,* p. 111.

political inclinations. Cullen addressed this challenge at the First Vatican Council where, on January 12, 1870, Pope Pius IX condemned and excommunicated the Fenians by name.[53]

Disdain for electoral politics echoed Cullen's contempt for outright rebellion. Plodding "piecemealism" might best describe his legislative philosophy, and he would take what he could get from either of a pair of bad choices. Britain's Liberals and Whigs supported Italian revolutionaries who wanted to fold papal lands into a cohesive state; Conservatives depended on northern Irish Orangemen for their majorities. Cullen accepted an alliance with the Liberal Party who entered government on the strength of Irish parliamentary support. During William Ewart Gladstone's first term as prime minister (1868–74) the disestablishment of the Church of Ireland (1869) and passage of the first Irish Land Act (1870) occurred, but the University Bill (1873) failed, because it embraced nondenominational enrollment and instruction. The great irony of the reforms that came from Gladstone's first government that addressed two of three of Cullen's political priorities was the prime minister's admission that they occurred in some part in reaction to Fenian activities.

Locally, Cullen's tepid support in the mid-1860s for the modest aims and peaceful tactics of the National Association of Ireland evolved in the 1870s into his outright opposition of the Home Rule movement (that is, an Irish parliament within the United Kingdom), its Protestant leader Isaac Butt, and the Independent Irish Party. Cullen backed the creation of the Catholic Union in October 1872, as he viewed it as a counterbalance to home government organizations. Agitation to grant amnesty for Fenian prisoners brought a portion of the IRB into the Home Rule camp. A new generation of Irish MPs dispensed with conciliation and embraced parliamentary obstructionism; they included Belfast-born Presbyterian and member of the IRB Supreme Council Joseph Biggar and the heir to an Anglo-Irish political legacy, Wicklow's Charles Stewart Parnell. Emmet Larkin detailed a political parade that had passed by both militant nationalists and the cardinal as it moved toward parliamentary independence.[54] The ten years between major political funerals saw the ineluctable advance of Irish constitutionalism.

---

[53]*Tablet*, February 5, 1870.
[54]Emmet J. Larkin, *The Roman Catholic Church and the Emergence of the Modern Irish Political System* (Washington, DC, 1996), p. 442.

cite this

In February 1877, the U.S. Fenian leader John O'Mahony died in New York City, and the transatlantic Fenian funeral machine swung into action. With constitutional Fenianism on the rise, the "ultras" sought to revitalize their fortunes with the tried and true tactic of the political funeral. Backed by U.S. money, the IRB intransigents purged their home rulers.[55] The confrontation between the home rulers and the ultra-Fenians played out in the pages of Dublin's daily newspapers. Home Ruler Alfred Webb acknowledged O'Mahony's devotion to country and his scholarly contributions to its heritage but then decried his advocacy of settling the differences between England and Ireland with the sword: "Home Rulers are now under special bonds to show the sincerity and straightforwardness of their convictions."[56] The honorary secretaries of the O'Mahony Funeral Committee, James O'Connor of the *Irishman* and Thomas Sexton of the *Nation*, responded that from its inception the campaign to repatriate the deceased Fenian had included Home Rulers. They said Irishmen who sought to assist in their country's "uprise" had more in common than in conflict: "No one can have any right to attribute a sectional or a special complexion to an act in which the participation of the nation at large is invited."[57] Webb's concerns about "coquetting with the 'party of action'"[58] illustrated the push and pull of political funerals and the strains within Irish nationalism.

Just as had been the case with McManus, when O'Mahony's remains reached Queenstown, Bishop John McCarthy of Cloyne permitted a Mass for the dead to be offered in the city's Pro-Cathedral and for the body to remain overnight. McCarthy later explained at length to Cullen how a delegation of the city's respectable Catholics had visited him, as well as assured Cullen that O'Mahony had died a true son of the Church and received the last sacraments: "I refused the High Mass because it would be regarded as a sort of Religious Sanction of the political demonstration which I knew was to follow."[59] McCarthy rationalized that since Fenians had been excommunicated by papal decree in 1870, it followed that O'Mahony, who had received the sacraments in New York, must have renounced his affiliation prior to his death. McCarthy also received assurances, which were kept, that the processions to and

[55]*Ibid.*, 207.
[56]*Freeman's Journal,* February 13, 1877, p. 5.
[57]*Freeman's Journal,* February 14, 1877, p. 7.
[58]*Freeman's Journal,* February 13, 1877, p. 5.
[59]John McCarthy to Cullen, March 5, 1877, Paul Cullen Papers, DDA Section 329/1, no. 24.

from the cathedral would be subdued with no political trappings. Still, the bishop acceded to the obvious Fenian ceremony in opposition to Cullen's expressed will and in sympathy with his flock.

Dublin's cardinal had become aware of O'Mahony in 1863 when he described him as the driving force behind the McManus funeral.[60] Two years later, writing to Archbishop Martin Spalding of Baltimore, Cullen compared O'Mahony to the Italian revolutionary Mazzini and accused both of living in quiet comfort while they sacrificed others to obtain their ends. With O'Mahony's death, the conflict between Cullen and the IRB reached its apogee. The cardinal and the funeral committee aired their positions publicly. On February 17, newspapers published a missive from the publicity-hungry funeral organizers that cited the ministrations of the Church given to O'Mahony in New York and requested "the lying-in-state of the remains for some brief period previous to the date of interment, either in the Pro-Cathedral or should your Eminence prefer, in any other church of the city."[61] Four days later Cullen responded. His letter detailed his beliefs as to the proper use of cemeteries, funeral processions, and solemn honors awarded to the dead: "It is to be regretted that in the present times, and in opposition to the feelings of all good Christians, cemeteries and funerals are diverted from their sacred purposes, and that in some countries, they die professing themselves unbelievers or Socialists or Red Republicans."[62]

Cullen traced the appropriate application of religious honors for the dead in Ireland from St. Patrick and Brian Boru to Daniel O'Connell. He questioned O'Mahony's Catholicism, noted his service as leader of the American Fenians, and wondered how O'Mahony could continue in such a role after the pope had condemned such activities: "Knowing these facts, were I to allow the remains of Mr. O'Mahony to lie in state in our Pro-Cathedral, I would seem to take on myself to approve his religious and public conduct and his projects in regard to Ireland, a responsibility which I am not inclined to assume."[63] In his best pastoral pose, Cullen urged prayer for O'Mahony's soul, and the burial went on without clerical involvement in Dublin. A witness to the funeral stated, "It was a tremendous gathering—the people very

[60]Cullen to Kirby, December 3, 1863; qtd. in MacSuibhne, *Paul Cullen and His Contemporaries* 4:158.

[61]*Cork Examiner,* February 18, 1877, p. 3.

[62]*Freeman's Journal,* February 22, 1877, p. 7.

[63]*Ibid.*

orderly, but I thought very bold and defiant looking. The Cardinal's most excellent letter has had no effect on the mob."[64] When Charles Kickham[65] gave his oration for O'Mahony outside Glasnevin Cemetery, he disputed the sentiments expressed by Dublin's cardinal and declared that generous people rejected and loathed the cold-hearted suggestion that honors should only be bestowed upon the victorious.[66] The Fenian C. G. Doran recited the prayers for the dead over O'Mahony's grave, which he would share for eternity with McManus.

Cullen received kudos not only from religious colleagues but also from pro-British portions of the press. The *Irish Times* editorialized: "He administers a severe rebuke to the men who strive, for some purpose or other, to keep up a fictitious discontent."[67] In London, the *Daily Mail* expressed relief that Cullen had refused to allow his cathedral to aid in the funerary theater: "It is not at all likely that this epistle will extinguish what remains of Fenianism, or its latest imitator Nationalism, as both are really the expression of a vague discontent made up of many discordant and fluctuating elements."[68] His supporters within the Church were effusive in their praise. Bishop MacEvilly of Galway wrote: "There is no lover of religion or sincere lover of country but must admire it and pray God fervently to grant your Eminence health and strength to defend both."[69] Archdeacon James Redmond said that a hesitant or faltering reply by Cullen would have been used as Dublin Castle's vehicle for new, restrictive legislation for Ireland and, surely alluding to Conservative Benjamin Disraeli (Britain's first prime minister of Jewish heritage), declared, "My Lord you have checkmated the Saxon, Heretical Jew."[70] Redmond wrote more fulsomely the following day, "By your reply . . . you broke up a diabolical programme intended for the prostitution of religion to the purposes of Communism."[71] Bishop Laurence Gillooly of Elphin exhibited some wishful thinking: "I think the O'Mahony interment is

---

[64]Keenan to Emly, March 4, 1877; qtd. in Larkin, *The Roman Catholic Church and the Emergence of the Modern Irish Political System*, p. 442.

[65]Rebel, patriot, poet, and journalist Charles Kickham is best known for his novel *Knocknagow, or the Homes of Tipperary* (Dublin, 1879).

[66]*Freeman's Journal*, March 5, 1877, p. 6.

[67]*Irish Times*, February 23, 1877, p. 4.

[68]*Daily Telegraph* (London), February 24, 1877, repr *Freeman's Journal*, February 26, 1877, p. 7.

[69]John MacEvilly to Cullen, February 25, 1877, Paul Cullen Papers, Section 329/1, no. 19.

[70]Redmond to Cullen, February 26, 1877, Paul Cullen Papers, Section 329/4.

[71]Redmond to Cullen, February 27, 1877, Paul Cullen Papers, Section 329/4.

London exploits the contradictions.

the last of the kind we are to be troubled with. Your Eminence's letter has shown to all who are not wilfully blind the true character of these profane exhibitions."[72] Cullen concurred: "I think we shall have no more Fenian Funerals from America."[73] The cardinal enjoyed a moment of partial prescience. No further Fenian funerals did arrive from America to trouble him, but, rather, a grand obsequial demonstration originated on his doorstep. When former British army color-sergeant Charles McCarthy passed away in Dublin on January 15, 1878, the cardinal's letter regarding O'Mahony's obsequies served as a blueprint for a public funeral that could circumvent his innate opposition to any such Fenian demonstration.

Court-martialed as an IRB organizer, McCarthy, who at age forty-four had a heart condition, had suffered badly during his twelve years as an inmate at Britain's most severe prisons. On January 13, the raucous receptions in Kingstown and Dublin held for him and his fellow former Fenian prisoners[74] caused his collapse; given McCarthy's broken health, his welcoming parades could be considered corteges attended by their subject while still alive. Less than forty-eight hours after his return to Irish soil, McCarthy attended a formal breakfast at Dublin's Morrison Hotel where he was the guest of Parnell and other parliamentarians. Shortly after his arrival, he asked for his colleague Michael Davitt, who helped him to a sofa, where he died. The indisputable public excitement attached to McCarthy's release from prison reinvigorated for his public funeral.

The prior of St. Teresa's Carmelite Church on Clarendon Street, Father Daniel Fogarty, intimated to McCarthy's friends that after the coroner finished the autopsy his chapel would receive the remains. Fogarty called on Cullen to explain his acquiescence and to seek his advice on how best to proceed. The cardinal instructed the Carmelite priest as follows: "I beg to state there must be no political exhibition of any kind in the case of McCarthy. . . . If the remains of the deceased be brought to your church, let them be kept in the chapel of the confraternity and let not be kept any longer than Thursday morning."[75]

[72]Laurence Gillooly to Cullen, March 4, 1877, Paul Cullen Papers, DDA Section 329/1.

[73]Cullen to Kirby, March 7, 1877; qtd. in Larkin, *The Roman Catholic Church and the Emergence of the Modern Irish Political System*, p. 442.

[74]Along with McCarthy, British authorities released Michael Davitt, Thomas Chambers, and Private John Patrick O'Brien from penal servitude.

[75]Cullen to Fogarty, January 15, 1878; qtd. in Larkin, *The Roman Catholic Church and the Emergence of the Modern Irish Political System*, p. 460.

Cullen also told Fogarty that he must first ascertain that McCarthy died in communion with the Church. Fogarty wrote to Cullen that McCarthy's fellow prisoners said he had taken Holy Communion at least once a month while in prison and wore the scapular of Our Lady of Mount Carmel.[76] In his negotiations with Cullen the Carmelite benefited from the public acclaim for McCarthy's fortitude and forbearance while in British custody and emphasized that the funeral organizers were not out to score points at the cardinal's expense. Fenian "ultras" had received little boost out of O'Mahony's funeral; IRB "opportunists" asserted themselves with McCarthy's obsequies.

In Fogarty's letter to Cullen of January 17, he revealed that the funeral committee had expected to return McCarthy's remains to Cork "until Mrs. McCarthy signified her wishes on yesterday that her husband shall be interred in Glasnevin. . . . In consequence of these peculiar circumstances we took the liberty of presuming the permission of your Eminence."[77] Cullen allowed McCarthy's remains to stay at St. Teresa's one additional night (through Friday), but would not allow them to interfere with Sunday services: "I hope the people[,] instead of indulging in useless display at the funeral, will pray fervently for the eternal repose of the departed soul. . . . I do not understand how his friends can justify him for having violated the oath of allegiance, which he took to the Queen, in order to join an association organised for the purpose of overthrowing her government."[78] Cullen's appreciation for order disconnected him from a large portion of public sentiment that saw McCarthy not as a man who went back on his word but as a hero who had suffered for Irish freedom. Cullen's blind spot would soon reappear.

For the three days McCarthy's remains lay in St. Teresa's Confraternity Room, all the services of his church were bestowed. Vast crowds paid their respects and reprised the sobriety and the reverence that had been common to all the nationalist funerals. When the Prisoners' Reception Committee met to make funeral arrangements, they agreed to facilitate the Carmelites and remove McCarthy's remains to the Bricklayers' Hall on the morning of Friday, January 18, for the last two days before his funeral. Breaking further still from the McManus and O'Mahony models, the committee declared its intention

---

[76]Fogarty to Cullen, January 18, 1878, Cullen Papers, DDA 326/329/7/2.

[77]Fogarty to Cullen, January 17, 1878, Cullen Papers, DDA 326/329/7/11/3.

[78]Cullen to Fogarty, January 17, 1878; qtd. in Larkin, *The Roman Catholic Church and the Emergence of the Modern Irish Political System,* p. 460.

for the funeral to partake more of a religious character and the burial service to be observed in its entirety.[79] In devising such arrangements the funeral planners admitted to the importance of having the Church, Home Rulers, and "opportunist" Fenians coming to compact. The committee forswore any oration connected to the funeral. However, when McCarthy's services ended in Glasnevin, Father Thomas, his confessor at Chatham Jail, who had moved to Dublin and served at St. Mary's on Church Street, broke both the cemetery's rules and Cullen's imperative and spoke briefly, although nonpolitically, over the grave. In so doing, local priests marked their divergence from their cardinal's preferred practices, a move that would hardly endear them to Cullen.

Further underscoring the deviation from Cullen's views, the *Freeman's Journal* published a letter to its editor, Edmund Gray, from Cashel's archbishop, Thomas William Croke. The latter included a cheque for £5 for the newly established fund for the former Fenian prisoners. Calling them the "Irish Political Prisoners" the archbishop continued, "They suffered long and much for the patriotic faith that was in them; . . . Poor M'Carthy's death presents one of the most tragic incidents in all this sad and sickening episode of our history; and I believe no true Irishman at home or abroad, can read of it without sympathy, or reflect on it without indignation."[80] Cullen lost no time in admonishing his younger colleague. On the day of the letter's publication he wrote to Croke: "I think it is not well for Your Grace to praise the Fenians who have been freed from prison. The only public work they have to boast of is that they violated their oath of allegiance to the Queen and joined a secret society directed against her."[81] Croke responded immediately to Cullen's rebuke. On January 25, he wrote to Cullen, vigorously defending his position and saying that any reading of "praise" in his letter to the *Freeman's Journal* was mistaken: "I simply state an undoubted fact, that they suffered much for what they considered the cause of Ireland, and that the country is not indifferent to their sufferings. I express an opinion moreover on McCarthy's case in particular, and I feel well assured that nine tenths of the Irish Catholic race all over the world will fully endorse."[82] Croke asserted his own convictions as well as an astuteness about his countrymen's

---

[79] *Freeman's Journal,* January 19, 1878, p. 4.

[80] *Freeman's Journal,* January 24, 1878, p. 5.

[81] Cullen to Croke, January 24, 1878, Archbishop William Croke Papers, NLI Ms/Reel 5711.

[82] Croke to Cullen, January 25, 1878; qtd. in Larkin, *The Roman Catholic Church and the Emergence of the Modern Irish Political System,* p. 462.

allegiances that were absent from Cullen's make-up. Cullen did not follow up with Croke.

The actions of the Dublin-based priests who orchestrated and conducted McCarthy's funeral services combined with the exchanges between Croke and Cullen previewed the coming close alliance between the Catholic clergy and a newly energized Home Rule movement. A review of the members of the McCarthy's reception and funeral committees—Parnell, Davitt, Patrick Egan, John Dillon, and so forth—foreshadowed the coming new departure in Irish politics in which militants and parliamentarians found common ground in the pursuit of Home Rule. After thirty-five years of this *realpolitik*, militant nationalists would return to the political funeral as a vehicle for both ideological espousal and revolutionary preview. When Jeremiah O'Donovan Rossa was returned to Ireland for burial in 1915 and a laying-in-state at Dublin's Pro-Cathedral that was approved by Archbishop William Walsh, much of the old Fenian's funeral committee was composed of the future leadership of the 1916 Easter Rising. The McManus and McCarthy obsequies bookended a period of conflict and consternation between the leader of the Archdiocese of Dublin and Irish nationalists, with inconclusive results as to which party actually gained the upper hand. For all of the nationalist funerals except for O'Mahony's, a priest led the concluding rites of the Christian burial service. Cullen attempted to deny Fenians the full honors of their Church at the political obsequies in his diocese, but clerical dissenters evaded some of his prohibitions, the potency of these public displays overrode his wishes, and Fenianism's endemic socializing effectiveness could not be inhibited. Conversely, Cullen's success in "Romanizing" the Irish Church endured for more than a century; thus, with such a record, the IRB memorial services could be considered by some as minor failures in Cullen's career. The cardinal died nine months after McCarthy's funeral, received an immense funeral of his own, and was buried, according to his wishes, below the high altar in Holy Cross College, Clonliffe.

But how did British officials view this internal conflict?

RE-EVALUATING THE ROLE OF "NATIONAL" IDENTITIES IN THE AMERICAN CATHOLIC CHURCH AT THE TURN OF THE TWENTIETH CENTURY: THE CASE OF LES PETITES FRANCISCAINES DE MARIE (PFM)

BY

FLORENCEMAE WALDRON[*]

Ethnic divisions and nationalism dominate the scholarship on the Church's efforts to incorporate immigrants in the decades around 1900. By studying nuns' perceptions of their place in the Church in their own words, the author argues that female religious may not have prioritized ethnic distinctions as highly as their male counterparts did. Examining how founding members of the Petites Franciscaines de Marie (PFM) understood their ethnic identity in relation to their identity as nuns, this article challenges prevailing interpretations of nationalism among ethnic Catholics in the United States, while suggesting the importance of incorporating women's views into a fuller understanding of church history.

Keywords: French Canadians; gender; nuns, nationalism; New England

Despite recent growth in interest and scholarship on North American female religious orders, much work remains with regard to incorporating these insights into the historical narrative of the U.S. Catholic Church or considering what an analysis sensitive to changing definitions of manhood and womanhood can add to this history. Because female religious had different positions and responsibilities within the Church, seeing the Church through their eyes can potentially offer new perspectives on the history of Catholicism in the

[*]Dr. Waldron is a research associate in the Department of History at Franklin & Marshall College in Lancaster, Pennsylvania. For helpful feedback on earlier versions of this essay, the author is indebted to Elaine Beretz, John McClymer, R. Emmet McLaughlin, and the anonymous reviewers of *The Catholic Historical Review*. Unless otherwise noted, all translations are the author's.

United States. French Canadian immigrant nuns remain especially marginalized in this historiography. By focusing on the Petites Franciscaines de Marie (PFM), an order established in the United States by French Canadian immigrants, this essay will consider how shifting our focus from male church officials to female religious can alter our understanding of the relationship between religious and ethnic identities. Moreover, its use of previously unavailable sources highlights the importance of exploring how nuns understood their position in Church and society through their own words and records.

On an organizational level, the Catholic Church is a universal institution whose loyalties supersede national boundaries. Yet within U.S. immigrant communities, ethnically homogeneous local parishes have often served as bulwarks of ethnic identity and sometimes as bases of collective action on behalf of political battles still being waged at home. Scholarship on French Canadian migration to the United States in the decades around 1900 contains numerous accounts of how important such "national" parishes, defined by common language and ancestry rather than geography, were to Quebecois[1] migrants. In the New England communities where they settled, priests and lay leaders alike fought to preserve their distinct French Canadian identity at the parochial level. Periodic skirmishes with bishops over the right to ethnically homogeneous congregations with priests from Quebec were part of this struggle. While interactions between Irish American bishops and their French Canadian constituents were not always antagonistic,[2] the ethnic presses of the late 1800s and early 1900s indicate that overall these relationships were, as one historian put it, "rarely amicable"—an assessment echoed by the bulk of the secondary literature.[3]

---

[1]*Québécois* and *Québécoise* have only recently become widespread self-identifiers among persons from Quebec; migrants *c.* 1900 called themselves *canadiens* and *canadiennes, canadiens-français* and *canadiennes-français,* and (especially after 1900 and among the U.S.-born) *franco-américains* and *franco-américaines.* In using the anglicized (unaccented) version *Quebecois* as both adjective and noun when referring to historical subjects, this essay follows the practice of Pierre Anctil, Yves Roby, C. D. Rolfe, Nive Voisine, and others in distinguishing Quebec migrants from Acadians (French-ancestry Canadians from the Maritimes).

[2]Yves Roby, "De Canadiens français des États-Unis à Franco-Américains: une analyse des discours de l'élite franco-américaine," in *Identité et cultures nationales: L'Amérique française en mutation,* ed. Simon Langlois (Sainte-Foy, Canada, 1995), pp. 207–32, here p. 209.

[3]In original: "rarement amicales"; Yves Frenette, "La genèse d'une communauté canadienne-française en Nouvelle-Angleterre: Lewiston, Maine, 1800–1880" (PhD dis-

In this regard, Quebecois émigrés had much in common with other Catholic immigrants at the time. By 1900, most U.S. bishops descended from earlier Irish immigrants,[4] who had never faced the language barrier that later non-English-speaking migrants encountered. These Irish American bishops were keenly aware of anti-Catholic currents in mainstream American society, which culminated in the xenophobic campaigns of the 1920s Ku Klux Klan revival.[5] By adopting English and acculturating to life in the United States, many bishops believed, the newer migrants would help to unite the U.S. Catholic Church and strengthen the Church in its battles against the dominant Protestant culture.[6] As a result, later generations of German, Italian, French Canadian, and Polish immigrants, along with Mexican Americans, all fought with U.S. bishops over how their ethnic group would practice their faith and how each parish would relate to the larger diocesan hierarchy.[7] Some Catholic immigrant groups had relatively harmonious relationships with Irish bishops,

---

sertation, Université Laval, 1988), p. 345. See also Yves Roby, "Les Franco-Américains et les évêques 'irlandais,'" in *Religion catholique et appartenance franco-américaine—Franco-Americans and Religion: Impact and Influence*, ed. Claire Quintal (Worcester, MA, 1993), pp. 11-16; *idem*, "Un demi-siècle de luttes: Les Franco-Américains et l'épiscopat de la Nouvelle-Angleterre," *Cap-aux-Diamants,* 61 (2000), 34-37; Michael J. Guignard, "Maine's Corporation Sole Controversy," in Quintal, *Religion catholique*, pp. 17-24; Mark Paul Richard, "From *Canadien* to American: The Acculturation of French-Canadian Descendants in Lewiston, Maine, 1860 to the Present" (PhD dissertation, Duke University, 2001), esp. chap. 3.

[4]Notable exceptions to this rule include the Spanish in the Southwest, French in Louisiana, and a heavily Germanic episcopate in the upper Midwest; see Robert D. Cross, *The Emergence of Liberal Catholicism in America* (Cambridge, MA, 1958), p. 22.

[5]For an overview of the Klan revival and the Americanization campaign it inspired within American Catholicism, see Jay Dolan, *In Search of an American Catholicism: A History of Religion and Culture in Tension* (Oxford, 2002), pp. 134-46.

[6]Frenette, "La genèse d'une communauté," pp. 273-74.

[7]Among the many works on these struggles, see Colman J. Barry, O.S.B., *The Catholic Church and the German-Americans* (Milwaukee, 1953); Theodore Andrews, *The Polish National Church in America and Poland* (London, 1953); Rudolph J. Vecoli, "Peasants and Prelates: Italian Immigrants and the Catholic Church," *Journal of Social History,* 2 (1969), 217-68; Richard M. Linkh, *American Catholics and European Immigrants 1900-1924* (New York, 1975); John J. Bukowczyk, "Mary the Messiah: Polish Immigrant Heresy and the Malleable Ideology of the Roman Catholic Church, 1880-1930," *Journal of American Ethnic History,* 4 (1985), 5-32; Jay P. Dolan and Gilberto M. Hinojosa, eds., *Mexican Americans and the Catholic Church, 1900-1965* (Notre Dame, 1994). In contrast, Wisconsin's Polish immigrants fought similar battles not with Irish bishops, but with bishops primarily of German, Austrian, or Swiss descent; Anthony J. Kuzniewski, *Faith and Fatherland: The Polish Church War in Wisconsin, 1896-1918* (Notre Dame, 1980).

and some communities also wrestled internally with championing ethnic consciousness versus submitting to church authority.[8] Bishops' overarching attempts to unite Catholics in the United States, and the backlash these "assimilationist" efforts inspired among ethnic priests and their parishioners, dominate the scholarly literature on this era's Catholic immigrants.

Did female religious side with male priests in defending their ethnic turf against bishops whom they perceived as hostile and assimilationist? Alternatively, could nuns not have cared less about connections between their religious identity and their ethnic identity? Or did they understand the relationship between the two in some other way completely? On these and similar questions, the scholarly record is silent. We know that despite—or perhaps in some cases, because of— the push to "Americanize," ethnic parishes not infrequently also served as sites of acculturation to American society, even while helping their members to preserve traditional worship practices, customs, and language.[9] We also know that nuns were key players in these processes. In New England's "Little Canadas," for example, French-speaking nuns ran the parochial schools in which Quebecois migrants' children studied religion and Canadian history in French while learning English through their classes on American history and government. But such data indicate little about how the nuns themselves understood their place within the U.S. Catholic Church or where they stood on its debates over national identity.

As a historian of gender and international migration, I first asked these questions while working on a larger project, which explores how ideas of gender shaped the migration process for New England's French Canadian immigrants from 1870–1930. Whether clergy or laity, men dominate the historiography on French Canadian national

---

[8]On amicable relationships, see June G. Alexander, *The Immigrant Church and Community: Pittsburgh's Slovak Catholics and Lutherans, 1880-1915* (Pittsburgh, 1987); for an example of internal conflicts, see Victor Greene, *For God and Country: The Rise of Polish and Lithuanian Ethnic Consciousness in America, 1860-1910* (Madison, 1975).

[9]This is the central argument of Richard's "From *Canadien* to American"; see also Stephen J. Shaw's *The Catholic Parish as a Way-Station of Ethnicity and Americanization: Chicago's Germans and Italians, 1903-1939* (Brooklyn, 1991), on similar dual functions in Chicago national parishes. For New England's French Canadians, parish naturalization clubs, which drew members from a parish's adult male population and met in the parish social hall, are just one example of parish-sanctioned Americanization.

parishes; previous works have ignored whether nuns and laywomen likewise bound their Catholic faith to their ethnic identity. A dearth of scholarship on how nuns conceptualized their identities as female religious, in their own words and from their own records, in part explains this omission. The tumultuous origins of the Petites Franciscaines de Marie (also known as the Little Franciscans of Mary or PFM) make this order an intriguing case study for examining such issues of self-identity and self-perception. Prior to my 2004 request to access the order's private annals, no outside researcher had ever read these documents. While nationalism may dominate the historical narrative of the U.S. Catholic Church at the turn of the twentieth century, a careful reading of the PFM's records indicates that this interpretation is at odds with how the order's founding members defined their place within the Church. In turn, this variance raises the possibility that the nationalistic focus so prominent in our understanding of American Catholicism during this era may have rung truer for male clerics and laymen than for women's religious orders and other female constituents.

The PFM are the oldest of three Catholic orders that French Canadian migrants founded in the United States.[10] When I began to explore their history, I realized that despite their close ties to fellow migrants and to Quebec, the PFM drew upon "national"[11] allegiances in ways very different from the patterns so well documented among Quebecois migrant priests and laymen. While the latter often linked their Catholic faith to their "national" identity as French Canadians,

---

[10]Quebecois migrants also founded the Sœurs de Sainte-Jeanne-d'Arc (SSJA) in Worcester in 1914 and the secular Institut Saint-Pie X (open to priests, laymen, and married couples) in Manchester, NH, in 1940. Yves Garon, A.A., "Religieuses franco-américaines: les Sœurs de Sainte-Jeanne d'Arc," in Quintal, *Religion catholique*, pp. 47–52, here p. 51; *ibid.*, "The Congregation of the Sisters of Saint Joan of Arc: A Franco-American Foundation," in *Steeples and Smokestacks: A Collection of Essays on the Franco-American Experience in New England,* ed. Claire Quintal (Worcester, 1996), pp. 217–23, here p. 222n7.

[11]Note that the "nations" involved were not the United States and Canada, but the United States and Quebec. Although Quebec remains a Canadian province, many French Canadians have long thought of Quebec as *la nation canadienne-française,* a phrase that evokes not just homeland but also sovereignty. In the late 1800s and early 1900s, references in the migrant press to *nationale* clubs and events (such as *sociétés nationaux,* ethnic organizations of Quebec émigrés, and the June 24 feast of St. John the Baptist, which French Canadians have long deemed their *"fête nationale"*), or to *notre nationalité* and *nos nationaux* (used for those still in Canada and fellow migrants alike), referred not to Canada or Canadians in general, but to French Canada (i.e., Quebec) and French Canadians.

from the outset the founding members of the PFM years invoked national allegiances only when immediate needs justified doing so, and their proclamations more often reflected expediency than principle. The PFM's early history, as the sisters themselves recorded it at the end of their first decade and in their correspondence from their early years, suggests that common bonds as Catholic women and female religious, rather than "national" ties, lay at the core of their identity.

* * *

The PFM mark 1889 as the year their order was born. That summer, Father Joseph Brouillet—head of Notre-Dame-des-Canadiens (NDDC), the first *canadien* parish in Worcester, Massachusetts—decided that his parish needed someone to care for its many orphans; to this end, he began to recruit young women from his parish for a new religious order he planned to establish.[12] Thus, while the PFM originated among Worcester's French Canadian émigrés, from its inception the order was characteristically American in several respects. First, whether Brouillet realized it or not, he was hardly the first Catholic clergyman in the United States to create a new order in response to pressing local needs; other bishops and priests had done so throughout the 1800s, establishing an indigenous precedent for communities engaged in active charitable works that contrasted sharply with the European tradition of cloistered contemplative orders.[13] Second, Brouillet indicated no desire to establish a two-tier membership within his foundation. The distinction between well-bred "choir nuns" and less-educated "lay sisters," women from slightly more modest backgrounds, had continued to flourish in Quebec's female religious communities, both indigenous and transplanted from Europe, as recently as 1800.[14] Yet this two-tier system was never a feature of orders founded in the United States, and it

---

[12]See Sister Marie-Michel-Archange (Michelle Garceau), P.F.M., *Par ce signe tu vivras: Histoire de la congregation des Petites franciscaines de Marie 1889-1955* (Baie-Saint-Paul, 1955), esp. chap. 1; reprinted in English as *By This Sign You Will Live: History of the Congregation of the Little Franciscans of Mary 1889-1955*, trans. Sister Marie-Octave, P.F.M., and Betty Dunn (Worcester, MA, 1964).

[13]Mary Ewens, O.P., *The Role of the Nun in Nineteenth-Century America* (New York, 1978), pp. 68-69, 128-30, 135, 213-14.

[14]Substantial dowries for new choir sisters (and with these dowries, the two-tier system within religious orders) remained the norm in Quebec until the early 1800s, when they began to fall by the wayside; Micheline D'Allaire, *Les dots des religieuses au Canada français, 1639-1800: Étude économique et sociale* (Montreal, 1986), p. 194.

remained problematic for those transplanted communities who attempted to preserve such distinctions.[15]

Although Brouillet's first recruit was the American-born daughter of Quebec immigrants, many of the other women he solicited had been born in Canada and later migrated as children. As word of the new order and its ministry spread, other women from nearby towns and as far away as Montreal flocked to Worcester to join.[16] While documentation on the family backgrounds of the order's founding members is scarce—and even less exists for those who eventually left the group without pronouncing vows—it appears that overall, those who heeded Brouillet's call were from modest means. Here, too, the new order had more in common with other nineteenth-century U.S. foundations than it did with contemporary orders in Quebec. The father of Sister Marie-Joseph, the only original member born in the United States, was a grocer; yet despite his relative prosperity, Marie-Louise Rondeau could only fulfill her childhood dream of finishing her education at a Quebec convent school by working first to earn the necessary tuition. Of the other founding members who lived in Worcester before joining the order, two were the daughters of carpenters, the fathers of two others worked as unskilled laborers, and another's father was a railroad engineer. Sister Marie-Dominique (Lumina Bolduc), who herself had worked before joining the group, left her widowed mother to enter the community. Of those from outside greater Worcester, Sister Marie-des-Sept-Douleurs (Emma Decelles) had lived on her own as a Fall River textile-mill worker before she joined the group at age thirty-two. Likewise, the Perron siblings—Zelie, age thirty-eight (Sister Marie-Frederic), and Agnes, age thirty-four (Sister Marie-de-Bon-Secours)—left jobs as paid lay employees at the Grey Nuns' orphanage in Montreal, where they had worked for more than half their lives, for the chance that the new Worcester order offered them to become full-fledged nuns.[17] That the Perron sisters

---

[15]Ewens, *Role of the Nun*, p. 279; Jo Ann Kay McNamara, *Sisters in Arms: Catholic Nuns through Two Millennia* (Cambridge, MA, 1996), pp. 581–82. Those communities that attempted a two-tier membership in the United States began to phase out such systems in the late 1800s and early 1900s; only with Vatican II was the two-tier system in female religious orders finally abolished globally in the 1960s.

[16]See Marie-Michel-Archange, *Par ce signe*, chaps. 2–3.

[17]Biographical data comes from the 1870, 1890, and 1891 editions of *Worcester Directory* (Worcester), and *Le Worcester Canadien: Directoire des canadiens-français de Worcester*, vol. XIV (Worcester, 1900), as well as Marie-Michel-Archange, *Par ce signe,* especially chap. 7, and the foundresses' necrology files preserved in the community's archives at the Maison-Mère, Baie-Saint-Paul, Quebec.

had worked so long in Montreal without taking vows suggests in part that they did not meet the financial requirements of an order that still collected dowries from prospective members; not until the twentieth century would candidates for female religious life in Quebec come primarily from the working classes.[18]

The small orphanage was overflowing with charges by spring 1890 (see figure 1), around the time a rift developed between Brouillet and his spiritual daughters on issues ranging from whom the orphanage would serve to when the women could progress with their religious vocations. As John McClymer has noted, while U.S. parishes and parochial schools often adhered to ethnic exclusivity at this time, this was never the case for Catholic orphanages or other charitable institutions in North America.[19] Despite this, Brouillet favored accepting only French Canadian children to the orphanage, even if their parents, alive and well, were simply seeking affordable child care.[20] Brouillet's vision of an "orphanage" that offered child care was a well-established practice in Quebec's growing cities by this time. Admitting other children for a small monthly fee was one source of needed revenue for orphanages; and despite cultural dictates stating that *canadienne* wives and mothers belonged at home, nuns in Montreal and other cities ran orphanage/day care centers to address the needs of a growing female workforce.

In contrast to Brouillet's view on who should occupy the limited slots in the women's chronically overcrowded home, the women preferred accepting parentless Catholics of all backgrounds over the children of *canadiens* who thought a mother's place was in the workforce, rather than at home caring for her children. While the women firmly believed that they had been called to mother the truly

---

[18]Danielle Jutreau and Nicole Laurin, *Un métier et une vocation: Le travail des religieuses au Québec, de 1901 à 1971* (Montreal, 1997); Lucia Ferretti and Chantal Bourassa, "L'éclosion de la vocation religieuse chez les sœurs dominicaines de Trois-Rivières: pour un complément aux perspectives de l'historiographie récente," *Histoire sociale/Social History*, 36 (2003), 225-53.

[19]See Micheline Dumont-Johnson, "Des garderies au XIXᵉ siècle: Les salles d'asile des sœurs grises de Montreal," *Revue d'histoire de l'Amérique française*, 34 (1980), 27-55; Bettina Bradbury, *Working Families: Age, Gender, and Daily Survival in Industrializing Montreal* (Toronto, 1993), esp. chap. 6; John McClymer, "'Rebellion against Priest': Making a Niche in a Late Nineteenth-Century American City," *The Massachusetts Historical Review*, 10 (2008), 1-22.

[20]Richard L. Gagnon, *A Parish Grows Around the Common: Notre-Dame-des-Canadiens, 1869-1995* (Worcester, 1995), p. 40.

FIGURE 1. Sisters and orphans at the Orphanage St. Francis of Assisi, Worcester, Massachusetts, early 1890s. Archives de la Maison-Mère, Baie-Saint-Paul, Quebec. Reproduced by permission of Les Petites Franciscaines de Marie.

orphaned, regardless of background, the practical motivations of finances also entered their calculations. As an active order that lived the Franciscan rule of poverty, the women's founding tenets included begging daily for alms to support themselves and their charges; but as word spread that Brouillet accepted children who were not orphans, donations from the French Canadian community dropped, as patrons agreed with the would-be nuns that mothers' place was in the home, not in the workforce—a somewhat anomalous situation, given the city's limited female job options.[21] Moreover, Brouillet had initially

[21]Even in the textile-dominated economies to which many Quebecois migrants gravitated, public opinion sided against outside employment for married women; the phenomenon's relative rarity in less female-oriented employment markets such as Worcester made French Canadians there less likely to tolerate such deviations from what they deemed appropriate gender roles among fellow migrants. See FlorenceMae Waldron, "'I never dreamed it was necessary to *marry!*': Women and Work in New England French Canadian Communities, 1870-1930," *Journal of American Ethnic History*, 24, no. 2 (2005), 34-64; see also Joy Parr, *The Gender of Breadwinners: Women, Men, and Change in Two Industrial Towns 1880-1950* (Toronto, 1990).

promised the women that they would make their first vows a year after adopting religious habits; yet as the first one-year anniversaries approached, his refusal to discuss the subject further strained his relations with the women.[22]

As donations continued to fall short of expenses, in August 1890 the young women—seeking to protect their communal property from Brouillet, and themselves and their families from creditors—incorporated their group in Massachusetts, with the stated mission of maintaining "a home for orphans and for the elderly who are in need" and educating "poor and abandoned children."[23] Then, perplexed because Brouillet still refused to discuss moving forward with their vocations, several of the women went to Springfield for an audience with Bishop Patrick T. O'Reilly, hoping he could convince Brouillet to commit to a date.[24] Only upon their arrival, when it soon became clear that O'Reilly had no idea who they were, did the would-be nuns learn that Brouillet had not secured O'Reilly's permission to start a new order.

As McClymer has observed, Brouillet never explicitly stated why he neglected even to consult his superior—let alone gain O'Reilly's approval—before calling young women to his new foundation. According to both the custom for U.S. nuns since their first appearance in 1790 and the women's own incorporation statement, ultimate responsibility for supporting a new community (financially and otherwise) rested not with Brouillet's parish but with the diocese; hence gaining episcopal sanction should have been Brouillet's first step.[25]

[22]See Marie-Michel-Archange, *Par ce signe,* chap. 3.

[23]In original:"un foyer pour les orphelins et les vieillards nécessiteux";"enfants pauvres et abandonnés." Marie-Michel-Archange, *Par ce signe,* p. 80.

[24]Prior to the Diocese of Worcester's formation, Worcester was under the jurisdiction of the Diocese of Springfield.

[25]The custom of U.S. orders answering directly to bishops stems in part from the fact that until 1908, when the country lost its designation as a "mission field," U.S.-based religious were under the authority of the Congregation of the Propaganda in Rome rather than canon law, and partly from the fact that—although Pope Benedict XIV acknowledged the beneficial works of noncloistered orders by legalizing their existence in 1749—active congregations were technically not true religious, according to Catholic law and in the minds of many church officials, prior to 1900. There is no indication, however, that O'Reilly and Beaven held the women's noncloistered status against them. Rather, it seems the bishops were reluctant to recognize the group first because Brouillet had not sought permission to establish a new order and later because they did not want the diocese to be financially liable for the group, especially given Brouillet's continued efforts to destroy it. See Ewens, chap. 1, and Marie-Michel-Archange, *Par ce signe,* chap. 3.

Moreover, while U.S. bishops had authority to establish new orders, priests generally did not. As one of the city's English-language newspapers reported, Brouillet believed he had once received such authority, as well as other privileges beyond those of ordinary priests, from a Father Frederick in Quebec (possibly Blessed Father Frédéric Janssoone, O.F.M.).[26] Then again, many of the sentiments Brouillet and other Quebecois priests in the United States supported—from their rights to ethnic or "national" parishes and the importance of parochial schools to their wariness of American Protestants—were at odds with the actions and beliefs of Worcester's Irish Catholic clergy, whose liberal interpretation of Catholicism in the late 1880s and early 1890s included forging ties with American Protestants and favoring public education over parochial schools.[27] These two distinct viewpoints represent facets of the larger battle between conservative and liberal forces in the American Catholic Church during the late 1800s; in this case, the women who became known as the PFM were caught in the middle.

That Brouillet found himself opposite local Irish clergy in such conflicts no doubt influenced his reluctance to trust fully in his Irish-born bishop. Even after becoming the first bishop of the new Diocese of Springfield in 1870, O'Reilly continued as pastor of St. John's parish in Worcester until 1885, two years after Brouillet had become pastor of NDDC.[28] Brouillet's assessment "that Irish and French could not get along well together,"[29] as reported in a local newspaper during coverage of Brouillet's disputes with his female recruits, suggests that Brouillet had a well-established (and no doubt well-founded) history of distrusting local Irish priests by the early 1890s. This distrust was likely fueled by everything from their willingness to cooperate with local Protestants to their reluctance to establish parish schools. For example, an 1884 mandate from the Third Plenary Council of Baltimore dictated that each U.S. parish should have its own school by 1886 or face pastoral reassignment and episcopal sanctions. O'Reilly's unwillingness to enforce this decree on his Worcester colleagues helps to explain why only one of

[26]"French Orphanage Facts," *Worcester* [MA] *Daily Telegram*, January 19, 1891, p. 4; McClymer, "'Rebellion.'"

[27]See Timothy J. Meagher, "'Irish All the Time': Ethnic Consciousness among the Irish in Worcester, Massachusetts, 1880-1905," *Journal of Social History*, 19 (1985), 273-303, here esp. 277-78, on the views of Worcester's Irish clergy.

[28]Gagnon, *A Parish Grows*, pp. 26, 35.

[29]"French Orphanage Facts."

the city's seven Irish parishes had a parochial school before 1893.[30] Brouillet, on the other hand, not only worked to expand NDDC's parish school during his tenure but also opened a school for St. Joseph's—a mission chapel affiliated with NDDC—five years before St. Joseph's became a separate parish.[31] Brouillet likely believed, as did many French Canadian priests in New England, that parish schools were key to maintaining Quebec's beliefs, customs, and language among the migrants' children.[32] Whatever his reasons, Brouillet's failure to consult O'Reilly in advance had dire implications for the women who responded to Brouillet's call. O'Reilly was not amused to discover that Brouillet had overstepped his authority, and Brouillet was furious that his protégées had consulted his superior. Learning that the women had incorporated their group without his knowledge or consent only fueled Brouillet's anger.

Thus began the women's seven-year fight to secure not only the right to exist as an order but also permission to remain in Worcester. As per their rules of incorporation and appropriate channels of command in the Church, the women continued to consult O'Reilly on how best to deal with Brouillet's demands that they either revoke their corporation or remove their habits and return to secular life. Both the bishop and their secular supporters, including a sympathetic French Canadian lawyer, urged them not to choose either path. Yet by refusing Brouillet's ultimatum and seeking outside counsel, thus intensifying Brouillet's trouble with his superior, the women's actions provoked Brouillet beyond the breaking point. In January 1891, during one of the coldest winters on record in Worcester, Brouillet locked the women out of the orphanage, confiscating their property and most of their orphans. Left with only the clothes on their backs, what followed tested the women's decision to model their religious lives upon the radical Franciscan ideal of literal poverty: for two months, the women and the four orphans still in their care lived in what they later dubbed the "House of Misery," a drafty, uninsulated barn, with insufficient food and clothing and without furniture or bedding (see figure 2). The combined effects of exposure to the elements and inadequate nour-

---

[30]Thomas C. McAvoy, C.S.C., *A History of the Catholic Church in the United States* (Notre Dame, 1969), pp. 259–60; Gagnon, *A Parish Grows*, p. 24; Timothy J. Meagher, *Inventing Irish America: Generation, Class, and Ethnic Identity in a New England City, 1880–1928* (Notre Dame, 2001), pp. 133, 159, 262.

[31]Gagnon, *A Parish Grows*, pp. 42–43; Kenneth R. Desautels, *History of Saint Joseph Parish, 1820–1992* (Worcester, MA, 1992), p. 18.

[32]See Roby, "De Canadiens français" (see above, n. 3), p. 212.

FIGURE 2. The "House of Misery," on the outskirts of Worcester, Massachusetts, *c.* 1891, Archives de la Maison-Mère Baie-Saint-Paul, Quebec. Reproduced by permission of Les Petites Franciscaines de Marie.

ishment led two of the women to premature deaths and left several others with lifelong ailments.[33]

Equally damaging to a group that begged for its daily bread, Brouillet sought to discredit the "Brown Nuns," as locals dubbed them because of their brown habits, both within Worcester and throughout the region. First, he brought in an established order from Canada to take over the orphanage that the young women had begun. Next, he refused to hear their confessions, denied them seats at Sunday Mass, would not allow them to receive Holy Communion, and ordered the priests in Notre Dame's mission chapels to follow suit. His refusal to absolve the women or give them communion led to rumors, which Brouillet did nothing to discourage, that the Little Franciscans had been excommunicated; on these grounds, Brouillet urged Worcester's French Canadians to support the newcomers from Quebec rather than the "rebellious" imposters.[34] This prompted many male house-

[33]See Marie-Michel-Archange, *Par ce signe*, chaps. 4 and 7.

[34]Variations on this epithet dogged the women in the months after their disputes with Brouillet became public knowledge. After breaking the story under the headline "Rebellion against Priest," the *Worcester Daily Telegram* (hereafter, *Telegram*) routinely

hold heads, who agreed with Brouillet's condemnations of the "Brown Nuns," to turn away the young women on their begging tours. As a result, wives—who were more likely to applaud the nuns' efforts on behalf of motherless children than heed Brouillet's slanderous words and actions—secretly sent their children running after the women with donations. On this basis, Brouillet subsequently charged the women with sowing familial discord, adding this to the grounds on which he denied them access to the sacraments.[35]

Wanting no part of what they saw as an internal community dispute, O'Reilly and his successor, Thomas D. Beaven, largely refused or ignored the women's repeated pleas to mediate. Before his death, O'Reilly tried to avoid dealing with them altogether by stating that because the Springfield diocese could not afford the financial burden of serving as headquarters for a new religious order, the PFM would get his approval to remain in Worcester only if they established their motherhouse elsewhere. But finding a base location for the new order became increasingly difficult, as Brouillet made his views on the PFM known throughout New England, while local English-language newspapers kept those outside Worcester's Quebecois migrant enclave abreast of the dispute, with coverage that did not always enhance the women's reputation.[36] That the women's infamy reached as far as Quebec became clear in March 1891, when the father of the Perron siblings became so upset by the stories he heard that he rushed to Worcester, demanding in vain that his daughters quit the order and return to Canada. Rumors regarding the PFM's actions and questionable character help to explain why the women only obtained permission to open a novitiate in late 1891, in the remote Quebec community of Baie-Saint-Paul, thanks in part to a priest who was desperate to staff his asylum for the poor and "feeble-

---

dubbed the women "rebelling" sisters or "rebels" in even their most positive accounts, following Brouillet's practice of calling the women "[les] rebelles" before other priests. See the articles "Rebellion against Priest," January 13, 1891, p. 1; "French Orphanage Squabble," January 16, 1891, p. 1; "They Are Poor but Happy," January 26, 1891, p. 1; see also Marie-Michel-Archange, *Par ce signe*, p. 112.

[35]See Marie-Michel-Archange, *Par ce signe,* chap. 5.

[36]Although some reports portrayed the women sympathetically, others in the *Telegram* and its rival, the *Worcester Daily Spy* (hereafter, *Spy*), hinted at alleged sexual improprieties among the founding members and similar shortcomings in Durocher, their spiritual guide until Brouillet dismissed him. For example, "Sisters Desert Orphanage," *Telegram*, January 14, 1891, p. 1; "Priest against Priest," *Spy*, January 16, 1891, p. 1. Durocher denied all charges against him in "French Orphanage Squabble."

minded."[37] In early 1892, Louis-Nazarre Bégin, bishop of the Diocese of Chicoutimi, sanctioned them as an order of Regular Franciscan Tertiates in his diocese;[38] with Bégin's approval, the women had taken the first step toward becoming an official religious order.[39]

Yet despite this permission, a series of circumstances, among them O'Reilly's death and Brouillet's ongoing rancor, continued to challenge the women's efforts to stay in Worcester, the city they called "the cradle of the Institute."[40] Following O'Reilly's death in May 1892, Beaven did his best to avoid upholding O'Reilly's bargain with the women. Although the Brown Nuns had Bégin's agreement to house their novitiate and motherhouse in his diocese, Brouillet's stance made Beaven reluctant to allow the women to continue their operations in Worcester, where they competed directly for donations with the order Brouillet had imported to replace them. Thus, for the next six years, even as they sought to clear the remaining hurdles standing between them and full canonical recognition, the ten surviving foundresses and their protégées waged a simultaneous battle to remain in the city that had given birth to their order.[41]

[37]Rev. Ambroise-Martial Fafard, Baie-Saint-Paul, telegram to Sisters in Worcester, n.d. (c. early November 1891), *Annales de la Fondation* (hereafter, *AF*), 1:160, Localisation B/11/4/6-B, Boîte B/2/1/1-A, Centre d'archives regional de Charlevoix (CARC), Baie-Saint-Paul, Quebec. Originally contained in three handwritten volumes, the *AF* were transcribed into seven typed volumes (1, 2A-2C, and 3A-3C) sometime in the first half of the twentieth century, when the condition of the originals (which included many pieces of original correspondence bound together) began to deteriorate. All citations to materials from the *AF* refer to the seven typed volumes held in the CARC, which houses the order's oldest and most fragile records.

[38]Bishop Louis-Nazaire Bégin, Chicoutimi, letter to Father Fafard, Baie-Saint-Paul, February 18, 1892, *AF* 2A:14. While emphasizing the women's dependence upon male secular clergy for their existence, the designation as third-order Franciscans stems from the fact that they were an active order, not a cloistered one, according to the needs and evolving traditions of the North American milieu whence they emerged; thus, from the start they had lived by the rule of the Third Order of St. Francis. By the late 1800s, North American clergy were too dependent upon active orders' charitable works to continue the Church's tradition of looking down on such groups or dwelling upon their technical status as "laity"—an outdated distinction Rome eliminated in 1900, in part because of the challenges America's active orders posed. Hence, when Bégin sought European Franciscans to guide the women's spiritual formation, he solicited only third-order communities. See Ewens, chaps. 1 and 6, and Marie-Michel-Archange, *Par ce signe*, chaps. 1 and 8.

[39]See Marie-Michel-Archange, *Par ce signe*, chap. 6.

[40]For example, Marie-Michel-Archange, *By This Sign You Will Live*, p. 3; in the French original, "la maison du Berceau," Marie-Michel-Archange, *Par ce signe*, p. 13.

[41]See Marie-Michel-Archange, *Par ce signe*, chap. 9.

* * *

Why were the nuns so determined to remain in Worcester, and what, if anything, does the way they pursued this goal reveal about their understandings of "national" identity? When I first learned of the order's tumultuous foundation, these questions haunted me as I tried to place the order's history within the model of ethnically-defined Catholicism so prevalent in scholarship on this era. Careful examination of the correspondence and commentary preserved in the order's *Annales de la Fondation*[42] leads to one clear conclusion, supported by a close reading of local church histories and newspaper accounts from the period: the women had very different views of the connection between their "national" identity and their calling as Catholic nuns, which diverged from that of Brouillet and many other migrant priests in the American Catholic Church at the time. If the women had considered themselves French Canadian above all else, one might expect that establishing a Quebec motherhouse would have been preferable to remaining in Worcester. Even the sole U.S.-born foundress had spent several years in Canada, where most of the group's first members had lived at least half of their lives; two had migrated with their families to the Worcester area less than a year before taking the habit. Thus, while many of the founding members had family in Worcester, their personal ties to the city were hardly permanent; and as the fledgling order expanded, women shuttled among its various locations according to staffing needs and the wishes of Bégin, the bishop who took them in. The women anchored their identity as Catholics not on their Quebecois ancestry, but on the needs they could fulfill as PFM.

Moreover, as their obedience to Bégin makes clear, the women were also not entirely opposed to male church authority—just authority that, in their view, would hamper or thwart their ability to accomplish the religious works to which they felt called by God. One prime example is the ongoing row among the women, O'Reilly, and Brouillet in 1891 over whether the women could continue to wear religious garb. At several points, both O'Reilly and Brouillet ordered the women to remove the brown habits they had been wearing and

---

[42]The *Annales de la Fondation,* compiled retrospectively in the late 1890s and consisting mostly of correspondence, includes letters among the sisters, and between the sisters and various priests and bishops, concerning the progress and development of their order and its missions; as well as letters among male clergy regarding the order's fate. The *AF* provide the bulk of the primary sources behind the chapters in the order's own published history, *Par ce signe,* on the order's founding years

return to secular dress. Each time the women demurred; the explanations they offered for their failure to comply ranged from the fact that
they had cut off their hair and could not bear the shame of appearing
publicly, without the socially-mandated long locks of the day, to their
poverty's precluding owning or buying other attire.[43] But the women
no doubt realized, in their ongoing fight to exist, the spiritual and
moral weight that religious robes conferred. To church officials,
Catholics more broadly, and the American public at large, the habit
had become *the* symbol of a bona-fide nun by the late 1800s, a fact
that an 1889 papal mandate reinforced.[44] As long as they wore their
brown robes, the women's attire imparted the authority to collect
alms and care for Worcester's foundlings. The fact that there always
seemed to be more poor and parentless children in Worcester than
they could accommodate—even after their January 1891 eviction, as
they started over while competing directly with their replacements
from Montreal—was their clear indication that they had, indeed, been
called by God to fulfill a need in the city. Hence they refused to let
Brouillet, the bishop of Springfield, or anyone else stand in their way.[45]

The women, therefore, joined the ranks of many female religious
orders in the nineteenth-century United States who found themselves
in power struggles with clergymen, from bishops to priests and other
male spiritual directors, over how they would live out their calling.[46]
At first glance, Brouillet's actions—from locking them out of the
orphanage and confiscating their property to doing his utmost to
drive the order he had started out of existence—might appear to be
simply a case of wounded pride, injured by women who went too far
in challenging religious and social hierarchies of the time. As their
priest and patron, Brouillet was the women's spiritual father, and they

[43]See Marie-Michel-Archange, *Par ce signe,* chaps. 3-5.

[44]Ewens, *Role of the Nun,* p. 281. Prior to the 1889 "Ecclesia Catholica," U.S. male
church officials had periodically fought to compel nuns to wear their habits in public,
while nuns sometimes preferred secular dress to avoid the very real dangers such
public self-identification posed in the face of earlier hostile American Protestant attitudes toward nuns. After nuns' service as Civil War nurses, however, Americans
regarded Catholic female religious much more highly, and nuns' habits became a
respected symbol.

[45]Similarly, when Bégin called Missionary Franciscans of Mary from France to provide a Franciscan religious foundation for his new Tertiates, the North Americans
refused to adopt the French order's white habit, considering it to be less practical for
active works of charity among the poor than their traditional brown habits, which
would not show dirt as easily. See Marie-Michel-Archange, *Par ce signe*, chap. 8.

[46]See Ewens, esp. pp. 211-14 and 284-87.

owed him all the deference and obedience any single woman owed to her earthly parents (or, for that matter, to her parish priest if Catholic) in the late 1800s, whether in Quebec or New England. By repeatedly acting without his consent and defying his wishes, the women's behavior was nothing short of insubordination, from Brouillet's perspective. For their part, the women had expected Brouillet, in the role that biological fathers or husbands would have filled had they not chosen religious callings, to protect them and to foster the vocations he had first nurtured. It was his failure to do so that had led them to go over his head, rather than a deliberate intention to subvert his authority by placing him at odds with the bishop. Nonetheless, it is easy to see how Brouillet might detect a disturbing emergent pattern in the women's failure to bow to his wishes in all matters concerning the new order he had first envisioned.

A closer look at this incident, however, reveals a much deeper and more complicated picture. At its heart are questions not only of gender relations but also of the complex interplay between religion and national identity for these and other French Canadian migrants to New England in the late-nineteenth and early-twentieth centuries. The nuns' struggle unfolded in an era when men's and women's relationships to the nation-state were undergoing significant transformations in the United States, at the end of a century in which many American-born Protestant women had wielded religious and moral arguments to establish a greater public and political role for themselves.[47] A study of the PFM's language and actions throughout their quest to remain in Worcester, while simultaneously establishing roots in Baie-Saint-Paul, suggests that their difficulties with Brouillet stemmed in part from their refusal to contain their Catholicism within the same narrow "national" boundaries that he himself used. Even as it illustrates a group of determined young women who defied clergymen's efforts to interfere with their religious calling, the history of the PFM's

[47]Among examples of the prolific literature on this subject, see Paula Baker, "The Domestication of Politics: Women and American Political Society, 1780-1920," *American Historical Review*, 89 (June, 1984), 620-47; Lori D. Ginzberg, *Women and the Work of Benevolence: Morality, Politics, and Class in the Nineteenth Century* (New Haven, 1992); Beth A. Salerno, *Sister Societies: Women's Antislavery Organizations in Antebellum America* (DeKalb, IL, 2005); Peggy Pascoe, *Relations of Rescue: The Search for Female Moral Authority in the American West, 1874-1939* (New York, 1990); Elizabeth Hayes Turner, *Women, Culture, and Community: Religion and Reform in Galveston, 1880-1920* (New York, 1997); Elizabeth Joyce Stebner, *The Women of Hull House: A Study in Spirituality, Vocation, and Friendship* (Albany, 1997).

battle to become a full-fledged order highlights the ways in which the women selectively invoked national allegiances and how their use of national identity differed from the views of priests like Brouillet. In this context, the radically different interpretations Brouillet and the Brown Nuns proffered of how religious faith linked to national allegiance highlights the dramatic differences between these Catholic men and women in their relationships with church and ethnic identity, in both Quebec and the United States, at the turn of the twentieth century.

Despite his own religious vocation, Brouillet—like many other male leaders in clerical and lay roles who migrated from Quebec to New England in the decades around 1900—seems to have perceived his loyalty as first and foremost to the French Canadian *nation*.[48] Like the Irish before them, but unlike other Catholic immigrants during this era—who, other scholars have argued, developed a distinct ethnic or "national" identity only upon arrival in the United States[49]— French Canadian immigrant priests and male lay leaders often emigrated with a well-developed identity as Catholic French Canadians. To them, ever since the fall of New France in the mid-1700s, their language, faith, and customs distinguished them from what they perceived as the hostility and Godlessness of the surrounding British

[48]In both Canada and the United States, many French Canadians in the 1800s considered themselves a nationality distinct from Americans and Anglo-Canadians; some Quebec leaders even dreamed of a day when French Canada would regain its sovereignty. An 1872 editorial published in Montreal's *L'Opinion Publique* and reprinted in *L'Étendard Nationale,* its edition for expatriates in the United States, exhorted French Canadians on both sides of the border to "travailler sans relâche, avec courage et patriotisme à former une nation distincte en Amérique" (to "work relentlessly, with patriotism and courage, *to form a distinct nation in America* [i.e., North America; emphasis added]"; *L'Etendard National* (Worcester, MA), January 4, 1872, 11. More common was the adjective *national(e)*, as in references to "les sociétés nationales des Canadiens-français [qui] retardent ou empêchent l'assimilation" ("the French Canadian national societies[, which] slow or prevent assimilation") by helping the migrants maintain their religious beliefs and "langue nationale" ("national language") "car c'est toujours un abaissement et une humiliation pour une nation de perdre sa langue" ("because it's always degrading and humiliating for a nation to lose its language"). *Le Jean-Baptiste* (Worcester, MA), February 8, 1890, p. 4.

[49]For example, Greene (see n. 5); Jonathan D. Sarna, "From Immigrants to Ethnics: Toward a New Theory of Ethnicization," *Ethnicity*, 5 (1978), 370-78; or more recently, Ewa Morawska, "Becoming Ethnic, Becoming American: Different Patterns and Configurations of the Assimilation of Eastern European Jews, 1890-1940," in *Divergent Jewish Cultures: Israel and America*, ed. Deborah Dash Moore and S. Ilan Troen (New Haven, 2001), pp. 277-303.

Protestant culture. After the failed 1837–38 rebellion against British rule, many Quebec clergy and lay leaders alike perpetuated a narrative of victimization—and, with it, an increasingly public struggle to maintain the distinct identity and culture of Catholic French Canadians—that had already become well entrenched in discourses on Quebec identity by the time Brouillet and his future postulants emigrated to the United States.[50]

Central to this effort was the concept of *survivance*, an unwavering commitment to preserving French Canadian identity and, with it, the future of the nation and race. Since the key tenets of *survivance* were maintaining the Catholic faith, use of the French language, and French Canadian *mœurs* or customs—often described as *les traditions de nos pères*[51]—Brouillet and others like him found it hard to separate their Catholic faith from their cultural heritage and ethnic (or, as they would have said, even in the 1800s, "national") identity as *canadiens*. While Catholicism was part of this identity, at its core the values and responsibilities of being a French Canadian man concerned civic obligations and political allegiance to an "imagined community"—a particularly apt description of the French Canadian "nation" in the nineteenth and twentieth centuries, considering (and despite) its lack of sovereignty.[52] For men like Brouillet, Catholicism was inextricably linked to a larger French Canadian identity and way of life.

Although women figured in this project as both literal and ideological reproducers of the French Canadian *nation* and its culture, they were not its authors, gained little if any power or authority from it, and thus stood to gain far less than Brouillet did from perpetuating its existence. Likewise, as women they had less access to political and civic participation in the United States prior to female suffrage becoming federal law in 1920. For the would-be nuns, then, to identify

[50]For example, Henri-Raymond Casgrain's 1866 call for a French Canadian "national" literature, as recounted in *Women and Narrative Identity: Rewriting the Quebec National Text*, ed. Mary Jean Green (Montreal, 2001), p. 5; see also Jocelyn Létourneau, *A History for the Future: Rewriting Memory and Identity in Quebec*, trans. Phyllis Aronoff and Howard Scott (Montreal, 2004).

[51]That is, "the traditions of our fathers"; for example, on the masthead of Worcester's *Le Jean-Baptiste*, beneath the paper's title, appear the words "*La Langue [the Language] et les Traditions de nos Pères.*"

[52]See Benedict Anderson, *Imagined Communities* (London, 1983). The key distinction between the nation that French Canadians imagined and the communities Anderson describes is that the latter are sovereign.

as "French Canadian" or "American" would mean very different things than it would have to Brouillet and other men, for the simple reason that such national allegiances in and of themselves were not a direct route to power, influence, or the ability to make a difference in either Quebec or New England at the time. Although the women recognized a sort of ancestral homecoming in their eventual establishment of a permanent home base in Baie-Saint-Paul, they saw no reason for this headquartering to mean that they should relinquish their claim to Worcester as the birthplace of the PFM. Unlike French Canadian clergymen such as Brouillet, who viewed everything through a lens of French Canadian identity, the PFM's words and actions suggest that, from the outset, they defined themselves as Catholic religious above all else, embracing an inclusive definition of Catholicism that more closely matched church tradition and history than did the more narrow definitions of Brouillet and other immigrant priests.[53]

In other words, for the PFM, their Catholicism was more closely linked to their identity as women than to their identity as French Canadians. Nuns are by definition female; and the particularly female nature of this order's work, from their initial orphan ministry to later forays into teaching and nursing, reinforced their gender identity as female caregivers rather than their "national" identity as *canadiennes-françaises*. It was as female religious that the PFM could have a voice in, and an impact on, the world around them—not as French Canadians or Americans. Hence, rather than placing "national" affiliations at the heart of their individual and group identities, the women drew upon these allegiances selectively. They were female religious above all else; their individual French Canadian ancestries and their order's American origins were secondary to their religious identity, rather than at its center.

* * *

The women thus continued to keep their doors open to anyone in need regardless of national background, and—unlike Brouillet—saw no shame in trying to work with others who were not French Canadian Catholics, from their Irish-born bishop to Worcester citizens outside the *canadien* émigré community. The Brown Nuns regularly took in orphans from the city's seven other Roman Catholic parishes, all of which were Irish-dominated. Since these parishes lacked their

---

[53]See Richard P. McBrien, *Catholicism* (Minneapolis, 1980), 2:1173-76. Thanks to Elaine Beretz for this reference.

own orphanages, their women's societies preferred to entrust their congregations' orphans to the care of fellow Catholics, rather than sending Catholic children to the city's Protestant-run children's home. This was especially true for St. John's parish, the former pastorate of O'Reilly, which was home to a particularly large number of orphans.[54] Given that there was no shortage of parentless children in Worcester, the would-be nuns were incensed at Brouillet's habit of admitting as paying boarders "a large number of children [whose parents] could well afford to keep them at home," which left fewer spaces available for destitute orphans from neighboring parishes. Consequently, despite their devotion to the life of mendicant poverty that came with adopting a Franciscan rule, the women cringed at the thought of soliciting the public without "the assurance that their efforts are for the support of solely orphan children" rather than "children which [sic] are not poor and destitute."[55]

Besides their orphanage's open-door policy, the women regularly accepted donations from Irish Catholic and Protestant women's church groups, and routinely nurtured functional working relationships across ethnic and religious boundaries. This policy and the warm welcome they extended to all orphans regardless of background netted the Brown Nuns substantial financial and material support from across Worcester—not from priests or male lay leaders of the city's English-speaking Catholic churches, but from women's organizations throughout the city. In return for the disproportionate number of orphans they sent the Brown Nuns, the Ladies Charitable Society of St. John's parish ranked among the women's main financial backers outside Worcester's *canadien* community; their donations included a horse and carriage for use on begging tours (see figure 3).[56] The would-be nuns' friendly relations with and openness toward non-French Catholics was one of the chief reasons that Brouillet ultimately turned on his protégées; as observers at the time noted, he regularly "maintained that Irish and French could not get along well together, and frowned upon the admission of any more Irish Catholics" to the orphanage. Donations of furniture, bedding, and money came not only from Catholic women's groups but also from Protestant American women's organizations—so much so that, at the time of the January 1891 lockout, the city's English-language press

[54]Gagnon, *A Parish Grows*, p. 40; Marie-Michel-Archange, *Par ce signe*, pp. 49–50.
[55]"Sisters Desert Orphanage."
[56]"French Orphanage Facts."

FIGURE 3. The begging vehicle, *c*. 1890s, Archives de la Maison-Mère, Baie-Saint-Paul, Quebec. Reproduced by permission of Les Petites Franciscaines de Marie.

reported that about three-fourths of the orphanage's "furniture and fixtures," all of which had been "donated by the public," had come from "Irish [Catholics] and Americans [i.e., Protestants]."[57]

Unlike Brouillet's refusal to dissociate his faith from his ethnic background, the only time the would-be nuns' "national" allegiances surfaced is when circumstances made it expedient for the women to choose sides and state where their loyalties lay. The official records of the first ten years of the order's history suggest that as an order and as individuals, many considered themselves to be both French Canadian and American. For example, one of the most explicit examples in which the sisters themselves spelled out their "national" identity described them, in their official chronicler's words, as "the little Sisters of Worcester, being [French] Canadian-Americans, children of St. Francis"[58]—hardly a ringing endorsement for an exclusive, let alone primary, devotion to one national allegiance over the other.

[57] *Ibid.*; "Rebellion against Priest."
[58] In original: "les petites Sœurs de Worcester étaient Canadiennes-Américaines, enfants de St François"; *AF* 1:32. "French" is inferred; at this time, French Canadian émigrés used *canadien* and *canadienne* solely to refer to Quebec-born French speakers.

Such instances were the exception rather than the rule; the annals of the order's foundation include very few references from the pens of the women themselves regarding whether they thought of themselves as *canadiennes, américaines,* or both. Instead, the women's letters to each other focused mostly upon their common group identity as female religious—women called together to serve God under a common purpose. Periodic references to being "Canadian" or "American" most often indicated the location of a given group of sisters at that moment, or an affiliation articulated to serve some larger immediate goal, rather than a statement of core identity.

In most other respects, the women's constant references to themselves as Catholic women, rather than French Canadian Catholic women, contrasts sharply with the ethnic turf battles that priests like Brouillet were waging at the time. Moreover, rather than using such labels themselves, the references to whether the sisters were "American" or "French Canadian" came more often in the letters written by various priests on their behalf—albeit at times in words apparently chosen according to the women's explicit instructions. A significant number of the letters in the order's *Annales de la Fondation,* particularly those involving the technicalities of establishing their permanent status as a regular order based in Baie-Saint-Paul and those that concerned maintaining their Worcester presence, were written to and/or from various priests and bishops—among them, Father Ambroise-Martial Fafard, the priest who welcomed the women to his Baie-Saint-Paul parish; Father Zotique Durocher, their original spiritual guide until Brouillet banished him from Worcester for siding with them; Darveni-Hugues Langlois, S.J., who replaced Durocher as the women's Worcester counselor; and Bégin and his successor, Michel-Thomas Labrecque, bishops of the Diocese of Chicoutimi, home to Baie-Saint-Paul. Hence, when first introducing them to Fafard in summer 1891, in the hopes that he would grant them a Quebec home for their motherhouse, Father Alexis Delphos—a sympathetic Worcester-area priest who had been involved in the order's founding from the start—strategically labeled the women "daughters of [French] Canada, born in Canada, but knowing English" and urged them to highlight their *canadienne* ancestry when contacting Fafard. Yet in Fafard's own letter of introduction to Bégin, Fafard described them as "American Franciscan sisters" to indicate whence they had come.[59]

[59]In original: "de filles Canadiennes, nées au Canada, et sachant l'anglais"; "Sœurs Franciscaines américaines." Alexis Delphos, East Douglas, MA, to Ambroise Fafard, Baie-

Despite the shortage of explicit references to national identities and allegiances from the Sisters themselves, the founding members of the order defined their group as simultaneously *canadienne* and American, in contrast to many of the Quebecois priests in the United States during this era. At the same time, it is clear that they deliberately deployed their dual attachments as tools in fulfilling their mission, rather than placing these allegiances at the core of their being. For example, the most U.S.-rooted foundress, Worcester-born Sister Marie-Joseph, willingly volunteered to leave the city where she had spent most of her life and move to Chicoutimi in 1894 when Labrecque—perhaps as a test of the women's filial loyalty—requested that two PFM come to keep house for him. While cheerfully settling into her new residence and role in Quebec, Marie-Joseph used her time in the bishop's house to lobby for Labrecque's assistance in their ongoing fight to stay in Worcester. As late as June 1894, Labrecque had said he wanted no part of the women's war with Beaven; by early November, scarcely two months after his housekeepers' arrival, Labrecque was writing letters on their behalf to Francesco Satolli, Rome's apostolic delegate in Washington, D.C., to whom the women had recently taken their ongoing fight against Beaven and Brouillet. Even though Marie-Joseph left Chicoutimi after three months due to illness, she continued to curry Labrecque's loyalty and support from Worcester, through flattering references in later letters to the "fond memories" she had of her time keeping house for him in Canada.[60]

The longer the women's struggle to receive the Springfield bishop's sanction dragged on, the more conscious they became, by necessity, of their dual identity as *canadiennes* and *américaines*— and the more regularly and forcefully they deployed one or the other allegiance to accomplish their larger goal of operating as a full-fledged order on both sides of the border. This strategy had first become apparent to the women at their initial 1890 audience with O'Reilly, who pointed out that because the women were not an official religious order with his approval, they were subject neither to his protection nor to his authority; as an incorporated body in Massachusetts, however, they were a civil body protected under and

---

Saint-Paul, July 7, 1891, *AF* 1:128; Delphos, East Douglas, to Sister Marie-Joseph, Worcester, June 22, 1891, *AF* 1:123; Fafard, Baie-Saint-Paul, to Louis-Nazaire Bégin, Chicoutimi, July 17, 1891, *AF* 1:135.

[60]In original: "un bon souvenir." Marie-Joseph, Worcester, letter to Labrecque, Chicoutimi, April 8, 1895, *AF* 3A:25.

subject to state laws. Hence, according to the local American press, when Brouillet evicted the women in January 1891 with a local sheriff's help, the women "asserted their prerogative to act as free and independent American subjects" with the right to go where they wished.[61] By 1894, unable to maintain their avoidance of national references, the PFM had begun to position themselves as either [French] Canadian or American depending on the most expedient course in any given situation. When appealing to their support base among fellow New England émigrés, who viewed the women's struggle as more evidence of Irish bishops' unjust discrimination, the PFM were "Canadians."[62] When making their case to higher-level church officials, although they positioned themselves as Americans with a constitutional right to stay in the United States, the women also noted that they provided critical services to the "Canadians" who "formed nearly one half" of the Springfield Diocese and who "are sorely in need of us."[63]

The women's 1894 appeal to Satolli, in the hope that papal intervention could convince Beaven to grant them permission to remain within his diocese, provides one example of this tactic. As acting Worcester superior Marie-Alexis explained when relaying news of Satolli's initial response to Fafard in Quebec, she and Langlois were convinced that they would prevail because, first and foremost, "We are American citizens, and only the State can make us leave." As all but one of the foundresses had been born in Canada, along with half the women who had joined since 1891, this was hardly the case for many of the PFM in an era when foreign-born women derived U.S. citizenship almost exclusively through either their fathers or, if married, their husbands. However, their group (having incorporated in Massachusetts long before its members considered establishing a motherhouse elsewhere) was indeed a "citizen" in Massachusetts. This legal fact was far more important to them than any constitutionally-protected rights of freedom of religion, which is the sort of argument that New England's Quebecois priests would invoke in defending their rights to French-language parishes staffed by French-speaking

[61]*Par ce signe,* chap. 3; "Sisters Desert Orphanage."

[62]For example, Sister Marie-Anne-de-Jesus, Baie-Saint-Paul, to the sisters in Worcester, March 21, 1895, *AF* 3A:18–19; Fafard, Baie-Saint-Paul, to Marie-Joseph, Worcester, June 5, 1896, *AF* 3A: 93–95.

[63]For example, Sister Marie-Alexis, Worcester, to Fafard, Baie-Saint-Paul, October 13, 1894, *AF* 2C:328–29; the Sisters of Worcester to Apostolic Delegate Satolli, Washington, DC, March 12, 1895, *AF* 3A:12–14.

clergy.[64] Like *canadien* priests' efforts to enforce national versions of Catholicism in the United States,[65] the women kept open both the option of redress through the Church and that of justice via the American legal system.

* * *

Under pressure from Satolli, Beaven eventually relented, recognizing the PFM as female religious within his diocese and sanctioning their presence in Worcester in late 1897. With his capitulation, the issue of whether they were *américaines* or *canadiennes* all but vanished from the official record of the order's existence.[66] However, this does not mean such identities either were unimportant to the women or remained unproblematic for them over the years. The nuns continued to define themselves collectively as both French Canadian and American, although these identities remained subordinated to their calling as Catholic nuns. Only in the latter part of the twentieth century did the order expand their mission field beyond the United States and Canada; until then, they established missions primarily in North American locations with significant populations of French Canadian ancestry (although, as noted above, they did not deny services to those in need from other ethnic groups).

As such, the PFM in the early-twentieth century continued to draw explicitly upon "national" identities when necessary to help them fulfill their larger calling to the work of the Church, all the while invoking these allegiances in a selective and calculated manner. Letters preserved in foundress Alphonse-Marie-de-Liguori's necrology file[67] were

[64] In original: "1o—que nous sommes citoyennes américaines, donc l'Etat seul peut nous chasser." Marie-Alexis, Worcester, to Fafard, Baie-Saint-Paul, November 17, 1894, *AF* 2C:328–29.

[65] In perhaps the best-known example, French Canadians in Maine appealed to Rome for a repeal of the state's Corporation Sole law only after efforts at legal change through the state legislature failed; see Guignard, "Maine's Corporation Sole Controversy."

[66] See "Articles of Agreement Between Les Petites Sœurs Franciscaines de Marie, having their Motherhouse at La Baie St. Paul, P.Q., and The Diocese of Springfield," signed by Beaven on December 7, 1897, *AF* 3B:238A–B; see also Marie-Michel-Archange, *Par ce signe*, chap. 10.

[67] PFM superiors notified the order's members of a sister's death by way of a lengthy epistolary obituary, which included details of the sister's final hours as well as her biographical background before joining the order and her history of service within it. The PFM Maison-Mère preserves each letter in a necrology file bearing that sister's name within the community's archives. The only additional materials contained in the necrology files of the other founding members are baptismal and confirmation records.

no doubt far from unique for members of the order, especially after U.S.-Canadian border crossings became increasingly difficult in the 1920s.[68] Born in Montreal in 1872 as Marie Alphonsine Albertine Riopel, Albertine (as she was known during her youth) moved to Worcester as a young girl and ran away from home at age seventeen to join the fledgling order. Although she spent most of her religious life in Worcester, she served in Baie-Saint-Paul from 1917–20, as well as at PFM sites in Montreal, New Brunswick, Maine, and Wisconsin, before her death in 1936.

Whether Sister Alphonse-Marie had become a naturalized U.S. citizen by the 1920s is unclear. Worcester records indicate that the Riopels resided in the city for at least fifteen years after their emigration, which took place at some point before twelve-year-old Albertine's 1884 confirmation in Brouillet's Worcester parish. Although Eusebe Riopel is still listed as a Worcester resident in the 1900 *Le Worcester Canadien*, the city directory of Worcester's French Canadian community, the family was apparently away on census day, as it does not appear in the 1900 manuscript census returns for Worcester. Albertine, now known as Sister Alphonse-Marie-de-Liguori, appears in the 1900 census as one of the PFM then staffing St. Francis Home, the community's mission in Worcester; but as census enumerators in 1900 were only instructed to record the citizenship status of adult males, the census entry for Sister "Mary Alphonsus" offers no information on her citizenship status.[69] Perhaps young Albertine's father had become a U.S. citizen, thereby conferring American citizenship upon her as well; or perhaps Alphonse-Marie had herself filed citizenship papers at some point.

The question of Alphonse-Marie's citizenship status becomes germane in light of her file in the PFM archives, which includes a series of letters written on her behalf and at her request. As the letters show, issues of national identity had become most salient for the nuns when their movement among the PFM's various mission fields involved crossing the U.S.-Canadian border; it was at these times that the

---

[68]On new visa rules and other regulations that complicated efforts to enter the United States from Canada, see Bruno Ramirez, *Crossing the 49th Parallel: Migration from Canada to the United States, 1900–1930* (Ithaca, 2001), esp. chap. 2, "The Rise of the Border."

[69]See *Le Worcester Canadien*, p. 111; *United States Manuscript Census of Population* 1900, reel 586, p. 118, line 46; on Albertine's confirmation, see her necrology file, Archives des PFM, Maison-mère, Baie-Saint-Paul, Quebec.

women were most likely to draw upon these identities, in a manner carefully calculated in advance. The first letter, dated December 15, 1926, was on official City of Worcester stationery and signed by former mayor Peter F. Sullivan; it read in part:

> To the Honorable, Immigration Commissioner, American-Canadian Border. . . . This letter will . . . introduce Sister Alphonse Marie, formerly Miss Albertine A. Riopel. . . . I have known her and her whole family as residents of Worcester for about 40 yrs. . . . During her administration in [the St. Francis] Home in Worcester she did noble work and Worcester Citizens were sorry when she was taken from Worcester and took up higher honors in Bay-St. Paul, Quebec.
>
> She is in my office at this moment and tells me of her difficulties in going and returning from Worcester to her new home in Canada.
>
> I told her I thought the American inspectors on the border would be glad to make it easier for her if they knew her as we do here in Worcester and so I asked her to take this letter, which I trust will aid her.[70]

That Sullivan directed his letter not to Canadian officials but to "American inspectors on the border" makes clear that the letter's purpose was not to establish Alphonse-Marie's credentials in entering Canada, but rather to facilitate her eventual reentry to the United States.

Despite Sullivan's assertion that the letter was his idea, the next two items in the sister's file suggest that she had requested the letter and shaped its contents. Just as Sullivan's letter sought to make clear the nun's right to belong in Worcester, in a 1930 proclamation on official stationery, Bruno Charbonneau established Alphonse-Marie's claim to Montreal residency:

> I the undersigned Acting Mayor of the City of Montreal . . . hereby certify that Reverend Sister Alphonse Marie . . . is a citizen of Montreal who has always enjoyed the respect and esteem of the community.
>
> As the said Reverend Sister Alphonse Marie is about to leave for United States [*sic*] I commend her to the kind offices of all persons she may meet, as being worthy of their courtesy and consideration.[71]

A subsequent letter, written less than a year later on Worcester stationery and signed by Mayor Michael J. O'Hara, addressed itself "TO WHOM IT MAY CONCERN" and stated:

---

[70]Peter F. Sullivan, Worcester, letter to American border officials, December 15, 1926, preserved in the necrology files of Mother Alphonse-Marie-de-Liguori.

[71]Official proclamation by Bruno Charbonneau, August 23, 1930, in *ibid*.

> This is to certify that Reverend Sister Alphonse-Marie, of the Little Franciscans of Mary order, St. Francis Home of the Aged, 37 Thorne Street, is a citizen of the United States.
>
> She is going to spend several months in Canada in connection with her religious duties and I shall appreciate any courtesies that may be extended to her.[72]

As with Sullivan's letter, O'Hara's missive sought to establish beyond question Alphonse-Marie's credentials as residing in the United States (in contrast to her temporary stay in Canada)—not to aid her in leaving the United States, but to lay the groundwork for her eventual return. With U.S. border officials increasingly requiring visas and/or proof of U.S. citizenship for those wishing to enter the United States for more than a short vacation, such advance measures were designed to make any reassignments that accompanied Alphonse-Marie's living out her vocation, as her order placed her where her skills could best be used at any moment, as seamless as possible.

* * *

As their selective and restricted use of national labels indicates, national identity was far from paramount in the minds of Alphonse-Marie and her fellow PFM, in contrast to the male counterparts in the late-nineteenth and early-twentieth centuries. For these women, their calling as Catholic nuns transcended national boundaries, as did their mission field; well into the twentieth century, the nuns defined themselves collectively as an order that was equally French Canadian and American, but preferred to think of themselves as female religious above all else. Alphonse-Marie drew upon her claims to both Canadianness and Americanness when circumstances forced her to do so, and then only as tools to aid her in fulfilling her vocation as a nun whose mission field happened to span an international border. For her and for other PFM, while national identity was important, nationality was subordinate to their calling as nuns, not the other way around. Moreover, unlike many of their male counterparts in the United States at the time, they did not let ethnic and national divisions interfere with their work as part of the Church universal. As such, the PFM's attitude, like that of liberal Catholics whose efforts to reform the American church in the late 1800s ultimately lost out to conservative voices both in the United States and in Rome, was a forerunner

---

[72]Michael J. O'Hara, Worcester, letter to American border officials, June 23, 1931, in *ibid.*

to "pan-ethnic Catholic" movements in Worcester and other U.S. cities in the twentieth century.[73]

In her 2001 essay "Religious History without Women," feminist French Canadian historian Micheline Dumont sharply criticized the persistent tendency among scholars of Quebec's religious history to ignore the subject of women and the methodological potential of a gendered analysis in their scholarship:

> The subject of all these works remains the religious man, whether missionary or parish priest, cleric or lay, believing or non-believing, obedient or rebellious, traditional or modern. Is it even possible to measure the theoretical impact of this absence [of female subjects and gender as an analytical category] on our overall knowledge?[74]

Understanding the story of the PFM's stubborn refusal to fit neatly into the ethnic categories used by Brouillet and his contemporaries to define themselves is one small step toward this larger end. Future scholarship on how nuns defined themselves in this era, particularly within communities of newly arrived immigrants, will shed further light on the extent to which the PFM's take on religious and national identity reflects the experiences of other women.

[73]For example, Robert Emmett Curran, "Prelude to 'Americanism': The New York Accademia and Clerical Radicalism in the Late Nineteenth Century," *Church History,* 47 (1978), 48–65; Meagher, *Inventing Irish America* (see n. 30), esp. chap. 5, "The Triumph of Militant, Pan-Ethnic, American Catholicism."

[74]In original: "Le sujet de tous ces ouvrages reste l'homme religieux, missionnaire ou pasteur, clerc ou laïc, croyant ou incroyant, obéissant ou révolté, traditionnel ou moderne. Serait-il possible de mesurer l'impact théorique de cette absence sur la connaissance?" Micheline Dumont, "L'histoire religieuse sans les femmes," *Études d'histoire religieuse,* 67 (2001), 197–208; here 207.

REVIEW ARTICLE

FURTHER LIGHT ON VATICAN COUNCIL II

BY

JARED WICKS, S.J.*

Carnets du Concile. By Henri de Lubac. Edited and annotated by Loïc Figoureux. 2 vols. (Paris: Éditions du Cerf. 2007. Vol. 1: Pp. 1, 567, €39,00 paperback, ISBN 978-2-204-08528-1. Vol. 2: Pp. 569, €36,00 paperback, ISBN 978-2-204-08529-8. Vols. 1 and 2: €75,00.)

Vatican II: A Sociological Analysis of Religious Change. By Melissa J. Wilde. (Princeton: Princeton University Press. 2007. Pp. xv, 196. $38.50. ISBN 978-0-691-11829-1.)

Vatican II. Herméneutique et réception. By Gilles Routhier. [Collection Héritage et projet, 69.] (Montréal: Éditions Fides. 2006. Pp. 468. C$39.95 paperback. ISBN 978-2-762-12685-3.)

This review article continues two earlier discussions of recent publications of sources and studies on Vatican Council II.[1] Presented here are (1) the personal diary kept from 1960 to 1965 by *peritus* Henri de Lubac, (2) a sociological study of how the Council came to make its major interventions favoring change in the Church, and (3) a collection of studies and reflections on the Catholic Church's reception over forty years of Vatican II.

The Vatican II Diary of Henri de Lubac (1896–1991)

The existence of de Lubac's Council diary[2] had been known, but few scholars had access to it, whether in the handwritten original or in the typed

---

*Father Wicks is writer-in-residence at John Carroll University, University Heights, Ohio.

[1]"New Light on Vatican Council II," *The Catholic Historical Review*, 92 (2006), 609–28, and "More Light on Vatican Council II," *The Catholic Historical Review*, 94 (2008), 75–101. Massimo Faggioli offers an ample survey of three years of recent work in all languages in "Council Vatican II: Bibliographical Overview 2005–2007," *Cristianesimo nella storia*, 24 (2008), 567–610.

[2]Leo Kenis treated the importance of personal diaries in historically oriented Vatican II studies at the 2005 congress held in Mechelen, Leuven, and Louvain-la-Neuve. See his "Diaries. Private Sources for a Study of the Second Vatican Council," in *The*

text dating from the early 1980s.[3] The published text now offers testimony that pinpoints problematic aspects of the Council's doctrinal preparation, with de Lubac's astute perceptions of conciliar action during the four working periods and his critical views, late in the Council, about how the Church should engage in dialogue with the world.[4]

1. Problems in Vatican II's Doctrinal Preparatory Work

In 1960 de Lubac was appointed, along with Father Yves Marie Joseph Congar, O.P., to work as a consultor of Vatican II's Preparatory Theological Commission. In this appointment de Lubac saw an indication by Pope John XXIII that it was time to set aside the Vatican difficulties of the early 1950s over theological opinions of certain French Jesuits and Dominicans.[5] The

---

Belgian Contribution to the Second Vatican Council, ed. Doris Donnelly, Joseph Famerée, Mathijs Lamberigts, and Karim Schelkens, [Bibliotheca Ephemeridium Theologicarum Lovaniensium, 216], (Leuven, 2008), pp. 29-53.

[3]Philippe Levillain used the original notebooks to good effect but preserved de Lubac's anonymity by citing them as *documents inédits* or *documents privés* throughout *Le méchanique politique de Vatican II: la majorité e l'unanimité dans un concile* (Paris, 1975). Karl H. Neufeld did not draw on the diary for his surveys, "In the Service of the Council. Bishops and Theologians at the Second Vatican Council," in *Vatican II: Assessment and Perspectives*, ed. René Latourelle, 3 vols. (New York, 1988), 1:74-105, esp. 88-98, and "Henri de Lubac S.J. als Konzilstheologe," *Theologisch-praktische Quartalschrift*, 134 (1996), 149-59. Giuseppe Ruggieri drew on the unpublished *Carnets* to document de Lubac's perceptions of what were for him disturbing currents circulating during 1964-65, in "Delusioni alla fine del concilio. Qualche atteggiamento nell'ambiente cattolico francese," in *Volti di fine concilio. Studi di storia e teologia sulla conclusione del Vaticano II*, ed. Joseph Doré and Alberto Melloni (Bologna, 2000), pp. 193-224, esp. pp. 207-18. Alexandra von Teuffenbach cited sixteen passages from early parts of de Lubac's diary in notes on Tromp's record of the work of the Preparatory Theological Commission; see Tromp's *Diarium Secretarii, Konzilstagebuch, mit Erläuterungen und Akten aus der Arbeit der Theologischen Kommission. II. Vatikanisches Konzil*, ed. Alexandra von Teuffenbach, vol. I/1-2 (1960-62) (Rome, 2006), pp. 503-66.

[4]Neufeld, in "H. de Lubac als Konzilstheologe," recalls that before the Council, de Lubac published major works on several topics taken up at Vatican II, such as ecclesiology renewed from early sources, Eucharist and Church, modern atheism, the graced human vocation, and the Christian relation to Buddhism.

[5]*At the Service of the Church. Henri de Lubac Reflects on the Circumstances That Occasioned His Writings*, trans. Anne E. Englund (San Francisco, 1993), p. 116, where de Lubac notes that shortly after becoming pope, John XXIII made a large donation to support Sources chrétiennes, the patristic editions directed by de Lubac and Jean Daniélou, and he sent de Lubac a warm personal letter. The pope knew of the "difficulties" from his service as papal nuncio in Paris from 1944 to 1953. In 1952, a visitor found Nuncio Roncalli with a copy in his hand of Congar's *Vraie et fausse réforme dans l'Église* (Paris, 1953). Congar heard this in 1965 and recorded it in his Vatican II diary (*Mon Journal du Concile* [Paris, 2002], 2:441-42).

Preparatory Commission prepared seven doctrinal and moral draft texts in 1960-62, which in time met incisive criticism by the Council's majority.[6] About the preparatory work, de Lubac wrote later that a complete chronicle "would not be lacking in picturesque scenes," but such a chronicle will probably not be written "since most of the participants would have no desire to transmit the memory of it to posterity."[7]

Among the scenes of 1960, de Lubac recorded meeting Joaquin Salaverri, S.J., a consultor from Madrid, at the Biblical Institute and candidly telling Salaverri how mistaken he had been about the Jesuit theologate of Fourvière in his critical articles of 1949-51. On November 15, 1960, de Lubac went to the Holy Office, where he met another consultor, Father Marie-Michel Labourdette, O.P., who had in 1946 criticized the Fourvière Jesuits (de Lubac, Jean Daniélou, Henri Bouillard, Gaston Fessard, and Hans Urs von Balthasar) with an article in *Revue Thomiste* on theology and its sources. Shortly afterward, de Lubac knelt before Cardinal Alfredo Ottaviani, who sat between two lighted candles with the book of Gospels in his lap, and took an oath to keep the preparatory work secret.[8]

Beyond picturesque scenes, de Lubac's diary describes the commission's controlling mentality, which clashed with convictions underlying de Lubac's own work of thirty years for theological *ressourcement*. His Belgian confrere and redactor of the commission's texts on revelation and faith, Edouard Dhanis of the Gregorian, "has no sense of the simple grandeur of the faith of the Church that we proclaim, and strangely diminishes faith in Jesus Christ."

[6]On the commission: Riccardo Burigana, "Progetto dogmatico del Vaticano II: la commissione teologica preparatoria (1960-1962)," in *Verso il Concilio Vaticano II (1960-1962). Passaggi e problemi della preparazione conciliare*, ed. Giuseppe Alberigo and Alberto Melloni (Genoa, 1993), pp. 141-206.

[7]*At the Service of the Church*, p. 117. The preparation brought de Lubac to Rome four times for a total of forty days of commission meetings, as related in *Carnets du Concile*, 1:7-88. Congar's diary for this period is of the same length (*Mon Journal du Concile*, 1:15-97).

[8]*Carnets du Concile*, 1:12 (meeting Salaverri), p. 13 (with Labourdette), and p. 14 (taking the oath). On Salaverri's critiques and on several other publications indicated in de Lubac's diary, the edition does not furnish references. Labourdette's 1946 criticism, targeting the series Sources chrétiennes and the series Théologie, which Réginald Garrigou-Lagrange soon took to a more threatening level, was treated by Étienne Fouilloux in "Dialogue théologique? (1946-1948)," in *Saint Thomas au XXᵉ siècle. Colloque du centenaire de la* Revue thomiste (Paris, 1994), pp. 153-95. Because of his oath of secrecy, de Lubac recorded in his diary few notes that illuminate the genesis of the Preparatory Commission's schemata. But von Teuffenbach's edition of Tromp's office diary, in the pages indicated above in n. 3, lists nine written comments that de Lubac handed in on draft chapters of the commission's doctrinal schemata. Congar's diary is more informative in areas such as the initial make-up of subcommissions for four schemata and the highlights of the plenary meeting of September 18-28, 1961 (*Mon Journal*, 1:34-36, 60-79).

Those overseeing the drafting of the schemata manifested negativity, a low intellectual level, and mean-spiritedness, while possessing little sense of the world that awaits the Gospel, as shown in the November 1960 public lecture by Monsignor Antonio Piolanti, the Lateran University rector, who called on the Council to condemn French Catholic neo-modernist theology by ratifying tenets of Pope Pius IX's *Syllabus of Errors* (1864) and Pope Pius XII's *Humani generis* (1950).[9]

According to de Lubac and Congar, the draft schemata came from men who seemed indifferent to Scripture, the Fathers, and the Eastern tradition, as well as unconcerned over modern currents of thought hostile to Christian faith. They privileged judgment and a small system of certitudes to the neglect of an understanding that could nourish believers and attract the world to the Gospel. They did not speak about central dogmas and the Christian mystery in its deep unity, as they pulverized it into assertions resting on magisterial texts of the past century. They worked energetically on issues of church government, but only superficially on the mystery of faith. These men were fixated on recent papal texts, which they patched together in draft texts that they wanted the Council to proclaim as the present-day faith.[10]

In the early phase of Vatican II doctrinal preparation, de Lubac clashed with his Jesuit confrere Dhanis over the latter's formulation of a censure of ideas of Pierre Teilhard de Chardin in draft chapters on creation and original

---

[9]*Carnets du Concile*, 1:21 (on Dhanis, November 19, 1960), p. 22 (Piolanti's address), and p. 24n4 (letter of the same day mentioning Piolanti). Dhanis and Piolanti were not consultors but members of the Preparatory Commission. From the latter, see "Magistero della chiesa e la scienza teologica," *Divinitas*, 5 (1961), 531-51, which cites deviations from the *Syllabus* and *Humani generis* in works by Bouillard, von Balthasar, Chenu, Daniélou, and de Lubac in *Surnaturel* (1946), *Corpus mysticum* (1949), and "Le mystère du surnaturel" (*Recherches de science religieuse*, 36 [1949], 80-121). The address corresponds to Piolanti's chapter on theology and the magisterium in the Lateran University's voluminous *votum* on topics for the Council submitted during the pre-preparatory canvas of 1959-60 (*Acta et Documenta Concilii Oecumenici Vaticani II Apparando*, ser. I [Antepreparatoria], IV/I/1:248-63). The Sacred Congregation on Seminaries took over Piolanti's text and, after dropping references by name to theologians and their works, submitted it as its own Council *votum* (*Acta et Documenta*, ser. I, III:321-28).

[10]*Carnets du Concile*, 1:34-36 (generalization of September 19-20, 1961), pp. 53-54 (typology dividing theologians between those immersed in the sources and those knitting together patches from recent encyclicals), and pp. 85-87 (final reflection on March 12, 1962, after sessions on the schema *De ecclesia*). De Lubac's typology of theologians anticipates Philips's statement, based on the preparation and beginning of Vatican II, "Deux tendances dans la théologie contemporaine," *Nouvelle Revue Théologique*, 85 (1963), 225-38. Congar framed his general assessment in August 1961 in a manner resembling de Lubac's analysis, while adding that the draft texts endangered any realization of John XXIII's objective of promoting ecumenical reconciliation (*Mon Journal*, 1:57-59).

sin in the schema on guarding the deposit of faith. At the time de Lubac had begun, under commission from his Jesuit superiors, his first book-length apologia for Teilhard, and he argued vigorously, in February 1961, in defense of Teilhard against Dhanis and Piolanti before the whole commission. Bishop Albert Stohr of Mainz intervened in support of Teilhard, and Monsignor Gérard Philips proposed a vote that showed a majority of commission members wanting to drop the anti-Teilhard passage. But in September 1961 the passage was still in the text, and de Lubac saw no mention of his own written interventions in the *relatio* explaining the September text.[11]

A second clash broke out over Dhanis's draft text on God's revelation, prepared for chapter IV of the schema on the deposit of faith. Dhanis presented this to the commission on September 22, 1961, and de Lubac immediately recognized two passages that in effect censured ideas proposed in his own writings.[12] Treating the way in which God's revelation attains its fullness in Christ, no. 20 insisted that nonetheless divine and Catholic faith is in itself assent to revealed truths and so must not be explained as a first intuitive experience of all revelation in the mystery of Christ, from which believers pass on to expressions of this in concepts and terms.[13] No. 22 censured "a recent form of relativism"—namely, the idea that in revealed truths the propositions and concepts are only approximations that are incapable of declaring

[11]*Carnets du Concile*, 1:31 ("un rude combat" with Piolanti and Dhanis, February 16, 1961), p. 37 (recalling, on September 21, 1961, Stohr's earlier support and sharp rebuke of Dhanis and Piolanti, "Ne quid nimis!"), and pp. 39–40 (recalling the February vote and noting the disregard of his texts giving passages of Teilhard saying the opposite of what the text censured). Stohr died in June 1961. In October 1961 de Lubac completed the manuscript of *La pensée religieuse du père Pierre Teilhard de Chardin* (Paris, 1961), translated as *The Religion of Teilhard de Chardin* (New York, 1967). De Lubac relates his series of pro-Teilhard projects in *At the Service of the Church*, pp. 103–12 (narration) and pp. 323–36 (documents).

[12]*Carnets du Concile*, 1:37 (the September 22 meeting: "À deux reprises, ce texte contient un passage destiné à me faire condamner par le concile."). Congar heard from de Lubac how deeply upsetting it was to be attacked in a text meant for the Council (*Mon Journal*, 1:77–78, entry of September 28). The passages are in *Acta Synodalia Concilii Oecumenici Vaticani Secundi*, I/4:664, 665. The genesis of *De deposito*, chap. IV, on revelation, was studied by Brendan Cahill in *The Renewal of Revelation Theology (1960–1962). The Development and Responses to the Fourth Chapter of the Preparatory Schema* De deposito Fidei (Rome, 1999), offering chap. IV in Latin and English on pp. 266–91.

[13]This opposes what de Lubac wrote in "Le Problème du développement du dogme," *Recherches de science religieuse,* 35 (1948), 130–60, at 156–58 on the mystery of Christ as primary in faith and as "le Tout du dogme." A reprint is in the collection *Théologie dans l'histoire* (Paris, 1990), pp. 38–70, translated in *Theology in History* (San Francisco, 1996), pp. 248–80 (n.b. pp. 273–76). In explaining *De deposito*, no. 20, in 1962, Smulders saw the passage targeting a similar idea expressed by Karl Rahner. See my "Pieter Smulders and *Dei Verbum*: 1. A Consultation on the Eve of Vatican II," *Gregorianum*, 82 (2001), 241–97, esp. 276–78 and 296–97.

divine realities and so must be subject to ongoing correction and change.[14] Later information confirmed de Lubac's belief that Dhanis wrote these censorious passages of the schema because they agreed with what the latter had had included in the Gregorian theology faculty's antepreparatory proposal of topics for the Council.[15]

Dhanis rebuffed de Lubac's request for a fraternal discussion on revelation and dogmatic terminology, so the accused applied to the commission's secretary, Father Sebastiaan Tromp, S.J., with the demand for a clarification. If this were not forthcoming, said de Lubac, he would resign from the commission, since he could not serve if the commission was going to judge his writings as doctrinally deviant.[16] The drama of this exchange intensified on September 26, 1961, when de Lubac attended a session of a congress on St. Paul held in Rome and heard Dom Christopher Butler speak on St. Paul's notion of faith, which in Butler's view bore an uncanny resemblance to the conception that Dhanis's text intended to declare erroneous, but that, for de Lubac, was the center of Christian faith.[17]

Butler, along with other biblical experts, was a glimmer of hope for the coming Council. In addition, de Lubac met individuals in 1960-62 quite different from those dominating the drafting of doctrinal schemata. Congar was

---

[14]In *Carnets du Concile*, 1:51, de Lubac says he had seen this accusation ten years before, in pages sent to him by the Jesuit father general as a consultor's view that the father general should not allow de Lubac to publish the essay now accessible as "La doctrine du Père Lebreton sur la Révélation et le dogme d'après ses écrits antimodernistes," in *Théologie dans l'histoire*, pp. 108-56; translated in *Theology in History*, pp. 317-66. Dhanis served Father General John Baptist Janssens, S.J., as counselor on issues of theology by French Jesuits.

[15]In November 1960, Henri Vignon of the Gregorian showed de Lubac passages resembling nos. 20 and 22 of *De deposito* that were Dhanis's contribution to the Gregorian University's antepreparatory *votum* for the Council. On September 28, 1961, de Lubac made his own copy of this early form of the censures (*Carnets*, 1:21, 51-52). These parts of the Gregorian proposal are in *Acta et Documenta* (as in n. 9, above), ser. I, IV/1:11-13.

[16]*Carnets du* Concile, 1:40 (Dhanis's refusal), p. 50n1 (letter to Tromp), p. 55 (Tromp's oral assurance that de Lubac was not targeted in the passages), and p. 56n3 (Tromp's written response regarding the commission, which calmed de Lubac somewhat, but did not convince him about Dhanis's aim and intent). Later, on March 2, 1963, de Lubac heard from Tromp that the question was moot, because the Coordinating Commission had removed the schema *De deposito fidei* from the Council's agenda (*Carnets*, 1:545).

[17]*Carnets du Concile*, 1:42-43. De Lubac's further notes during Vatican II's four periods record several sound interventions by Butler, who joined the Council's Doctrinal Commission at the end of Period II. Butler's 1961 lecture was "The Object of Faith according to St. Paul's Letters," published in *Studiorum Paulinorum Congressus Internationalis Catholicus 1961*, 2 vols., [Analecta Biblica, 17-18], (Rome, 1963), 1:15-30.

an ally from the beginning. Cardinal Augustin Bea held promise for the
Council. Father Bernard Häring made good interventions, such as highlighting
charity in the moral schemata. Philips was effective in moderating otherwise
severe texts because of his source-based theology and calm demeanor. Bishop
James Griffiths, auxiliary of New York, made brief but memorable cautionary
statements against the Roman theologians, and Maxim Hermaniuk, C.Ss.R., the
Ukrainian-born bishop of Winnipeg, spoke effectively on the episcopate to
counter exaggerated accounts of the papal magisterium. On the horizon,
briefly noted, was the Council's Central Preparatory Commission with its out-
spoken cardinals and archbishops (Bea, Franz König, Josef Frings, Bernard
Alfrink, Julius August Döpfner, Paul-Émile Léger, Denis Hurley, and similar individuals) who in November 1961 began subjecting the prepared doctrinal
drafts to incisive negative criticism.[18]

2. Insights amidst Daily Life at Vatican II

De Lubac wrote later that his role during the Council "was not considerable," but limited to attending meetings of the Doctrinal Commission; to many
conversations with bishops; and to conferences for groups of bishops in
which he could tell them, for example, about the "not very happy" work of
the Preparatory Theological Commission. In drafting the Council's texts, he
contributed only a few details.[19] Nonetheless, de Lubac's *Carnets* offer many
astute remarks on Vatican II events and personages.

Like other diaries of *periti*, de Lubac's contains notes made in St. Peter's on
the Fathers' discourses, but there are also judgments and points of background. Cardinal Eugene Tisserant informed the Fathers on October 24, 1962,
about several Vatican-approved, Roman-rite missals in different vernacular
languages (Slavonic, Croatian, Syriac), in a "dryly delivered, precise, and erudite" talk of ten minutes without a wasted word. Two days later, the Dutch
bishop Willem Bekkers pointed out that most objections to the liturgy draft

[18]Before the preparation began, Congar visited de Lubac in Lyon to strategize (*Mon
Journal*, 1:21–22). In *Carnets du Concile*, de Lubac mentioned his positive impressions
of Bea (1:16), Häring (pp. 40–41, 79), Philips (pp. 66, 70–71), Griffiths (p. 70, on the
Spirit of Pentecost not coming down on the Roman theologians, and p. 74, on avoiding
a new Galileo case regarding overpopulation), Hermaniuk (p. 68), and the Central
Preparatory Commission (pp. 61–62). Congar recorded how Ottaviani told the
Theological Commission on March 5, 1962, about the Central Commission's chilly
reception of the theological schemata, to which Congar added that this was understandable because the texts exuded the atmosphere of the Holy Office and that the
Central Commission could be anticipating how the full Council would, in time, judge
these texts (*Mon Journal*, 1:88–89).
[19]Letter to Hubert Schnackers, given in *At the Service of the Church* (as in n. 5,
above), p. 362. The letter would be from around 1975, when Schnackers was in doctoral
studies at Regensburg. His dissertation is *Kirche als Sacrament und Mutter: zur
Ekklesiologie von Henri de Lubac* (Frankfurt am Main, 1978).

were coming from Council members speaking only for themselves, whereas several who praised the draft spoke in the name of whole episcopates. On November 14, 1962, the first day of interventions on *De fontibus revelationis*, Archbishop Gabriel Manek made, on behalf of the bishops of Indonesia, an incisive case against the schema, in which de Lubac identified arguments drawn up by *peritus* Piet Smulders in a text that had been circulating. But two days later, Bishop Émile Guerry of Cambrai descended to the level of an imprecise *ferverino* and concluded in an ambiguous manner that would encourage partisans of *De fontibus*. De Lubac added what he heard the next day about the dissatisfaction of many French bishops with Guerry.[20]

On December 2, 1963, on the Marian chapter of *De ecclesia*, General Secretary Pericle Felici and Cardinal Ernesto Ruffini both spoke of going "to God through Mary," showing no sense that all Christian prayer has a trinitarian shape and is through Jesus Christ. Cardinal Leo Jozef Suenens's intervention on Mary on September 17, 1964, was simplistic in doctrine and tended to promote an activist spirituality.[21] On October 26, 1964, when Dom Jean Prou, abbot of Solesmes, criticized Schema XIII, he had in mind Teilhard, but wrongly so. His real target was an unfortunate amalgamation of Church and world proposed by *periti* Marie-Dominique Chenu and Edward Schillebeeckx. On September 24, 1965, Cardinal Frings and Bishop Hermann Volk mounted "the German offensive" against doctrinal lacunae in the revised Schema XIII, making points that are "*justes et capitales*," but what influence can they have on the incompetent and superficial backers of the draft?[22]

De Lubac's *Carnets* contain notes taken at meetings, especially of the Council's Doctrinal Commission, of which the minutes are not in Vatican II's *Acta Synodalia*. On November 18, 1962, he recorded proposals advanced at a session convened by Volk of mainly French and German members and *periti* to plan alternatives to the doctrinal schemata on revelation and the deposit of faith. De Lubac, on October 11, 1963, recorded how the Doctrinal Commission reviewed an early draft on religious liberty. From the second intersession, the diary offers an ample record of the same commission's review, on June 1-6, 1964, of its subcommissions' revised drafts on the Blessed

[20]*Carnets du Concile*, 1:153, 163, 284, and 302.

[21]*Carnets du Concile*, 2:54, 121. On September 28, 1965, a long conversation with Suenens left de Lubac saddened over the cardinal's superficiality, pretensions, and lack of awareness of the spread of atheism (2:418-19). An ample account of the cardinal's Council roles and interventions, along with his interactions with other leading figures (John XXIII, Döpfner, Lercaro, Dossetti, Montini/Paul VI, and Léger), can be found in six papers of *The Belgian Contribution to the Second Vatican Council* (as in n. 2, above), pp. 59-357.

[22]*Carnets du Concile*, 2:251, 414. Three days after Frings and Volk spoke, de Lubac read the critical written observations on the draft of Schema XIII by the German and Scandinavian bishops, adding his regret that the French bishops never produce work like this, in spite of their real but often unenlightened pastoral zeal (2:417).

Virgin, revelation and tradition, episcopal collegiality (including treatment of suggestions from Pope Paul VI), and matrimony. The *Carnets* for Period III (1964) include notes made both during the Doctrinal Commission's methodical and often tense treatment of the final *modi* on *De ecclesia* and during the Mixed Commission's work to revise Schema XIII after its first discussion in the Aula. From Period IV de Lubac gives details of six hours of meetings on November 23, 1965, at which the Mixed Commission dealt with the *modi* generated during voting on the schema on the Church in the modern world.[23]

Accounts of Vatican II commonly highlight the conferences given by *periti* to update the bishops on theological and biblical topics. De Lubac's diary indicates that he gave fifteen such conferences, especially during Periods I and IV, to the bishops of France, Madagascar and francophone Africa, and Argentina, and to Brazilians and others at Domus Mariae.[24] The topics reflect the movement of the Council from early critiques of the prepared texts *De fontibus* and *De deposito fidei* to later accounts of nature and the supernatural in relation to Schema XIII. De Lubac notes giving just as many talks to seminarians and graduate students in Rome at national colleges (French, Belgian, English, and Portuguese) and religious houses (Holy Cross, Jesuit, and Salesian). In these, he treated the Creed early on, but in 1965 took up *Dei Verbum* as foundational in renewal.[25] In Rome, Florence, Bologna, and Milan, de Lubac lectured during the Council's Periods, especially on Teilhard.[26]

---

[23]*Carnets du Concile*, 1:322–29 (at Volk's meeting, de Lubac expressed pessimism about reaching any understanding with the Ottaviani-Tromp group, but Philips observed that the first month of the Council had made them less assured, while Rahner urged all to be ready to join in revising the preparatory schemata, except the impossible *De deposito fidei*, by tenacious preparation, line by line, of reformulations); 2:20–26 (October 11, 1963, where Griffiths insisted on the issue being *immunitas a coactione* and that John XXIII had said in *Pacem in terris* what the draft proposes; later, J. C. Murray made an excellent point); pp. 63–105 (June 1964; on Paul VI's suggestions, given as an appendix to the *Carnets* [2:506–09], but no reference to this appendix occurs in the text; pp. 85–100, that records the discussion and voting on them); pp. 227, 237–62 (determinations on *modi* on *De ecclesia*); pp. 316–18 (on Schema XIII, where disorder reigns because the co-chairs, Cardinals Ottaviani and Cento, are incompetent and tolerate airy discourses but cut off good interventions, like one by McGrath); and pp. 462–63 (six hours on the *modi* offered for the atheism section; doctrinal incompetence abounded, but Cardinal Franjo Seper of Zagreb combined good sense with moderation).

[24]De Lubac's Vatican II work with the bishops of France was not extensive. He noted that he had no part in their organized preparations of interventions and no regular contact with Archbishop Gabriel-Marie Garrone, the French member of the Doctrinal Commission (November 26, 1963; *Carnets du Concile*, 2:48). Congar lamented that the French bishops were not profiting from de Lubac's considerable stature as a theologian in their Council work (note of October 15, 1964; *Mon Journal*, 2:205). But de Lubac's own lament, late in Vatican II, was that no one had thought to involve von Balthasar: "The Church thus deprived itself of its best theologian" (November 11, 1965; *Carnets* 2:456).

The *Carnets* refer to three moments in which de Lubac sought to influence the development of what became the Pastoral Constitution on the Church in the Modern World, *Gaudium et spes*. At a meeting of the responsible commission (combined from the Doctrinal and Lay Apostolate commissions), de Lubac gave Bishop Marcos McGrath on June 5, 1964, some pages expressing his dissatisfaction with an early draft drawn up mainly by Häring. McGrath gave the text to Häring, who asked de Lubac the next day to help revise and further develop the text.[27] In September 1964 de Lubac participated in a workshop of French bishops and *periti* that met twice to evaluate the previously distributed text of Schema XIII that was soon to be discussed in the Aula. The *Carnets* include de Lubac's critical letter written between the two meetings on the present schema's timidity and unfocused ideas of nature and the supernatural. The text needs "apostolic audacity." The diary also gives his notes on proposals at the second meeting; de Lubac spoke last, calling for a text that spoke from the start out of Christian hope and, while light on doctrine, would still exude the conviction that Christianity carries in itself the truth necessary for life in this world.[28]

[25]The 1962 talks were developing parts of *La Foi chrétienne* (1969), translated as *The Christian Faith: An Essay on the Structure of the Apostles' Creed* (San Francisco, 1986). At the end of the Council, de Lubac was glad to write on *Dei Verbum*, both briefly in his preface to the commentary by Roger Schutz and Max Thurian (in French, 1966), translated as *Revelation: A Protestant View* (Westminster, MD, 1968), and more fully in his commentary on DV, nos. 1-6, in *La Révélation divine*, ed. B.-D. Dupuy, [Unam sanctam 70], (Paris, 1968). This commentary was published separately as *Dieu se dit dans l'histoire* (1974) and, with additions, as *La Révélation divine*, [Traditions chrétiennes], (Paris, 1983). On the last page of the *Carnets*, de Lubac recorded speaking on December 7, 1965, at the launch of the Italian edition of the encyclopedic collective volume of sixty contributions edited by Guilherme Baraúna on *Lumen gentium*, at which de Lubac spoke on how the Council's two dogmatic constitutions must be the bases of postconciliar reform and renewal (2:483). The substance of the conference came out in de Lubac's eloquent "*Liminaire*," in *L'Église de Vatican II*, ed. Guilherme Baraúna and Yves Congar, 3 vols. (Paris, 1967), 2:25-31.

[26]In Rome, on September 11, 1965, he spoke at the International Thomistic Congress, on "Tradition et nouveauté dans la position du problem de Dieu chez le P. Teilhard de Chardin," *De Deo in Philosophia S. Thomae et in hodierna philosophia*, 2 vols. (Rome, 1966), 2:212-20. When the *Carnets* mention this event, they add that two days later de Lubac took part in a meeting of the Secretariat for Non-Christians where he gave a paper on the absolute character of faith and the principles by which to judge the religions (2:399-400).

[27]*Carnets du Concile*, 2:82, 89. Study of the inventory of the McGrath Vatican II papers at the University of Notre Dame has not yet uncovered de Lubac's critical comments of June 1964.

[28]*Carnets du Concile*, 2:132 (first meeting, on September 21, at the French Seminary, with twelve bishops and eight theologians present, where de Lubac sensed a prevailing *faiblesse de pensée*), pp. 141-42 (de Lubac's written reaction, sent before or on September 25 to the group's secretary, Henri Denis, who had summarized comments made on September 21), and pp. 148-52 (notes on the second meeting, September 28).

Finally, during Period IV of the Council, on October 6, 1965, de Lubac consulted with Volk and McGrath on the need to somehow ensure that certain fundamental considerations urged in the Aula receive serious consideration for adoption in the revised text that would then be proposed for a vote. With McGrath, de Lubac hit on the idea of asking Professor Joseph Ratzinger, who combined competence with congeniality, for his involvement in the redaction. This led to new accents in what is now *Gaudium et spes*, no. 10, especially its concluding confession of Jesus Christ as "the key, the center, and the purpose of the whole of human history."[29]

3. De Lubac's Criticism of Currents in and around the Council

The *Carnets du Concile* help toward understanding one aspect of Catholic theology in last third of the twentieth century: the wave of criticism and laments voiced by some leading theologians (de Lubac, von Balthasar, Louis Bouyer, Daniélou, and Ratzinger) over a wide swath of post-Vatican II phenomena.[30] The *Carnets* of Council Periods III and IV, 1964-65, witness to de Lubac's critical turn, as he wrote negative evaluations of allegedly progressive ideas circulating at the Council, along with premonitions of coming theological decline in spite of the fine teaching of Vatican II's main texts.[31] In

---

The McGrath papers at Notre Dame preserve, in section CMCG 1/02, a copy of the outcome of this work, "Remarques sur le Schema XIII," mimeographed in eight single-spaced pages, coming from the *periti* de Lubac, Georges Cottier, Henri Denis, Jean Frisque, M. Hua, Marie-Joseph Le Guillou, Gustave Martelet, and Paul de Surgy. Among eight criticisms of the schema's content, no. 3 reflects the thought of de Lubac: "Un dualisme spontané conduisant à un extrinsécisme du surnaturel" (p. 4), as does no. 7, "Le schema souffre de l'absence d'une vue théologique ou biblique du dessein de Dieu," containing the assertion, "Il faudrait retrouver l'unité dans le Mystère du Christ" (p. 7).

[29]*Carnets du Concile*, 2:431. On Ratzinger's role at this stage of Schema XIII, I gave details to introduce a text that he composed in mid-October, 1965, and gave to the principal redactor, Pierre Haubtmann. "Six Texts by Prof. Joseph Ratzinger as *peritus* before and during Vatican Council II," *Gregorianum*, 89 (2008), 233-311, here pp. 246-48, with the text at pp. 291-93 (English) and pp, 309-10 (original Latin).

[30]Some exemplary titles include Hans Urs von Balthasar, *Cordula, oder der Ernstfall* (Einsiedeln, 1966; trans. *The Moment of Christian Witness* [Glen Rock, NJ, 1969]) and *Der antirömischer Affekt* (Freiburg im Breisgau, 1974; trans., *The Office of Peter and the Structure of the Church* [San Francisco, 1986]); Louis Bouyer, *The Decomposition of Catholicism* (Chicago, 1969); Jean Daniélou, *Tests* (Paris, 1968) and *Crise de l'Église, crise de l'homme* (Paris, 1972); Joseph Ratzinger, "Catholicism after the Council," *The Furrow*, 18 (1967), 3-23, "Der Weltdienst der Kirche," in *Zehn Jahre Vaticanum II*, ed. Andreas Bauch, Alfred Glässer, and Michael Seybold (Regensburg, 1976), and *The Ratzinger Report: An Exclusive Interview on the State of the Church* (San Francisco, 1985).

[31]After the Council, de Lubac spoke out in this vein in several works, such as "The Church in Crisis," *Theology Digest*, 17 (1969), 312-25; *L'Église dans la crise actuelle*

these passages, the *Carnets* document, first, the fracturing of the reforming group of bishops and theologians who at Vatican II led the majority to reject the magisterial positivism evident in the draft texts of 1962. But after this development had reoriented the Council, fissures emerged between exponents of different conceptions of directions to take, regarding both strategy and doctrinal content.[32] Second, de Lubac's diary notes give early expression to sharp judgments delivered after Vatican II by influential French, Swiss, and German critics of inauthentic and religiously destructive receptions and applications of the Council.

De Lubac's *Carnets* of June 1964 show an overlap of his reformist views with a new critical concern about where the Council was going. The Doctrinal Commission met June 1-6 to complete several revised schemata that the Fathers would consider during the coming Third Period. De Lubac's June 2 diary entry expresses once again his dismay over the efforts of the antireformist group in the commission, a small Roman "clan" that claimed a monopoly over formulating the faith and convinced some who should know better that they proposed the only orthodoxy.[33]

(Paris, 1969); "Problèmes actuels d'ecclésiologie," *Documentation catholique*, 71 (1974), 228-29; and in works from 1974 or earlier published as appendices to *A Brief Catechesis on Nature and Grace* (San Francisco, 1984 [original, 1980]): "The 'Sacrament of the World'?" (pp. 191-234, on texts of Schillebeeckx) and "The Council and the Para-Council" (pp. 235-60). On de Lubac in this phase, see Christopher J. Walsh, "De Lubac's Critique of the Postconciliar Church," *Communio*, 19 (1992), 404-32, which draws on the author's 1993 dissertation, under the supervision of Avery Dulles, S.J., at The Catholic University of America, "Henri de Lubac and the Ecclesiology of the Post-Conciliar Church: An Analysis of His Later Writings (1965-1991)."

[32]Joseph Komonchak described this 1964-65 differentiation among important Vatican II intellectual leaders in "Recapturing the Great Tradition. In Memoriam Henri de Lubac," *Commonweal*, January 31, 1992, 14-17, and, on a broader canvas, in "Le valutazioni sulla *Gaudium et spes*: Chenu, Dossetti, Ratzinger," in *Volti di fine concilio* (as in n. 3, above), pp. 115-53. In the framework of the second essay, de Lubac belongs with Ratzinger as critical of the social-historical anthropology of Chenu, perceived as secularizing, and of drafts of Schema XIII, while not sharing the evangelical radicality, especially on nuclear arms and peace, of Giuseppe Dossetti, the *peritus* of Lercaro and mentor of Giuseppe Alberigo. At the congress on the Belgians (see n. 2, above), Jan Grootaers treated insightfully these differences within the Council majority in his paper, "Diversité des tendences à l'intérieur de la majorité conciliaire. Gérard Philips et Giuseppe Dossetti," *The Belgian Contribution*, pp. 529-62. This analysis shows the inadequacy of many conservative versus progressive characterizations of the dynamics of Vatican II, especially those that do not look carefully beyond Periods I and II of 1962-63.

[33]*Carnets du Concile*, 2:69-70, about Ottaviani; Michael Browne, O.P.; Pietro Parente; Frane Franic; Rosaire Gagnebet, O.P.; Dino Staffa; Ugo Lattanzi; and similar individuals: "Nothing is more demoralizing than to see up close their spiritual and intellectual mediocrity" (p. 70). The danger is that bishops who oppose them take on a

But at the same time, de Lubac's criticism turned in another direction. On June 5, he circulated observations on the current draft of Schema XIII, on the church in the modern world, with an attached letter of warning that the text should not encourage an "opening to the world" that would let believers be invaded by the world and then attend to secular concerns in such a way as to neglect truths of faith about human existence. In his view, the schema was too reticent on God as man's final happiness. Revisions should state from the beginning the Christian faith about human beings: "A few words would suffice. The eternal and divine vocation of man should be emphasized." The schema would thereby make it possible to take up the world's problems—family life, culture, economic and political life, and world peace—in the light of mankind's true human destiny and according to the Church's proper mission, but it must take care to avoid an opening toward the secularization of Christian life.[34]

In September 1964, just before de Lubac went to Rome for the Council's Period III, a diary entry notes that since the previous winter he has noted signs of doctrinal ambiguity and even anarchy breaking out under cover of slogans about the Church's opening herself to the world. In de Lubac's view, some individuals speak and write about profoundly transforming theological teaching, but upon closer examination their aim is to suppress dogmas of Christian faith. In Rome, de Lubac contributed (as noted above) to the French seminar on Schema XIII and wrote on September 24 that the text engendered confusion and impeded a robust assurance about the word of God and its truth. His entry the next day includes his letter to Henri Denis, the seminar convener, with the lament that in seeking common cause with unbelievers concerning the world the new text distances human beings from their true identity: "If we are not convinced a priori, by an outlook of faith, about a pre-established harmony between revelation in Christ taken in its fullness and the hidden expectation planted by God in the depths of the human person of every age, we will lack the apostolic boldness that alone has a chance of reaching people of our age." Then, on October 4, he noted what the Brazilian Dominican, Bernardo Catão, told him about how some French confreres had accused Catão of outmoded ideas because in retreat conferences he insisted

---

revolutionary allure that disturbs the peace of the church. Earlier, as Council Periods I and II were ending, de Lubac expressed his fears to Congar that this Roman group would revise the texts according to their views (Congar, *Mon Journal*, 1:25, November 26, 1962, and 1:573, November 25, 1963, when de Lubac spoke unguardedly about the Romans as "gangsters").

[34]On de Lubac's June 1964 observations on Schema XIII, see above on p. 555. His words on "the eternal and divine vocation of man," showing that his judgment rests on the one supernatural end of humans, are from *At the Service of the Church*, p. 342. On June 4, de Lubac had told Congar that the present draft of Schema XIII lacked Christian boldness based on the church's assurance of knowing in Jesus Christ "the truth about man" (Congar, *Mon Journal*, 2:98).

on prayer and interior intimacy with God. For Catão's hearers, the new movement was toward concrete, historical human beings without imposing any "idealistic" superstructure.[35]

Before the Aula debate on Schema XIII began on October 20, 1964, de Lubac wrote a letter about his concerns over deeper misunderstandings of the Council's renewal program. On October 17, he gave the letter to Cardinal Léger of Montreal and heard two days later that the cardinal wanted to speak in the Aula about de Lubac's issues.[36] De Lubac pointed out that the Council majority, because of its absorbing need to constantly defend texts against undermining by the antireformist minority, seemed unaware that the Council's proposals of reform—*aggiornamento*, openness to the world, ecumenism, and religious freedom—could easily be misunderstood. De Lubac believed that the opponents promoted misunderstanding when they branded the new currents the fruits of religious indifference, amorphous liberalism, concessions to a worldly spirit, and the near abandonment of faith and morality. In his view, journalists were not capable of presenting the new directions as in fact arising from a "purified and deepened Christian spirit." Then, too, the descent into juridical arguments over episcopal collegiality detracted from the desired spiritual density in several texts that were now being adopted. According to de Lubac, Schema XIII posed new risks, such as engaging the Church with problems of the temporal order so much as to leave "silence or timidity in the schema about the eternal vocation of man," which could abet a turning away from the realities of the faith.[37]

One troubling idea that de Lubac pointed out to Léger was a theoretical account of the relationship of church and world, "according to which there would no longer even be any true evangelization in the future, since the so-called 'profane' world is already Christian in reality, independently of any evangelical revelation."[38]

---

[35]*Carnets du Concile*, 2:2, 111 (note of September 10, before the trip to Rome), p. 138 (September 24, on Schema XIII impeding the apostolic audacity of Paul in 2 Cor 4:1-2), pp. 141-42 (September 25, with letter to Denis, citing p. 142), and pp. 170-71 (with Bernardo Catão, O.P., whose Strasbourg dissertation on St. Thomas's soteriology was published in the series Théologie in 1964).

[36]*Carnets du Concile*, 2:205 (composing the letter on October 13), p. 221 (letter "sur les interprétations frauduleuses du concile" completed on October 17 and given to Léger), and p. 222 (Léger wants to present de Lubac's ideas in a coming intervention).

[37]The letter to Léger is in *At the Service of the Church*, pp. 340-41, in which de Lubac says that he presented to Léger a problem "whose seriousness has worried me for a long time."

[38]*At the Service of the Church*, p. 341. On October 16, de Lubac had spoken with Father Emile Berrar of Paris, one of the priests invited to be a Council auditor, who asked de Lubac's opinion on a theory spreading among the priests of Paris—that is, "le monde serait chrétien depuis toujours; la révélation Chrétienne ne ferait que nous le dire, simple passage de l'implicite à l'explicite, etc." De Lubac answered sharply that this

De Lubac's critical concerns of autumn 1964 came to be focused on a conception of the world as implicitly Christian by God's hidden but grace-giving influence amid the human experience of existence and responsible action in developing the world and society. God's gratuitous nearness and empowerment thus often reach individuals before they encounter the Church, which discloses explicitly God's gracious nearness. De Lubac encountered this conception in Schillebeeckx's lecture on "Church and World," which was delivered at the Dutch Documentation Center on September 16, 1964, and then circulated in printed form. The lecture aimed to give Schema XIII a better theological basis than it had in the text that would be discussed in the Aula beginning on October 20.[39] Later, de Lubac heard another lecture by Schillebeeckx, which was not as extreme as the one on church and world, but de Lubac believed it still lacked a dimension of depth regarding genuine renewal in the Catholic Church. However, despite de Lubac's misgivings, he published a critical study of Schille-beeckx's lecture texts only after the Council.[40]

---

amounts to a betrayal of the Gospel, but the idea was circulating in Rome from a talk by Schillebeeckx and seemed to be favored in the recent article of Marie-Dominique Chenu, "Consecratio mundi," in *Nouvelle Revue Théologique,* 86 (1964), 608-18. See *Carnets du Concile,* 2:218. Chenu says the layperson's task in science, politics, and social promotion is not to consecrate the world, as an earlier schema stated this (*De ecclesia* of 1962, chap. IV). To consecrate would be to set creatures apart from their own finality as a sign of God's sovereignty. Instead, in the Christian economy of incar-nation and sanctification, Christians act in faith, hope, and charity to bring creation to its own finality according to its immanent aims and in service of human flourishing.

[39] The lecture appeared in English as "Church and World," in Edward Schillebeeckx, *World and Church* (New York, 1971), pp. 97-114. De Lubac's critical comments appear in *Carnets du Concile,* 2:218 (October 16, 1964), p. 220 (October 17), p. 251 (October 26), and p. 261 (October 29). The first mention adds the exclamation, "Combien plus sérieuse, plus Chrétien, plus réfléchie, la doctrine d'un Teilhard!". On October 17, de Lubac wrote to Karl Rahner that his opposition to Schillebeeckx's ideas made it impos-sible for him to serve with Schillebeeckx on the editorial board of the new journal *Concilium.* Again, the contrast is with Teilhard, who would never say that revelation only articulates the implicit Christianity of the profane world. Rahner persuaded de Lubac to delay his resignation from the *Concilium* board, but after reading the first five issues, he wrote to Rahner that the journal was dominated by extreme views not in har-mony with the Council (letter of May 24, 1965; *Carnets,* 2:395-96). De Lubac ultimately resigned from the *Concilium* board on November 10, 1965 (*Carnets,* 2:455).

[40] *Carnets du Concile,* 2:327, in an entry of November 18, 1964, after hearing Schillebeeckx, whose forceful speaking style was striking, but "Rien dans son discours pour rappeler les conditions de base de tout aggiornamento vraiment évangélique et catholique." Later, de Lubac added appendix B on Schillebeeckx (pp. 191-234) to his *Brief Catechesis on Nature and Grace* (as in n. 31, above) that begins with problems in the latter's designation of the Church as *sacramentum mundi* and takes up the 1964 lecture on church and world both in itself and in contrast with the final form of *Gaudium et spes.*

In spring 1965 de Lubac attended commission meetings on Schema XIII, during which the interventions of Karol Wojtyla, archbishop of Krakow, impressed him deeply, but he lamented that Wojtyla's positions were not having the impact they deserved. De Lubac read at this time an article in *Commonweal* by Hans Küng, which left him distressed over Küng's superficiality, demagogic formulations, and hostility to Paul VI. As these meetings were ending, de Lubac wrote that one current of thought was taking *aggiornamento* wrongly as a worldliness without evangelical vigor, instead of a cultural deepening that liberates from old clerical narrowness and egotism.[41]

During Period IV of Vatican II, de Lubac made no mention in diary entries about the growth and consolidation of the strong Christological texts of part I of *Gaudium et spes*, the Pastoral Constitution.[42] He was heartened by Father Pedro Arrupe, the new Jesuit general superior, with whom he talked for fifty minutes on October 8, 1965, and who seemed to understand the gravity of the day's spiritual crisis.[43] But the critical remarks continued, for example, about the lack of understanding by some bishops and *periti* of the true sense of major positions taken by the Council.[44] A typical remark of these days was de

[41]Appreciative references to Wojtyla are spread throughout the entries from March 31 to April 7, 1965 (*Carnets du Concile*, 2:357-58, 361, 363, 364, 375, 391-92, 394). The first entry is to Wojtyla's view that the Church is present in the world to make the world attend to the "eternal questions," a point seconded by the German bishops Hermann Volk and Joseph Schröffer, but that Philips did not grasp in its depth and importance. On Küng, "The Council, End or Beginning," in *Commonweal*, February 12, 1965: *Carnets*, 2:344-45. On a mistaken *aggiornamento*: *Carnets*, 2:374 (April 5, 1965).

[42]See GS 10 (2nd paragraph), 22, 32, 38, and 45, studied by Thomas Gertler in *Jesus Christus—Die Antwort der Kirche auf die Frage nach dem Menschsein*, [Erfurt Theologische Studien, 52], (Leipzig, 1986). The Constitution honors de Lubac's concern in GS 41 in characterizing what the Church manifests to people of the modern world, that is, "the mystery of God who is their final destiny; in doing so it discloses to them the meaning of their own existence, the innermost truth about themselves. The church knows well that God alone . . . can satisfy the deepest cravings of the human heart."

[43]*Carnets du Concile*, 2:435-36. De Lubac told Arrupe that twenty years earlier the Holy Office and the Roman theologians had created a doctrinal desert, which explains the explosiveness of today's outbreaks. On September 10, de Lubac heard Tromp's lament over the doctrinal confusion of the day, which occasioned de Lubac's reflection that opposition to renewal by Tromp and other Romans had made Vatican II's first actions seem revolutionary and is now occasioning *un désordre para-conciliaire* (*Carnets*, 2:398).

[44]A French bishop was surprised on October 25, 1965, at de Lubac's approval of the *modus* adding to *De revelatione*, no. 9, the affirmation that the Church's certitude about doctrine does not arise from Scripture alone. The bishop thought that the rejection of the "two sources" of the first schema led to affirming *sola Scriptura* (*Carnets*, 2:446). Two days later, de Lubac noted the circulation of crude misconceptions of the Council's teaching on the source/sources of revelation, episcopal collegiality, the universal priesthood, and religious liberty (*Carnets*, 2:448). On November 23: several bishops and *periti* are doctrinally incompetent and ignorant of the real situation (*Carnets*, 2:422).

Lubac's reference to the intensified action on the margins of Vatican II by "pseudo-theologians" who leave their mark on bishops who are weak on doctrine and often distracted from the Council's actual work.[45]

De Lubac's Vatican II *Carnets,* Congar's Council *Journal,* and the diarylike letters of Dom Helder Pessoa Camara are vivid texts to read—rich troves of theological wisdom and enduring testimonies from within the event to the great reform effort that was Vatican Council II.

A Sociological Analysis of Vatican II as an Engine of Church Reform

For those with church-historical or theological background and interests, Melissa Wilde casts new light on Vatican Council II. Her study confronts, with the tools of social-institutional analysis, the question of just how the unwieldy body of about 2500 Council members formulated a refashioning of the Catholic Church, especially in the face of powerful Curial officials who were lukewarm about or opposed to most elements of the emerging reformist agenda, whether liturgical, biblical, catechetical, ecumenical, or oriented to elevating the lay-apostolate or episcopal roles in the Church.

Wilde goes beyond a "great man" causal analysis, as she qualifies John XXIII as providing the opportunity for promotion of the reform agenda, but lacking influence in its successful implementation that occurred step-by-step during thirty months of Council action after his death. More important was a distinct movement within Vatican II—namely, the low-profile meetings of single delegates from episcopal conferences who had collegial exchanges on Council topics at Domus Mariae on Via Aurelia late every Friday afternoon during the four working periods of Vatican II.[46] From these meetings, approximately 1900 Council members, or 75 percent of the Council, received information on and formulated opinions from positions that emerged in the conferences.[47] It is

[45]*Carnets du Concile,* 2:450 (October 29, 1965). On December 1, de Lubac wrote to Jacques Guillet, S.J., of Fourvière about the urgency of solid study of Vatican II, centering on its dogmatic constitutions, without infection by tendentious readings that would abort the Council's reform and compromise the foundations of the faith. One has to oppose a secularizing program that takes as nonexistent the doctrinal, spiritual, and apostolic themes of Vatican II (*Carnets,* 2: 473). Later, de Lubac added "The Council and the Para-Council," a more systematic appendix C to his *Brief Catechesis on Nature and Grace* (pp. 235–60), on twisted readings of Vatican II's texts.

[46]In "More Light on Vatican Council II," 81n22, I referenced Jan Grootaers's study of the Domus Mariae meetings in *Revue d'Histoire ecclésiastique,* 91 (1996), 66–112, a study enhanced by appendices giving texts of the petitions prepared and submitted to the pope and the leadership bodies by this group during the Council periods of 1962 and 1963.

[47]Wilde, *Sociological Analysis,* pp. 61–68, with a diagram on p. 65 of the connections between conferences in and around the delegates to the Domus Mariae meetings.

common wisdom that episcopal conferences functioned influentially at the Council, beginning on the first working day, when they were designated to prepare and circulate lists of candidates for the conciliar commissions. But Wilde carries this insight further by showing the simple yet innovative mechanics of ongoing information gathering and consensus building from and for numerous conferences by the delegates to the Domus Mariae meetings.

Wilde develops the procedural profile and an understanding of the effectiveness of the Domus Mariae delegates by contrast with the antireformist efforts of the *Coetus internationalis patrum*, which began functioning during Period II (1963) under the triumvirate of Luigi Carli (Segni, Italy); Marcel Lefebvre, C.S.Sp. (emeritus, of Dakar, Senegal); and Geraldo de Proença Sigaud, S.V.D. (Diamantina, Brazil). This trio emerged as authors of letters to Council members urging votes against reformist portions of drafts on the Church and episcopal ministry, which they saw as subverting papal prerogatives or traditional doctrines. But they were generally not effective in garnering enough adherents to halt the reform drive, or later in promoting votes *placet juxta modum*, accompanied by moderating amendments. Their weakness was due in no small measure to their approaches to individual Council members rather than conferences, since they opposed episcopal collegiality. For the *Coetus*, authority in church governance was concentrated at the two poles of the pope and the individual diocesan bishop.

A second major contribution of Wilde's book, based on the Vatican Archives records of emblematic Vatican II votes, is her identification and characterization of four principal groups of Council members: (1) the Spanish, Italian, and Irish bishops of traditionally Catholic countries; (2) the bishops of the northern, religiously pluralist lands of Europe and North America; (3) the Latin American bishops; and (4) the young churches' bishops from Africa and Asia.[48]

While the stability of Italian, Spanish, and Irish church life left few local bishops feeling a need for reform, the Latin Americans faced crises brought to

---

The secretary of the Domus Mariae group was Roger Etchegaray, who ran the secretariat of the French episcopal conference and as Vatican II began was directed by Cardinal Achille Liénart to make contacts with other conferences. Etchegaray found allies in his project in the two vice presidents of CELAM, Dom Helder Pessoa Camara and Manuel Larraín (bishop of Talca, Chile), and soon had twenty-two delegates participating in the weekly exchanges, including Helder and Larrain representing most Latin American national conferences and two others from FACE, the Federation of African conferences. Wilde gives the stable membership of the delegates' meetings in a table on p. 136.

[48]On the four groups, see Wilde, *Sociological Analysis*, pp. 32–42 and pp. 47–51. The numerical membership of the groups is as follows: Group 1: 519 or 20 percent of the Vatican II fathers; group 2: 633 or 25.5 percent; group 3: 570 or 22 percent; and group 4: 579 or 22 percent.

light by the success in their lands of Protestant missionaries and Marxist ideology. Thus, they were open to reformist proposals—liturgical, biblical, and
ecumenical—of bishops from northern pluralist backgrounds. To be sure, the
Latin American bishops were not ecumenically oriented toward Protestants in
their lands, but they embraced reforms likely to strengthen Latin American
Catholics against Protestant and Marxist competition.[49] The bishops of the
fourth group also embraced the reform program as likely to make their
churches apostolically more effective by lessening the scandal of Christian
divisions and by enabling their churches to take on more easily an incultur-
ated Catholic identity freed from European forms.

A first, unexpected indication of the strength of the northern pluralist
reform agenda was the vote taken on November 20, 1962, just a week after the
first exchange among the delegates at Domus Mariae. The vote came after a
week of general evaluations of the draft text on Scripture and tradition as
"sources of revelation." The motion was to end discussion and send the text to
a commission for revision, instead of moving on to treat each of the draft's five
chapters in detail. Sixty-two percent (1368 Council members) voted to halt discussion of the text, which had been criticized as an obstacle to better ecumenical relations *ad extra* and to productive biblical scholarship in the Church.
Only 822 voted to keep the draft on the table for more detailed discussion.[50]
Here was a first striking sign that the "northerners" were gaining adherents to
their reform agenda among the bishops of Latin America, Africa, and Asia.

This developing dynamic of wider receptiveness to reform proposals was
then confirmed during Period II by the vote of October 29, 1963, which, by a
small majority of just forty, decided that the Council would treat the Blessed
Virgin Mary not in a distinct constitution but within Vatican II's constitution

---

[49]Wilde cites an interview given early in Vatican II by Cardinal Raul Silva Henriquez
of Santiago, Chile, who lists elements of decline in the Latin American church: shortage
of priests, neglect of the laity, worship that is not understood, moralistic and devotional
catechesis, and the scandal of wealthy Catholics oblivious to systemic injustices from
which they profit. See *Sociological Analysis*, p. 44, with further analysis on pp. 48-49.

[50]Wilde, *Sociological Analysis*, pp. 21-22 and p. 131, with tables on pp. 33-42 showing that the four groups backed ending discussion of *De fontibus revelationis* to the
following extent: Group 1 (Italy, Spain, Ireland) 23 percent, group 2 (Northern Europe
and North America) 77 percent, group 3 (Latin America) 66 percent, and group 4
(Africa) 80 percent and (Asia) 72 percent. Because the 1368 votes to remove the text
fell short of a two-thirds majority, John XXIII intervened on November 21 to consign
the text for revision by a newly created mixed commission (Doctrine and the
Secretariat for Promoting Christian Unity). For understanding the northern European
opposition to the schema, see the critical theological analysis of the text presented by
Ratzinger to the German-speaking bishops on the eve of Vatican II's opening, in Jared
Wicks, "Six Texts by Prof. Joseph Ratzinger as *peritus*" (as in n. 29, above), pp. 269-85
(English translation) and pp. 295-309 (German original of Ratzinger's October 10,
1962, conference).

on the Church.[51] The next day, 81 percent of the members voted to affirm in *De ecclesia* the collegial sharing of the world episcopate with the pope in the leadership of the whole Church.[52]

Wilde also includes sociologically based accounts of the success of the promoters of the declaration on religious freedom and the failure of the relatively few promoters of a revised teaching on artificial contraception.[53]

Two observations can add to the factors treated by Wilde. First, a major source of reform promotion at Vatican II was the Secretariat for Promoting Christian Unity, instituted by John XXIII in early June 1960 and made an active participant, albeit on the margin, in the preparation of Vatican II draft texts. Not only was the secretariat headed by the widely respected insider Bea, but it also gathered a corps of capable theologian-consultors from major university and pastoral centers. This new institutional reality at the center served as a channel for desires voiced by the World Council of Churches and the Council's non-Catholic observers. It also brought clarity over several reform goals and was effective in working for them during the early defining moments of Vatican II.[54]

Second, because of the Catholic Church's creedal-doctrinal-theological basis, the institution's intellectuals played key roles in articulating, communicating, and defending the many-sided reform program. The demanding practice of the episcopal ministry by the Council members left many of them uninformed theologically and inept in textual analysis of draft texts based on doctrine. Here the *periti* entered in key ways into the dynamic of consensus building. What the delegates heard from the episcopal conferences of the northern pluralist lands at the Domus Mariae meetings of 1962 and 1963 were largely the views first expressed by *periti* in afternoon episcopal conference study sessions and then appropriated by a conference majority or even unanimously. *Periti* associated with the Curia, the theological preparatory commission, or the Italian or Spanish episcopates received few invitations to present analyses of early draft texts, while large numbers of members were reading and hearing critical disquisitions, with alternative proposals by

[51]Wilde, *Sociological Analysis*, pp. 33–40 (tables of votes on Mary by the four groups) and pp. 102–15 (narrative and analysis).

[52]Wilde, *Sociological Analysis*, pp. 60–62 (the problematic), p. 64 (procollegiality at Domus Mariae), and pp. 70–74 (the anticollegiality minority).

[53]Wilde, *Sociological Analysis*, pp. 85–101 (religious liberty) and pp. 116–28 (birth control).

[54]Another institutional body that is not covered by Wilde's study is the Commission (of seven cardinals) for Coordinating the Work of the Council, created by John XXIII in December 1962, which functioned as an active directorate over the preparation of revised schemata in 1963, for example, with Suenens overseeing *De ecclesia* and the fusion of "social" drafts into Schema XIII, Liénart covering *De revelatione*, and Döpfner overseeing, although with little success, the revision of the draft on episcopal ministry.

Schillebeeckx, Rahner, Ratzinger, Congar, and others. A band of intellectuals worked influentially, as Vatican II began, to solidify reformist positions, and soon many theologians entered the service of the Council's commissions to give essential aid in drafting revised texts expressing the emerging majority viewpoint and positions.[55]

Receiving and Interpreting Vatican Council II

Gilles Routhier's collection of a dozen essays, all but one from the new century, surveys the impact of Vatican II on the Catholic Church and proposes illuminating approaches to the ongoing interpretation of the conciliar event and texts.[56] The topics include an account of phases in receiving Vatican II down to the 1985 Extraordinary Episcopal Synod on the Council; contemporary theologies of reception; media-generated expectations and images of Vatican II; liturgical renewal in the midst of a changing world; ecclesiology under the impact of Vatican II texts and the conciliar experience; the Council's moves toward decentralizing church government; Marian devotion after Vatican II; the Council's reception in its phases, areas, levels, and agents; Vatican II's reception in the thirteen dioceses of Québec; a dialogue with Walter Kasper on conciliar hermeneutics; the needed movement in interpreting Vatican II from the genesis of the texts to perceiving them as a corpus; and councils in Catholic history and the synodal principle in today's Church.

The collection is most welcome as commemorations approach a half-century after the Council's dramatic unfolding, which ended the long Tridentine era and began refashioning Catholicism as a world church. Routhier addresses himself naturally to the band of seasoned scholars of the Council, but also to a new generation, which can take fresh approaches to receiving Vatican II with a degree of freedom from the conflicts and turmoil marking the early phase of its reception (1965–80).

---

[55]I surveyed the many-sided contribution of Vatican II's *periti* in "I teologi al Vaticano II: Momenti e modalità del loro contributo al concilio," *Humanitas* (Brescia), 59 (2004), 1012–38. I returned to the topic in "*De revelatione* under Revision (March–April, 1964). Contributions of C. Moeller and other Belgian Theologians," in *The Belgian Contribution* (as in n. 2, above), pp. 461–94. A revised and expanded version of the *Humanitas* article will appear in appendix 5, "Theologians at Vatican II," in Jared Wicks, *Doing Theology* (New York, 2009), pp. 187–223.

[56]The essays appeared first in a variety of French publications, with the exception of "Vatican II: The First Stage of an Unfinished Process of Reversing the Centralized Government of the Catholic Church," *The Jurist*, 64 (2004), 247–83. Related works by the author include *La réception d'un concile* (Paris, 1993) and *L'Église canadienne et Vatican II* (Saint-Laurent, 1997). He edited *Vatican II au Canada: enracinement et réception* (Saint-Laurent, 2001) and *Réceptions de Vatican II. Le Concile au risque de l'histoire et des espaces humains* (Leuven, 2004). Routhier contributed as well the engaging account "Léger et Suenens: les relations difficiles de deux princes de l'Église," *The Belgian Contribution* (as in n. 2, above), pp. 325–57.

The ecclesiologist of Laval in Quebec defines *reception* as the process by which an ecclesial subject—above all, a local church—appropriates to itself, assimilates, and integrates into its life an outside spiritual gift, determining the gift's place in its own life. The process is less the passing on of new norms of practice than the stirring of participation in a mentality that draws on fresh sources of self-understanding and action.[57] In another passage, the "spiritual gift" gains in precision, for its assimilation entails less the modernization of institutional aspects than deep conversion and reform on the part of the receiving corporate subject, which the Council calls to be a more transparent sign of God's saving presence in the world.[58] Another key element in reception appeared in the author's diagnosis that the churchwide reception of Vatican II in worship and catechesis has only in part shaped the new spirituality needed to ground deeply the Council's renewal of religious life, ministry, mission, and lay service in the world. The needed period of incubation was cut short by the cultural turmoil that affected the Western world in the late 1960s and throughout the 1970s, when the conciliar refashioning was just starting to shape understandings and foster new spiritual vigor.[59] On Vatican II in Quebec, Routhier makes a point of much wider application—namely, that initial changes in worship and instruction were not matched by a deeper renewal from the biblical, patristic, and liturgical sources. The Vatican II refashioning took place in a Church long centered on Catholic practices but unaccustomed to deeper study and reflection.[60]

Considering reception more deeply, Routhier points out that in the midst of all that is proposed by Vatican II there are key elements, admittedly brief and scattered, that provide an environment favoring deep reception of a refurbished identity. The Council does take tradition holistically as a vital heritage, open to dynamic growth amid ever new reception, of doctrine, life, and worship (*Dei Verbum*, 8). The Council contains a doctrine of local churches as subjects of action that are in communion with each other laterally while being one by their communion with the Church where St. Peter's successor is chief pastor (*Sacrosanctum Concilium*, 41–42; *Lumen gentium*, 13 and 23; *Unitatis redintegratio*, 14). More fundamentally, pneumatological perspectives repeatedly break through into visibility all through the Vatican II documentary corpus.[61]

---

[57]Routhier, *Herméneutique et réception*, pp. 90, 139, 255.

[58]*Herméneutique et réception*, pp. 225. In a later remark Routhier recalls that Catholic theology has not studied "reform" in the deserved depth and breadth since Congar's *Vraie et fausse réforme* (1950), which helps explain why so few have taken account of the high demands of the Vatican II program (p. 267).

[59]*Herméneutique et réception*, pp. 27–30.

[60]*Herméneutique et réception*, p. 302.

[61]*Herméneutique et réception*, pp. 64–68 and 248. On these elements, the author repeatedly refers to Yves Congar, "La réception comme réalité ecclésiologique," *Revue des sciences philosophiques et théologiques,* 56 (1972), 369–403, esp. 391–93.

On the question of interpreting Vatican II, Routhier engages in exchanges on the pattern of "Yes, but . . ." with Kasper's enunciation of principles for interpreting Vatican II's teaching.[62] Whereas Kasper proposes an integral reading that avoids selective privileging of particular statements in the Vatican II corpus, Routhier calls attention to the need of a "transversal" read-ing of the documents to search out the recurrent and unifying themes. The Council's commissions developed the individual documents for the most part independently of each other, and the first commentaries treated them diachronically in the light of their genesis through successive drafts. Thus, Vatican II did not articulate its own systematic center or cluster of unifying themes. The latter must be discovered by careful synchronic reading.[63]

Second, Kasper holds that interpretation must not take letter and spirit as opposed but as correlated with each other. But Routhier observes that to divine the "spirit" of Vatican II, certain particular points must be examined. These include (1) taking account of Vatican II's overall aim of reform and renewal of the Church, (2) drawing upon the intentions articulated in the *relationes* in which the commissions explained their successive drafts to the assembly, and (3) realizing that the documents arose amidst an intense expe-rience of collegial give-and-take within the assembled world episcopate.[64]

Kasper's third principle is that interpretation must honor the Council's intention to teach and decree within the tradition of preceding councils of the Catholic Church. Vatican II did not sketch the plan of a new Church, nor did it recover the long-lost Gospel, but it proposed the renewal of an existing tradition, acting in intentional continuity with the early creedal affirmations of the Trinity and Incarnation. To this, Routhier adds in confirmation that a manichaean contrast of before/after Vatican II is ruled out by the ways in which influential movements of reform—liturgical, biblical, patristic—did mark the Catholic Church before the Council. Still, one has to keep in mind the witness given by Council participants to their experiences of breaking with an inheritance proposed to them as "the tradition." Such dramatic

---

[62]Walter Kasper, "The Continuing Challenge of the Second Vatican Council. The Hermeneutics of the Conciliar Statements," in *Theology and Church* (New York, 1989), pp. 166–76, esp. p. 172.

[63]Routhier suggests that the following are themes recurring in Vatican II documents: the people of God as participating subject, regard for non-Catholics, respect for differ-ent cultures, readiness for and promotion of dialogue, and constant use of biblical themes and terms. *Herméneutique et réception*, pp. 330–33. A later passage reviews proposals on the unifying center of the Council, offered by Giuseppe Alberigo, Peter Hünermann, and Christoph Theobald, concluding on John O'Malley's early proposal of Vatican II's interior coherence through its preferred rhetorical discourse—encourag-ing, congratulatory, dialogical—in proposing doctrine and a reformed practice (pp. 388–99). O'Malley's thesis has now been fully developed in *What Happened at Vatican II* (Cambridge, MA, 2008).

[64]*Herméneutique et réception*, pp. 334–38.

moments occurred when they accepted, by a large majority, the schema on liturgy as a basic text (November 14, 1962); when they voted to stop discussing *De fontibus revelationis* (November 20, 1962); when they backed episcopal collegiality (October 30, 1963); and when they finally accepted, as basis of discussion, the revised draft on religious liberty (September 21, 1965). As a consequence, Routhier insists, interpretations have to take account of terms, themes, and affirmations on which the Vatican II documents intentionally observe a respectful silence. For this central step in interpretation, one must ferret out of the *Acta Synodalia* the initially prepared schemata of 1962-63 to identify and evaluate what was set aside as Vatican II developed its texts of renewed Catholic teaching and practice.[65]

Routhier wrote the conclusion of his essay collection in late summer 2005, just after TV coverage of Pope Benedict XVI's meeting with the youth of the world at Cologne, where the pope celebrated a liturgy that would have been inconceivable in 1960. Further, at Cologne the pope met Protestants and a Jewish delegation for exchanges that today seem customary, but only because of Vatican II. Many of the young people who greeted Benedict are influenced by new spiritual movements that have taken up with gusto *Dei Verbum*'s proposals on Scripture reading and a prayerful *lectio divina* in daily life. Even before it completed its Constitution on Divine Revelation, the Council itself expressed what it came to teach through the daily rite of "enthroning" and leaving open the book of the Gospels before the assembly as it prepared to enter deliberations and voting on schemata and documents.

Engaged reflection on an adequate interpretation and churchwide reception of Vatican II, as practiced by Routhier, is not a flight from issues of the day in 2009. This Council still has immense potential, when rightly interpreted and received, both in shaping the personal lives of Catholics and in maintaining the ongoing cultural and even political significance of the Catholic Church in today's world.[66]

---

[65]*Herméneutique et réception*, pp. 339-41 and 346-52.
[66]See Massimo Faggioli's pertinent remarks on the Vatican II Church as perceived and able to act in the global public domain in "Vatican II Comes of Age," *The Tablet*, April 11, 2009, 16-17.

BOOK REVIEWS

General and Miscellaneous

Magic and Superstition in Europe: A Concise History from Antiquity to the Present. By Michael D. Bailey. [Critical Issues in History.] (New York: Rowman & Littlefield. 2007. Pp. x, 275. $75.00 clothbound, ISBN 978-0-742-53386-8; $24.95 paperback, ISBN 978-0-742-53387-5.)

This book provides an ambitious survey of the history of magic from the ancient world to the modern West. The broad scope of the book gives readers a useful comparative perspective on how different Western societies viewed and categorized magic and superstition, and how magical traditions changed and adapted to different historical circumstances. It allows Michael D. Bailey to ask such questions as "Can we also speak of witchcraft and witches in the ancient world?" (p. 30) and to correct popular misconceptions concerning (for example) the association of magic with paganism in the late Middle Ages (p. 126), or the numbers of those legally executed for witchcraft (p. 175). According to Bailey, the greatest importance of the categories of magic and superstition lies in their deployment to define the limits of acceptable belief or action (p. 4). Bailey stresses the importance of magic as a field of study, although the book focuses more on how magic and superstition were created by, rather than shaped, their historical circumstances.

Bailey explains historical problems and contexts clearly and chooses interesting examples. He shows admirable command and understanding of a wide range of material, and his scholarly expertise in witchcraft is used to good effect in the lucid chapter on this complex subject. The book is aimed at the general reader or student with a particular interest in the history of magic. This means that the historical backdrop is presented in a very introductory way, and the limited footnotes will frustrate readers interested in following up particular examples or historiographical arguments. It is also a pity that the "further reading" bibliography contains only works in English when the book is likely to attract some readers, at least, with other languages. The bibliography thus omits important French and Italian scholarship in this field, a bias also reflected in the book's content. For example, the significant corpus of occult literature attributed to Hermes circulating in the late Middle Ages and explored by Paolo Lucentini and Vittoria Perrone Compagni (among others) is ignored. This leads, in my opinion, to the author overstating the differences between medieval and Renaissance learned magic.

Nevertheless, the book incorporates an impressive amount of source material and current historiography on the history of magic. Although at times I felt that the wood was lost for the trees, Bailey is an excellent scholar in the history of magic, and amid the historical and narrative detail are some provocative and interesting arguments. In chapter 6, for example, Bailey subverts the argument that skepticism about witchcraft and magic was the result of the Scientific Revolution, the triumph of mechanical philosophy, and the Enlightenment "Disenchantment of the world" and argues that this skepticism was in fact a causal factor in these developments. The book ends with an interesting chapter on magic in the modern West, which shows how modern groups adopted magical rites to confront and criticize aspects of contemporary culture, thus subverting the historical use of the labels *magic* and *superstition* to condemn practices that religious and secular authorities perceived as threatening.

University College London SOPHIE PAGE

Kirchengeschichte. Alte und neue Wege. Festschrift für Christoph Weber. Edited by Gisela Fleckenstein, Michael Klöcker and Norbert Schloßmacher. 2 vols. (Frankfurt am Main: Peter Lang. 2008. Pp. viii, 1009. $141.95. ISBN 978-3-631-57712-7.)

Thirty-nine essays by as many authors deal with five broad overlapping fields in which the honoree, Christoph Weber, has labored over the years. The largest number of contributions comes under the heading "History of the Papacy, the Roman Curia, and the College of Cardinals," covering episodes from AD 530 to 1933. There follow five chapters on mostly nineteenth-century ultramontanism and liberal Catholicism, including also one treatment of celibacy among Italian clerical composers (Vivaldi *et al.*) in the seventeenth and eighteenth centuries. Nine essays focus mainly on local history in the Catholic Rhineland in early-modern and modern times. Under the heading "history of historiography" come investigations dealing with Bernhard Jansen, S.J. (1877–1942); Johannes Jørgenson (1866–1956); and one Heinrich Schnee (1895–1968), as well as Erwin Gatz's contextualization of the project he is leading for a new atlas of church history. Five concluding essays range from Thomas Mergel's inaugural lecture on assuming his professorship at the University of Basel in 2007 (on the interrelationship of religious and national identity in the period before and after World War I) to Gerhard Menzel on ecclesiastical developments vis-à-vis Vodoun practices in Haiti. There is no index.

Many of the essays reflect the approaches characteristic of Weber, born in 1943 and for many years university professor in Düsseldorf. The bibliography of his publications and of the dissertations presented under his direction (pp. 991–1009) gives evidence of these orientations. For example, the prosopographical element of Weber's two-volume work, *Kardinäle und Prälaten in den letzten Jahrzehnten des Kirchenstaates* (Stuttgart, 1978) and his *Genealogien zur Papstgeschichte* (Stuttgart, 1999, 2001–04) is also prominent in the essays by Georg Denzler, Georg Schwaiger, Herman H. Schwedt, and Norbert Schloßmacher.

Also notable is the careful exploitation of archives (*Quellenforschung*, to use the emphatic German expression) throughout the twenty-nine books he has written or edited. Combining this archival emphasis with the biographical one, four noted researchers contribute studies of modern figures. Otto Weiss has discovered the personal papers of Constantin von Schaezler (1827–80), which reveal this convert's development into a proponent before the Holy Office in Rome of the posthumous condemnation of an enlightened Catholic bishop, Johann Michael Sailer (1751–1832). Similarly, Claus Arnold turns up new sources for the drafting of the 1907 antimodernist encyclical *Pascendi Dominici Gregis* by Joseph Lemius. Hubert Wolf (on Eugenio Pacelli as nuncio in Munich) and Thomas Brechenmacher (on a conversation between Pacelli and Pope Pius XI in early 1933 à propos of Nazi anti-semitism), take soundings of newly accessible Vatican sources. The copious notes are highly informative of the latest researches and publications on the current controversies regarding Pius XII.

Weber edited and annotated some works by Franz Xaver Kraus (*Liberaler Katholizismus* [Tübingen, 1983]) and the letters of Heinrich Brüning to Henricus Poels in the Netherlands (*Zwischen Hitler und Pius XII* [Hamburg, 2007]). Here one may see indirect American connections. Poels was the Scripture professor at The Catholic University of America from 1904 to 1910, who was fired on suspicions of modernism, but on his return to the Netherlands was a very prominent instigator of social Catholicism. An essay that links Kraus and the Catholic University is by Robert Ayers, which reveals that when Kraus (1840–1901) wrote on affairs at the Catholic University in his famous "Spectator-Briefe" in the *Allgemeine Zeitung*, his chief informant was Charles P. Grannan (1846–1924), also a Scripture scholar and professor at the Catholic University.

The vicissitudes of German Catholicism claim more attention, naturally. The *Kulturkampf* and more generally the issue of Catholic-Protestant relations loom large in essays by Jörg Engelbrecht, Karl Joseph Rivinius, and Ernst Heinen. Cologne was a center of Catholic culture, but in modern times had to depend on Bonn for a local university. In the 1894 *Katholikentag* (Heinen), the issue of discrimination against Catholics in civil service and higher education received renewed attention, as did the problem of the education gap between Catholics and Protestants first noted in 1869 by Georg von Hertling. After the new University of Cologne was founded, the Görresgesellschaft and the prominent Catholic daily edited by the Bachems in Cologne waged a campaign in 1930 to achieve "parity" in appointments, as Michael Klöcker's essay elucidates. He cites the case of Theodor Brauer (1880–1942), denied a full professorship in Cologne. This was the theoretician for the Catholic labor movement who joined the emigration in1935 and took refuge in the United States at the College of St. Thomas in St. Paul.

It is clearly impossible in a brief review to do justice to the solid studies gathered here in homage. Georg Schwaiger makes the case that Dioscurus should be included in the list of duly elected popes for the year 530. Neither he nor Pope Constantine II (767-68) should be relegated, as is still customary, to the category of antipopes.

Marquette University (Emeritus) PAUL MISNER

The Fathers and Beyond: Church Fathers between Ancient and Medieval Thought. By Marcia L. Colish. [Variorum Collected Studies Series, 896.] (Burlington, VT: Ashgate Publishing Company. 2008. Pp. xiv, 332. $124.95. ISBN 978-0-754-65944-0.)

The "beyond" of the patristic authors referred to in the title of this collection "looks backward, and sideways, as they reflected on and made diverse applications of their classical and early Christian heritage." It also, writes Marcia L. Colish, "looks forward, to the ways in which the fathers themselves served as *polyvalent* sources and authorities . . . and hence stimuli for critical thought to their high medieval successors" (p. vii).

The papers are arranged under four headings. The first group of eight articles (I-VIII) studies the Latin patristic writers and their use of their sources. The second group (IX-XI) focuses on Carolingian intellectual history. The third group (XII-XIV) centers around, or culminates in, the thought of Anselm of Canterbury. The fourth group (XV-XVII) traces the patristic legacy as it impacts the thought of the high Middle Ages.

The first group centers on the thought of Marius Victorinus, St. Augustine, and Ambrose. Paper V, "Cicero, Ambrose, and Stoic Ethics: Transmission or Transformation?," characterizes much of the post-Burkhardtian reading of the Middle Ages "as an authentic bridge between the ancient and modern worlds and as an integral part of a Western tradition whose fidelity to its classical roots is its very definition" (V, p. 96). Colish, however, would "move beyond the idea of a Middle Ages as a conveyer belt of classical sources . . . [and] move beyond the idea that . . . classicism was a donor only. It was a beneficiary as well" (V, p. 97).

The first paper in the second group is an excellent demonstration of this position. "Carolingian Debates over *Nihil* and *Tenebrae*: A Study of Theological Methods" begins with Augustine's "conviction that the liberal arts can shed light on the concept of nothingness" (IX, p. 757). Carolingian authors, Colish shows, exhibited great "freedom and flexibility" in their use or rejection of classical and patristic sources (IX, p. 758).

Among the third, or Anselmian, group of papers, "The Stoic Theory of Verbal Signification and the Problem of Lies and False Statements from Antiquity to St. Anselm" provides a comprehensive history of an important philosophical question. That question is raised by the Stoic insistence that words "signify their referents naturally and automatically." But in such a system "how is it possible to tell a lie or to make a false statement?" (XIV, p. 21). Colish's consideration of the history of the question, emphasizing Augustine and Anselm, demonstrates the contribution of early medieval thinkers to the theory of verbal signification, to logic as an autonomous discipline, to intentionality as the norm of moral acts, and to the role of judgment in cognition (XIV, p. 41).

Of the three papers in Colish's fourth group, the most interesting is the third, "The Virtuous Pagan: Dante and the Christian Tradition." There was a broad range of theories about the possibility of pagans' salvation in Dante's time, "both in the high theological culture of medieval Christianity, and in the tradition of popular Christian literature, both in Latin and the vernaculars" (XVII, p. 1). Some authors addressing the question Colish calls ecumenical maximalists, those holding that salvation is literally universal. Others "place more stringent conditions on access to heaven" (XVII, p. 1). A common position among the early Fathers was that pagans living before the time of Christ received from God a special revelation. "A more radical approach . . . was the argument that they held, by reason, the same truths that Christianity teaches, and that their moral conduct, guided by natural law, was on a par with Christian standards" (XVII, p. 18). On the other hand, "in the *City of God* and other works, Augustine rejects the idea that pagans can be saved (XVII, p. 19). Dante, it turns out, "is more of rigorist than any theologian or popular author up to his time. The one exception is his lowering of the requirements for the admission of philosophers to his limbo of virtuous pagans" (XVII, pp. 39-40).

Some of the articles are challenging. I pondered, perhaps unsuccessfully, the statement of the Carolingian thinker Fredigisius that "*nihil* cannot not be something" (IX, p. 760). On the other hand, Colish's erudition was for me a source of all sorts of information and insights.

University of Dallas   JOHN R. SOMMERFELDT

Piety and Plague: From Byzantium to the Baroque. Edited by Franco Mormando and Thomas Worcester. [Sixteenth Century Essays and Studies, Vol. 78.] (Kirksville, MO: Truman State University Press. 2007. Pp xii, 330. $55.00. ISBN 978-1-931-11273-4.)

That the plague was a shaping force in European history is difficult to deny. The challenge facing scholars through the centuries has been to establish precisely the influences and effects of the disease. The nine essays in *Piety and Plague* explore religious explanations and cultural responses of the plague, which range from the positive and pedagogical to the cautionary and commercial.

Five essays concentrate on the sixteenth and seventeenth centuries, and there is a lingering focus on Italy. This bias is unsurprising given that the volume developed out of the conference that accompanied the 2005 "Hope and Healing in Early Modern Italy" exhibition. Three contributors from the 2005 exhibition catalog also appear in this volume. Franco Mormando (on Michael Sweerts's painting *Plague in an Ancient City,* which adorns the cover) and Thomas Worcester (in his essay on three writings by Etienne Binet) develop subjects covered briefly in the catalog. Sheila Barker's fascinating discussion of the imagery of St. Sebastian complements Worcester's essay on St. Roch in the 2005 publication.

Although the piety considered in the volume is solely Christian and mainly Catholic, there is some originality in the plagues that are studied. Only two essays focus upon particular epidemics: Anthony Kaldallis is critical of what he finds to be a surprising incoherence in sixth-century Byzantine explanations of the plague and its divine causation. Ronald Rittgers's excellent essay on Nürnberg in 1562–63 illustrates that Protestants provided different explanations of the purpose of the plague in God's plan to those of Catholic tradition. Two essays focus upon the Plague of Ashdod: Elizabeth Hipps examines Poussin's painting of the same name, and Pamela Berger presents an ambitious but rather unfocused essay on the iconography associated with this biblical outbreak. William Eamon analyzes the sixteenth-century plague of the pox in Venice. Despite this variety (or perhaps because of it) neither the individual authors nor the editors wade into the swampy debate regarding the nature of the disease under consideration, leaving the reader to grapple with potential comparisons between the episodes that are described.

The essays are of varying lengths as well as quality—Mormando's aforementioned essay, for example, takes up nearly a quarter of the volume. Unsurprising given its heritage, a genuine strength of the volume is its contribution to our understanding of plague iconography and metaphor—a subject specifically addressed by six of the essays. This is not a new area for research within studies of the plague; however, it is refreshing to see a variety of source material being utilized, ranging from manuscript illuminations to transi tombs in Elina Gertsman's useful essay on the macabre.

The volume lacks an introduction. The brief preface provided by the editors does not highlight themes beyond those indicated in the title, which is a shame. This weakens the independent contribution made by the work and the historiographical punch of the volume. In terms of chronological spread, the volume does not surpass the valuable conference proceedings *Epidemics and Ideas: Essays on the Historical Perception of Pestilence* (New York, 1992). Nevertheless, individual essays will prove useful for specialists, offering insights into the variety of ways in which contemporaries responded (and scholars can study) the uncertainty and devastation caused by the plague.

Society for Renaissance Studies   JANE STEVENS

Biblical Poetics before Humanism and Reformation. By Christopher Ocker. (New York: Cambridge University Press. 2002. Pp. xvi, 265. $90.00. ISBN 978-0-521-81046-3.)

Since at least the publication of Beryl Smalley's *The Study of the Bible in the Middle Ages* (Oxford, 1940), scholars have been fully on notice that the Middle Ages was a time of considerable ferment, development, and creativity regarding the manner in which Christian readers ought to approach the Bible as Holy Scripture and find therein divine truth. How are the words of Scripture to be understood, and however can such words make God known? What kind of speech is this? A plethora of studies in the years since Smalley's now-classic work have given us a much better understanding of the development of biblical science in the long Middle Ages. The present work makes an original and energetic contribution to this important conversation, one that should inform not just medievalists but Reformation scholars and practitioners of theological exegesis as well.

Ocker's argument is sophisticated and subtle, so much so that I hesitate even to try to sketch it out here. Basing his analysis on an impressively wide reading in both the sources and the secondary literature, he makes a case for a later medieval change in "textual attitude" that looked to the human words of Scripture as the locus of divine revelation. This "textual attitude" was based perhaps most importantly on St. Thomas Aquinas's well-known dictum that from the literal sense alone "argument can be made." This meant that meaning, the material of theological argument and ecclesial proclamation, was to be found in the human words of Scripture: "verbal signification." This contrasted, as Ocker tells the story, with the Victorine idea (drawn from Augustine) that meaning is heavenly: the text as sign points to a natural object, which in turn points beyond itself to the object of knowledge properly so called. Meaning, on this old scheme, is located not in the *verba* of the biblical text, but lies beyond it, in the realm of intellectual or spiritual reality.

The new way of conceptualizing textual meaning paved the way, or, perhaps better, went hand in hand with developments in grammar, rhetoric, and philosophy that helped make it possible to treat Scripture itself as a divine word. In two extraordinarily wide-ranging chapters, which treat an almost dizzying array of little-known later medieval expositors, preachers, theologians, and postillators, Ocker carefully elucidates case studies in miniature of the transition to a "new textual attitude," a "biblical poetic" that brought Scripture into a wide-ranging nexus of relations with such works as Lombard's *Sentences,* canon law, the *Glossa Ordinaria*, patristic and other sacred literature, and so on.

This would be a fine work if Ocker had simply traced out this later medieval transition. Not content to leave it as a merely medieval story, however, he moves on in the chapter "Reformation" to sketch out some of the continuities and the deep dependence of Protestant exegesis and biblicism on the "textual attitude" created in the later Middle Ages. Theologians like Philip Melanchthon and John Calvin were, in Ocker's account, building on medieval developments, even when they rejected aspects of the theology and practice that had been developed by their western forebears. Most intriguingly, at least for this reader, this means that Luther's oft-trumpeted "hermeneutical breakthrough" did not at all signal a radical break with the Catholic Middle Ages. To the contrary, as Ocker puts it, it was a quintessentially later medieval protest against a false hegemony of the "spiritual senses" in favor of the true "spirituality of the letter" (p. 219).

Marquette University   MICKEY L. MATTOX

The Blessed and the Damned: Sinful Women and Unbaptised Children in Irish Folklore. By Anne O'Connor. (New York: Peter Lang. 2005. Pp. 260. $73.95 paperback. ISBN 978-3-039-10541-8.)

Historians and folklorists do not necessarily make good bedfellows. One is concerned mainly with the busyness of everyday political, economic, religious, and cultural life, while the other tries to penetrate below the daily round to the underlying structures of thought that shaped motives and actions. Inevitably the historian is involved in a world of continual change while the folklorist's cosmos appears almost static over time and space. However, the possibilities for the exchange of ideas are greater than one might expect, and this book is a fine example of such cross-disciplinary activity. It is a successor to Anne O'Connor's earlier fine study *Child Murderess and Dead Child Traditions* (Helsinki, 1991). While both books draw on a similar corpus of evidence, they treat it in very different ways. The earlier work, as befits a book based on a dissertation, contains not only an analysis of stories about unbaptized and ghostly children in the Irish and European folklore tradition but also a series of texts and the scholarly apparatus of motif numbers among which unwary historians are likely to become confused and disorientated. This book, while dealing with a similar body of material, is a less empirical and more reflective work. It is intended not to lay out the evidence but rather to consider what the evidence of folklore about unbaptized children and child murderesses may tell us about religion and the supernatural in societies that told those stories. It is therefore a rereading of this evidence within a series of frames different from those that were employed in the earlier work. Thus a range of reading strategies is deployed from feminist theory through contexts provided by cultural studies to the more traditional historical-geographical method of folklore analysis. The result is an extremely interesting and stimulating book that enlightens a whole range of issues in the

Irish past as well as addressing a more contemporary range of concerns about religious identities and memory. A case in point is the suggestion that many of the apparently medieval *exempla* in these stories are, in fact, products of Tridentine reform (pp. 188–97). This seems highly likely given that preachers in Irish, such as Geoffrey Keating, resorted to works such as the *Magna Exemplorum* for at least some of their illustrative material. However, this also suggests the traditional nature of what passed for Tridentine reform in Ireland and hints at the use of conservative strategies by which bridges between traditional and Tridentine forms of spirituality were created. Again the similarities between Irish and Breton (and more generally French) traditions (pp. 208–09) highlighted in this book may well reveal something of a shift in Catholic Tridentine religious sensibilities. While the early-seventeenth century was dominated by religious works from a Spanish tradition, and particularly that of the Low Countries, in the later seventeenth century when Bishop Luke Wadding of Ferns imported religious books for his diocese it was to France that he looked for his supply of works. Such story traditions may have traveled a similar route. This, as these two examples indicate, is a richly suggestive book for historians interested in the religious cultures of Ireland over time. It demonstrates the importance of multiple readings and approaches to the sometimes intractable evidence that makes up the raw material for interpreting religious identities in Ireland.

National University of Ireland, Maynooth   RAYMOND GILLESPIE

Iconoclasm and Iconoclash: Struggle for Religious Identity. Edited by Willem van Asselt, Paul van Geest, Daniela Müller, and Theo Salemink. [Jewish and Christian Perspectives, 14.] (Boston: Brill. 2007. Pp. viii, 506. $239.00. ISBN 978-9-004-16195-5.)

This is a collection of thought-provoking contributions—the result of a 2005 conference at the University of Utrecht on iconoclasm (the breaking of physical images as an opposition to representing the divine) and iconoclash (the collision between visual or mental presuppositions and attitudes toward images that evolves into a strategy of suppressing such mental or conceptual images and their agents, and a device for identifying the construction of religious identity). Mercifully the introduction (pp. 1–14) and the "Overview of the Contributions" (pp. 15–29) offer guidance over the intricate problematics of the conference with a précis of each article. The stated conclusions in most articles also offer a bird's-eye view of each entry and additional literature for further reading.

The joint consideration of iconoclasm and iconoclash is an imaginative one, however, and in spite of their coincidence in historical and ideological context, they are not inherently and automatically consequential. They do, however, pertain to essential identity, especially identity of faith. With regard to the Christian tradition, the possibility and even the necessity of *image*, and in difference to the Exodus 20:4-6 prohibition against *pèsèl* ("graven" images), flows from and witnesses to the fundamental premise of the incarnation of God-the-Word—a *sine qua non* antidocetic theology that simultaneously leads to a fresh, Christian anthropology that reaffirms and explains the "icon of God" in humanity, renders holiness demonstrable in humans, and allows a foretaste of an eschatological "communion of saints" from here and now. These two inherent and contextual derivatives of the image (or, better, icon) are not sufficiently presented in the volume. One should also take exception to "[t]he fact that Christianity is about the Word, or Logos, makes it . . . a religion of words, or books, or better still: a religion featuring a whole library" (p. 33). The *Logos* embraces and supersedes words; otherwise an icon would render the *Logos* redundant. Strictly speaking, the *word* or *book* notion is an inherent essential characteristic of Islam rather than of Christianity where the divine word is revealed in recital (*qu'rān*) rather than in flesh (*sarx*). Not that the Christian community has historically presented any unified position toward this fundamental premise, as the diverse positions regarding images show (a real iconoclash and an identity crisis) and as the volume has abundantly made evident.

The Christian East preferred the notion *icon* (from speaking of fashioning and portraying in the perfect tense as a completed fact; *cf.* here the intense analysis of the complex notion in John of Damascus, *imag.* 3.16-23 and *passim*) to *image* precisely to point to the significance of the relationship between God and human, rather than to any mental or external depiction. The notions *icon/image* and *iconoclasm/iconoclash* carry a host of doctrinal, social, ethical, liturgical, and artistic consequences and speak more to and about anthropology than to and about theology, which is made clear by the twenty-four papers in the volume; they are organized under the sections "Word and Image: Fundamental Questions," "Jewish and Christian Debates on Images until the Reformation," "Protestant Reformation and Catholic Reformation," and "Modern Times."

There seems to be a prevailing appreciation of the image, in and beyond the Christian tradition: its manifold manifestations (pictorial, three-dimensional, architectural, and even written), its significance in religious life and thought, and its inherent relationship to the word. Of special interest in this discussion is the timeless thought on seeing the divine of Abraham J. Heschel brought to the forefront by Even-Chen. Jan Hallebeek's paper, "Papal Prohibitions Midway Between Rigor and Laxity. On the Issue of Depicting the Holy Trinity," taking the clue from official papal positions on the case of depicting nonincarnate persons in the Trinity and not only Christ, is a good case of a simultaneous iconoclasm and iconoclash. Given its undeniable power that it has revealed in the visual communication age of ours, there is little misapprehension as to the significance of the image as a tool in the humanities and in the field of religion and spirituality. If there is a redeeming practical value in a volume such as this, it can be sought in the fact that in its broadness and seeming laxity, there are certain contributions that, with their punctuality and insight, are forcing us to revise long-held "iconoclastic" views about others, such as the stereotypical "Protestant image breaker" (Willem van Asselt, "The Prohibition of Image and Protestant Identity"). That in itself is a contribution.

University of Waterloo (Emeritus)   DANIEL J. SAHAS

The Peculiar Life of Sundays. By Stephen Miller. (Cambridge, MA: Harvard University Press. 2008. Pp. x, 310. $27.95. ISBN 978-0-674-03168-5.)

Stephen Miller's *The Peculiar Life of Sundays* is a general-interest book that provides snapshots of the Sundays of a handful of Anglo-American figures based on their personal diaries and public utterances. The title refers to Wallace Stevens's characterization of Sunday in a personal letter. The book opens with a description of Billie Holiday's classic rendition of "Gloomy Sunday," but then contrasts Sunday gloom (and even suicide) with a recent poll's discovery that more than three-quarters of Americans find Sunday "the most enjoyable day of the week" (p. 2). The introductory chapter moves without resolution between tropes of *Sunday Gladness* and *Sunday Gloom*, a pattern that characterizes the book as a whole. Woven into the book is an overview of the civic and religious regulation of Sunday since Constantine. The book's central chapters survey the Sundays of a dozen or so historical figures, wherein Miller demonstrates his strength as a gentle interlocutor and synthesizer. The final chapter, about contemporary Sundays, quietly laments the loss of the Sabbath.

The Peculiar Life of Sundays is not a book that scholars should add to their shelves, as it makes no new contribution to our scholarly understanding of Sunday, religion, Sabbatarianism, or Anglo-American culture. What is more, it is peculiar in its preoccupation with all things "pagan." The book is laced with the word: for example, "Emersonian paganism" (p. 247), "a pagan great awakening" (p. 197), and Stevens's embrace of "paganism" (p. 214). The lengthy list of entries under *paganism* in the index, at three-and-a-half inches long, outstrips the other entries, including those for *Lord's Day*, *Sabbatarianism*, and *Puritanism*. It seems that Miller is aware that "pagan" is inaccurate: he notes that it "was initially a pejorative term" that "some historians are wary of using" (p. 58). Would that he had been.

Nevertheless, Miller is a sympathetic reader of diaries, letters, essays, memoirs, and poetry. His discussion about Samuel Johnson's Sunday dilemmas, including a transcription of 1755 resolutions forming, in Johnson's words, "a scheme of life for the day" (pp. 101–02), is fascinating. However, Miller's interpretations founder because he employs a typology of Christian commitment that in the end does little to explain why Sunday poses so much hope and so much despair for so many people. In his view, those who despaired in Sunday had little faith and were even pagans. Had Miller looked more carefully at the rhythm of work and rest that his historical subjects encountered, rather than at where they belonged on a calculus of Christian commitment, he might have been better able to explain their particular outlooks concerning Sunday. For example, doing so likely would have enhanced Miller's interpretation of Thoreau's sly affront to the Sunday-Sabbath, for in nearly every written word, Thoreau challenged the American devotion to a narrowly defined field of work.

In all, *The Peculiar Life of Sundays* exemplifies one problem with nonfiction trade publications, particularly those undertaken by university presses: because the authors do not know enough about the subject that they have decided to write about, they lean too heavily on inappropriate sources (*The Wall Street Journal* for ideas about religion, for example), borrow too liberally from the work of others, and use anachronistic terms. None of these alone is a grievous misstep, but in the end together they point to the failure of an underprepared author and a profit-driven press to do justice to a subject and thus to the reading public as well as the scholarly community.

Southern Methodist University   ALEXIS MCCROSSEN

Converting Colonialism: Visions and Realities in Mission History, 1706–1914. Edited by Dana L. Robert. [Studies in the History of Christian Missions.] (Grand Rapids, MI: William B. Eerdmans Publishing Co. 2008. Pp. x, 304. $40.00 paperback. ISBN 978-0-802-81763-1.)

In a political and rhetorical climate in which colonialism is thought to be both oppressive and illegitimate, Dana Robert and her contributors aim to untangle the study of Christian missions from the study of colonial governmentality. They refuse, writes Robert in her introduction, to accept the "time-worn generalizations about the destructive impact of missionaries as carriers of Western ideas into Africa and Asia" (p. 6). Instead, Robert and her colleagues show, through a series of case studies, that missionaries aimed to "convert" colonialism, co-opting aspects of imperial government while also challenging that which was prejudicial to "gospel values" (p. 4). The book's singular focus on missionary agencies allows the contributors to illuminate the creative work in which evangelists were engaged, but also obscures the intellectual and political labors of African and Asian converts.

There are at least three areas in which Robert's book usefully advances our understanding of Christianity and imperialism. First, Robert and her contributors show that mission organizations were forums of knowledge production, not bastions of conformity. Missionaries performed anthropological research, learned vernacular languages, and published their work. Among nineteenth-century British missionaries the impulse toward political and ethnographic analysis was fed, as Andrew Porter's chapter shows, by missionaries' conviction that the new millennium was close at hand. Evangelicals kept an eye on the events of world, especially on the upheavals of the Ottoman Empire, looking for evidence heralding Christ's return. They also argued over the politics of missiology. Peter Williams's essay shows how during the late-nineteenth century Anglicans promoting a racially integrated church challenged the missiological theory of Henry Venn, who had in an earlier time hoped for autonomous African and Asian churches. Mission agencies were not simply vehicles of religious indoctrination but were platforms from which Europeans and their converts generated novel forms of theological and political reasoning.

Roberts and her colleagues make a second contribution by showing mission organizations to be networks of exchange, binding Christians in Europe together with co-travelers in South Asia, Africa, and other fields. Daniel Jeyaraj's excellent chapter shows how Protestant missionaries in southern India shaped the intellectual milieu of eighteenth-century central Europe. Agents of the mission in Tranquebar regularly published reports on their work, which were circulated widely among the German-speaking intelligentsia in Europe. Their linguistic and ethnographic work informed European scholars' developing view of oriental cultures. For German Protestants, missionary work constituted a circuit of exchanges through which novel ideas about language and religion flowed.

These essays make a third contribution by highlighting the role that Indian, African, and Chinese agents played in the propagation of the Christian faith. It may not be controversial to think, with R. G. Tiedemann, that China or any other part of the world was "not evangelized by missionaries, but largely by the Chinese themselves" (p. 240). But it is good that this book presents some evidence that challenges missionary-centered interpretations of Christianity in Africa and Asia. Eleanor Jackson offers a series of pithy biographies for the Bengali Christians who worked to advance the faith in their homeland during the nineteenth century; Jacob Ajayi highlights Christian converts' efforts to influence government institutions in nineteenth-century western Africa; and Tiedemann shows how long-established Christian communities in nineteenth-century China vied with a new wave of European missionaries for ecclesiastical and practical authority.

This book can profitably be read as a contribution to the growing historiography that expands the boundaries of European and American history. Robert and her colleagues show that missionaries were not simply extending an already existing culture to colonized territories. Their scholarly and religious work was collaborative in nature, drawing Africans and Asians into a transcontinental discourse about language and religion. However, these historians work mostly with documents produced in European languages by missionary organizations and rarely cite material produced in Swahili, Bengali, or Hawaiian by converts themselves. Their narrow source base poses problems for a balanced study of converts' intellectual and political work with missionaries' texts and ideas. Robert's chapter, for example, studies the "Christian home" as a focus of evangelistic endeavor among female American missionaries in the South Pacific. Robert says nothing about how missionaries' model of companionate marriage related to older forms of conjugality, and neither does she explore how Hawaiian converts invested in the novel forms of matrimony that missionaries propounded. Eleanor Jackson's portrait of Bengali converts' lives likewise says little about where converts stood in relation to older forms of religious and social authority; and Roy Bridges's study of missionary communities in mid-nineteenth-century eastern Africa ignores the forms of sociability that Swahili and other African peoples were creating alongside and within mission stations.

If the study of missionary endeavor is to take seriously the role that native agents played in the propagation of the faith, then historians need also to reorient their research methodology. They need to move outside the confines of the missionary archive and study the imaginative and interpretive work that African and Asian converts did in the vernacular.

Selwyn College, University of Cambridge   DEREK R. PETERSON

Martyrdom in an Ecumenical Perspective: A Mennonite-Catholic Conversation. Edited by Peter C. Erb. [The Bridgefolk Series.] (Kitchener, Canada: Pandora Press. 2007. Pp. 211. $20.00 paperback. ISBN 978-1-894-71081-7.)

This collection consists mostly of papers and responses by Catholic and Mennonite scholars who explored the theme of martyrdom at St. John's Abbey, Collegeville, Minnesota, in 2003 and 2004. Brad Gregory's keynote presentation at the 2004 meeting identifies the issues and sets the tone for the book. In the background is Gregory's magisterial study, *Salvation at Stake, Christian Martyrdom in Early Modern Europe* (Cambridge, MA, 1999).

Gregory laments the Catholic persecution of Anabaptists in the Reformation era, but insists that Catholic authorities were animated by understandable pastoral concerns. Gregory is a winsome participant in social ecumenical exchanges. But he remains conservative in his historiographical assumptions and in his opposition to any form of doctrinal relativism. He is pessimistic about the prospects for Catholic-Mennonite doctrinal reconciliation in view of their respective unbridgeable truth claims.

Neal Blough, a Mennonite mission worker in France, argues in response to Gregory that Catholic doctrine on some points has evolved over the centuries, rather than existing as a fixed and unchanging deposit. Before the fourth century, the Church did not put heretics to death. Both Catholics and Mennonites, Blough says, need to "broaden our narratives" to make space to accommodate the other (p. 50). Blough is more optimistic than Gregory that social ecumenism can foster doctrinal ecumenism.

Helmut Harder, a Canadian Mennonite theologian, suggests that Gregory gives too high priority to "doctrinal ecumenism" as a goal of ecumenical dialogue. A more fruitful focus, says Harder, citing John Howard Yoder's call for greater unity of ethical commitment, would be "ethical ecumenism" (p. 53).

Margaret O'Gara, a Catholic specialist in ecumenical theology, believes that "growth in understanding" (which she says need not involve change in doctrine) can proceed from genuine confession of sin, conversion, and purification of memories (p. 65). Answering Gregory, she argues that significant progress has already been made toward doctrinal ecumenism, without succumbing to doctrinal relativism.

Mennonite scholars Arnold Snyder and John Roth present case studies of Anabaptist martyrs Hans Schlaffer and Hans Landis, without directly engaging Gregory's challenges. Whereas the Catholic call has been for "purification of memories," Roth reports from recent Lutheran-Mennonite conversations a movement from "healing of memories" to "right remembering" (p. 102).

Helmut Harder (Mennonite) and Drew Christensen (Catholic) offer reflections arising from a project of the monastic community of Bose, Italy, to produce an ecumenical martyrology that includes the stories of martyrs from non-Catholic as well as Catholic traditions.

This volume concludes with essays, originally published elsewhere, by Mennonite scholars Chris K. Huebner and Jeremy M. Bergen. Huebner proposes an alternative epistemology in which a particular understanding of martyrdom is the key to truth. Although Huebner approvingly quotes Gregory's *Salvation at Stake*, there are significant disagreements in their philosophical assumptions that are not directly addressed in this volume. Gregory is quite averse to poststructuralist theory, but this collection does not include a response to Huebner on this issue.

Bergen's concluding essay welcomes evidence of recent Catholic moves toward a more inclusive and ecumenical understanding of martyrdom and admonishes Mennonites to abandon a confessional martyrdom that tends to exclude other religious traditions.

This volume is part of the Bridgefolk series, which is sponsored by a body of Mennonites and Roman Catholics who are interested in ecumenical conversation and celebration. It creatively reflects the shape of recent Catholic-Mennonite dialogue.

Bethel College, Kansas   JAMES C. JUHNKE

Ancient Church

The Oxford Handbook of Early Christian Studies. Edited by Susan Ashbrook
Harvey and David G. Hunter. (New York: Oxford University Press. 2008. Pp.
xxviii, 1020. $150.00. ISBN 978-0-199-27156-6.)

In books of this kind, two features count for the most: coverage and structure. The structure here, clearly, has been the object of great care. After three
chapters headed "Prolegomena" and a splendidly practical section on material
and textual evidence (archaeology, epigraphy, codicology, and so on), there
are six sections devoted to (1) identities; (2) regions; (3) structure and authority; (4) cultural expressions; (5) rituals, piety, and practice; and (6) theological
themes. However, it is not a handbook about early Christianity, with "cogent
summary introductions" as the editors put it (p. 2), but about the *study* of
early Christianity. The content of each section consists for the most part in an
account of how the modern view of early Christianity has been determined
by the methods and preoccupations of those who have studied it:
"Contributors were asked to reflect on the main questions or issues that have
animated research, to provide an introduction to the relevant primary
sources, and to offer some guidance on the directions in which future
research might be profitably pursued" (p. 2).

The tone is inevitably set, therefore, by Elizabeth Clark's introductory
chapter "From Patristics to Early Christian Studies" (pp. 8–41, including a 13-
page bibliography). The story is of a dissolving of disciplinary boundaries. As
in the case of "Late Antiquity," the centuries that are covered no longer dis-
close their integral meaning to the specialized scrutiny of theologians or clas-
sicists, the hands-on expositors of material culture, or even of historians. Most
of the more than forty contributors to the volume have led much of their academic lives within exactly those enclaves. Yet, each chapter here echoes with
the industry of its neighbors. Indeed, one may argue, early Christian "studies"
are governed as much by loyalty to ancestors and associates as by adherence
to the structural principles of a newly defined discipline.

Clark's account of multiplicity is matched by the accompanying chapters
on textuality (by Mark Vessey, pp. 42–65) and on the complex variety of belief
and practice that "early Christianity" represents (by Karen King, pp. 66–84).
For Vessey, the range of genres and the relational fabric of "textual communities" now familiar to the student of the period are very much in the eyes of
the modern beholders, themselves the masters of differing genres and
enrolled in textual communities of their own. We are now students of form.
How one presented the Christian position—to what audience, through what
medium, in what venue—mattered as much as the thought deployed. The
result was an increasingly unfettered engagement with the *litterati* of the age.
The voice on the page was a Christian voice, but it was "part of a history
unconfined by the Church" (p. 51). The mark of purpose in a text was its
desire to renegotiate the boundary between those who spoke and those who

listened—always with a sense of precarious and conditional encroachment or withdrawal. King's argument follows from that. Inquiry governed by academic ecumenism lays bare a fluidity of circumstance that precisely made necessary (or at least useful) a corresponding rigidity of discourse. The articulation of "orthodoxy" was a formal reaction to obscure or shifting boundaries, not their outcome or nemesis. Early Christianity was not, in other words, a single entity, nor indeed a static one. "Negotiation" was conducted by early Christians as much with one another as with those who did not share their beliefs. That is not to suggest mere chaos or raw competition, nor did it mean defeat for the multiple and victory for the hegemonic. Early Christians justly laid claim to a single arena, but they constantly moved within it according to a complex choreography of argument and historical appeal.

In the section on "Identities," chapters on Jews (Andrew Jacobs), pagans (Michele Salzman), gnostics (Antti Marjanen), and Manichees (Samuel Lieu) are followed by treatments of Arians (Rebecca Lyman) and Pelagians (Mathijs Lamberigts). The first four are concerned with negotiated boundaries and fluid definitions that force us to ask, as King would wish, what those juxtapositions do to our notion of what "Christian" might mean—when was a Christian not Jewish, in other words, or not pagan? The last two are focused on boundaries more obviously *within* the Christian body. (Jacobs's chapter on the Jews illustrates well the more general way in which modern scholars visit their preoccupations on the past. Our task is not to find "real evidence" that can justify what was in fact an artificial rhetoric of distinctiveness. We are not concerned to rifle texts for facts, but rather to decode them.) Similarly welcome is the chapter on the gnostics, which provides an admirable account not only of discovery but also of categorization, as calculated as that of Irenaeus; and our future attention, Marjanen tells us, should focus on gnostic praxis.

The question immediately arises: If Arius and Pelagius are covered, why not Nestorius? After all, the controversies surrounding Ephesus and Chalcedon imposed more lasting "identities" on the Christian scene. At this point, the structure breaks down. Index references to Nestorius and Miaphysites are not helpful and cluster in the following section. Raymond Van Dam's chapter on the regional character of Greece and Asia Minor makes Nestorius's "heresy" (rightly) less than central (pp. 332-36). David Brakke handles the issue more fully, in the context of Egypt and Palestine (pp. 355-58). Lucas Van Rompay, writing similarly on Syria and Mesopotamia, is interested chiefly in the subsequent schools of Edessa and Nisibis (pp. 376-79). But only Brian Daley, on "Christ and Christology," explores (much later) the issue at length (pp. 895-99) and then under the banner of theology. This leads one to more general reflections. Where is the full-blown debate over "heresy"? King makes clear the importance of Walter Bauer's work (p. 69), and the allusion is repeated briefly by Jacobs (p. 171) and by Lewis Ayres and Andrew Radde-Gallwitz on the "Doctrine of God" (p. 865); but discussions of "heresy" and "orthodoxy" are thinly scattered. Marjanen asks whether gnosticism is appro-priately thought of as a heresy (pp. 204-05), and the categories are present but tangential in Lamberigts's treatment of Pelagius. Francine Cardman, in her chapter on ethics, gives a nod to perceived errors about the body (p. 938). But only Karen Torjesen ("Clergy and Laity") and Stephen Shoemaker ("Early Christian Apocryphal Literature") pursue the issue further—Torjesen with interesting reflections on the way in which the attribution of heresy has ham-pered a balanced understanding of heterodox clergy and Montanist women (pp. 391-92, 395); Shoemaker in relation to suspicions about the very genre with which he is concerned (pp. 522, 525-27, 534). Little of this has to do with identity.

The issue of language also is a concern. There is no distinct discussion of the extent to which language—Greek, Latin, Syriac, or Coptic—could be regarded as a marker of identity. Coptic is virtually absent from the book, in spite of reference to Shenoute by William Harmless ("Monasticism," p. 505) and Rebecca Krawiec ("Asceticism," p. 776). Indeed, most of the language-ori-ented chapters are concerned with poetry and hymns (Michael Roberts, John McGuckin, and Sebastian Brock). Van Rompay comments on what he calls "the increasing Hellenization of Syriac Christianity" (pp. 375-76). Van Dam, echo-ing Fergus Millar's recent emphasis, discusses the unrelenting Greekness of the East (pp. 325-28). Mark Humphries—on Italy, Gaul, and Spain—has no wish to suggest "that Christianity in western Europe developed in isolation from the rest of the Christian world" (p. 294), but both his chapter and the others in the "regions" section present remarkably separated impressions of the areas they discuss. Pierre Courcelle, for example, is referred to sparsely, but in no case (save in a footnote by Vessey) in relation to *Les Lettres grec-ques en Occident*.

It has to be stressed, of course, that this meander in search of "identity" serves only to reveal, more positively, the wealth of material that the book contains. However, it is strange that the secular is largely unaddressed, and the word *secular* does not even appear in the index. In a discussion of modern method, especially when acknowledging the waning or transformation of a theological or even of a specifically religious interest, it would seem natural to assess the degree to which a secularization of European scholarship has affected not only the preoccupations of the contemporary academy but also the choice of past phenomena that are allowed to awaken its current inter-est. I was prompted by this reflection to trace references to the work of Robert Markus, whose first major contribution was precisely to an under-standing of St. Augustine's attitude to the "world"—an attitude that was, in many regards, strikingly neutral—and whose more recent work has explored precisely the extent to which the "secular" sphere in the late Roman period was "invaded"—indeed, "drained" of its character—by the growth of ascetic culture. Krawiec alludes to the notion briefly, but with more concern for the ascetic alternative (p. 771), and William Adler ("Early Christian Historiography") relates the trend narrowly to Socrates of Constantinople (p. 597); but the natural recognition of Markus throughout the book gives this insight otherwise no attention.

The relation between asceticism and monasticism also is worthy of consideration. Harmless's chapter on the latter is listed under "Structures," whereas Krawiec's treatment of asceticism is a study of "Practice." This is a modern distinction (and a little *passé*), and monasticism could almost as well be thought of as a practice, while asceticism, even in Krawiec's eyes, is surely just as much an "expression of culture." Harmless knows there is a problem— indeed, an "urgent issue" (p. 509). "Future scholarship," he writes, "may wish to re-evaluate realities behind the nomenclature, to understand how, within the wider umbrella of Christian asceticism, monasticism finds its proper specificity." The relation suggested between reality and nomenclature presents its own problems, but whatever failure is being referred to here most likely has been caused by a modern shift of understanding or interest. Even ascetics in the late empire found monasticism somewhat problematic, but many modern students have taken for granted the legitimacy of their desire to uncover the firmly delineated origins of later institutions. Harmless shows how changing interests have unearthed new information, but says less about the impact of those interests on the interpretation of the results. Just as they did in late antiquity itself, ideological imperatives and biases have often governed the inquiry. Krawiec's chapter quickly homes in on the issue of the self, in relation to both the body and society (she is more successful than Harmless in understanding Peter Brown's transition to the "social world"): asceticism "creates both a new self and a new social order" (p. 774). Within the chapter more generally, Krawiec moves with assurance from self to discourse to text to authority and power, as well as comments on Harmless's urgent issue: "The asceticism that transforms the individual body can be linked to the communal body of the monastery," and the purity or pollution of the one affects directly the health of the other (p. 776).

The reader's conclusion remains a simple one. A book that acknowledges these issues (and there are many others) and that forces the mind along so many fruitful paths of inquiry can only be hailed as a valuable addition to the many works of reference now pouring from our presses. This one will remain among the leaders, at once authoritative and provoking.

The Catholic University of America   PHILIP ROUSSEAU

The Power of Sacrifice: Roman and Christian Discourses in Conflict. By George Heyman. (Washington, DC: The Catholic University of America Press. 2007. Pp. xxviii, 256. $69.95. ISBN 978-0-813-21489-4.)

George Heyman's thesis is that "[t]he conflict between Rome and the early Church was ultimately a collision of sacrificial discourses" (p. xvii). While early Christians refused to participate in Roman sacrifices, their concept of sacrifice was structurally the same: "[W]hile the 'content' of what constituted a sacrifice may have changed, the importance of sacrificial rhetoric did not" (p. 147). The author recurs to the definition of sacrifice as derived from the Latin "to make" (*facere*) something "sacred" (*sacer*); hence a sacrifice was the removal or separation of something from the ordinary, to make something valuable "expendable" (p. xv).

Heyman sees the uniqueness of his book in the connection made between martyrdom and the rhetoric of sacrifice (p. xxiv). This is an overstatement, for I and others have pointed to the early Christian view of martyrdom as a sacrificial death, but we have not made it central the way Heyman does. He also claims that other scholars have not made a comprehensive analysis of the impact of the discourse of the Roman imperial cult on early Christianity, but such a presentation fits the increasing attention to the political dimension of the context of early Christianity (as for instance the work of Warren Carter on the New Testament).

Chapter 1 uses discourse theory to present the nature of religion and the organization of religious personnel in Rome. Sacrifice constituted Roman identity: "To be Roman was to be religious. To be religious was to sacrifice in a variety of specified and ritually controlled ways" (p. 43).

Chapter 2 on the imperial cult demonstrates the continuity from Roman state religion to the cult of Caesar. What changed was not "traditional Roman religion, but the direction through which religious discourse was controlled" (p. 54).

Chapter 3 discusses the New Testament texts that employ the rhetoric of sacrifice, especially as applied to the death of Jesus. The New Testament presents no coherent "theology" of sacrifice, but the author argues that a sacrifice can be both expiatory and communion-oriented at the same time. The terminology of "spiritual sacrifice" for various Christian activities can be misleading, for not all sacrifices involved killing animals but might be the offering of grain or the pouring out of a libation, and the Christian "sacrifices" might be material, as in benevolence; but the terminology does point to a valid distinction.

Chapter 4 takes up the rhetoric of martyrdom as one thread in sacrificial discourse in the context of pagan and Jewish examples of "noble death." Because of the focus on the conflict between Rome and the Church, the author does not treat other activities besides martyrdom that early Christians regarded as sacrifices. The distinctively Christian idea was that the martyr died "like Jesus," in imitation of him. The martyrs' deaths were sacrificial like Christ's; Jesus and the martyrs freely sacrificed their lives. The author argues that emperor worship was at the heart of the persecution of Christians.

There are some problematic interpretations. Martyrs are said to be a creation of those who wrote about them (p. xxii), but the cult of a martyr often preceded the martyrology."Ransom" is said to assuage the divine rage (p. 125), but in usage the word pointed to the liberty accomplished. That the allusions to sacrifice in reference to Jesus' death at the Last Supper mean the re-enactment of the Last Supper was a further means of atonement (p. 130) reads later theological ideas back into the Gospels. Instead of being "perplexing" (p. 147) Paul's use of *logikē* in Romans 12:1 accords with philosophical language of the time for worship that proceeds from the reasoning part of a person. Were Clement of Alexandria's comments on martyrdom a grudging concession? (p. 233). The assertion, "The struggle between the power of Rome and the Church was played out vis-à-vis a clash within sacrificial discourses and not a collision of competing systematic theologies" (p. 223), sets up a false contrast by the insertion of the word *systematic*. The first half of the sentence is correct, but sacrificial discourse was set in the context of contrasting ideologies that may be called theological.

The book is marred by some minor errors. To mention a few: my name has become Evert (p. 146, n. 128); Allen Brent has become Allen; Basilides has wrongly become a Valentinian (p. 203).

In keeping with the electronic age many of the sources can be accessed via Web sites.

Heyman is to be congratulated for showing how "[t]he early Christians adapted Graeco-Roman sacrificial and imperial ideology to produce their own unique discourse that challenged the hegemony of Rome" (p. 11).

Abilene Christian University   EVERETT FERGUSON

Medieval

The Hidden History of Women's Ordination: Female Clergy in the Medieval West. By Gary Macy. (New York: Oxford University Press. 2007. Pp. xiv, 260. $29.95. ISBN 978-0-195-18970-4.)

What more could be written or said about the ordination of women? A great deal, as we find in Gary Macy's *Hidden History*. His first point is that *Order* has not meant the same thing over the centuries in the East or West. Macy finds it unhelpful to take a modern, refined canonical understanding of *Order* and then look backward into history to see if it appears in some form. Initially, ordination meant to be engaged in ministry, to bring grace to the baptized—the grace of forgiveness, healing, teaching, feeding, and leading the worship service in a Christian community. Macy asks: Did women do any of these things in the ancient and early-medieval Church? They certainly did all these things and were given titles from their contemporaries of *epsicopae, presbyterae, diaconae,* or *abbatissa,* reflecting their work in their local communities. They may have been given names (it is and was widely agreed that such names did appear in the ancient literature), but were they ceremonially ordained as men were routinely and ceremonially ordained to perform the same sorts of functions? Macy presents much evidence to show that women as well as men were ritually ordained in this sense or in a parallel way. One great strength of his book is its wealth of Latin citations, demonstrating that women were doing ministry and were recognized as doing so. For those whose Latin is rusty or nonexistent, he provides English translations and a wealth of footnotes to give them a context. The context Macy provides shows that these titles were not mere honorifics. If women were occasionally titled *episcopae* and more frequently *diaconissae* until the early-twelfth century, why did this practice die out? If women ministers were so prevalent, why did they disappear from historical records to become almost invisible? Macy points the finger at reformers under Pope Gregory VII as culprits. We all know of the eleventh- and twelfth-century battles of ecclesiastical reformers who were intent on removing lay (read "royal") interference with church property and church life. It was then that the notion of *Order* was changed to carry the specialized meaning of having power to consecrate the Eucharist and preside. In the course of church reform, clergy were separated from laity, the clergy becoming more monastic in lifestyle, and the laity marginalized in the "church." It was in this century that women were vilified as temptresses and the cause of the Fall of the human race, flighty, and inferior in intellect. Women were further infantilized, no longer capable of being ordained, excluded from the nascent universities, and placed under tutelage of their husbands or fathers. Ordination was closed to women even if their *ministry* (their good offices) continued in the Church.

Macy's excellent *Hidden History* is both a scholars' book and a comfortable read that is hard to put down. Two points, however, require clarification. To describe *order* as that which a minister did in a community makes it difficult to distinguish the ordination of a bishop from a priest or deacon, or even from a teacher or a healer. When everyone is *ordained,* the sacramental notion of ministry seems absorbed into a general notion of function that could be performed by anyone either appointed or elected. Second, the notion that before the Gregorian Reform (or thereabouts) persons were ordained only for service to their local community still needs proof. Surely priests and deacons wandered all over the Mediterranean world in the patristic period ministering with powers independent of what the local community had given them.

Dominican School of Philosophy and Theology   JOHN HILARY MARTIN, O.P.
Berkeley, CA

Commentary on the Rule of St. Benedict. By Smaragdus of Saint-Mihiel.
Translated by David Barry, O.S.B. Introductory essays by Terence Kardong,
O.S.B.; Jean Leclercq, O.S.B.; and Daniel LaCorte. [Cistercian Studies Series,
212.] (Kalamazoo: Cistercian Publications; Collegeville, MN: St. John's
Abbey. 2007. Pp. vi, 568. $49.95 paperback. ISBN 978-0-879-07212-4.)

In the early-ninth century Smaragdus, abbot of the monastery of St. Mihiel
on the river Meuse, wrote the first extensive commentary on the Rule of
Benedict that has been preserved, as part of the program of monastic reform
associated with "the second Benedict": St. Benedict of Aniane. Since the aim
of this reform program was a return to the proper form of monastic life as it
had been laid down by St. Benedict of Nursia, it was necessary to understand
the text of the father of Western monasticism as fully as possible. Smaragdus
set to work to explain particular features of this text, but his work also, by
necessity, entailed a reinterpretation of particular parts of Benedict's Rule. As
such, it provides the modern reader with a fascinating view on ninth-century
Frankish monasticism.

Reading the smooth translation offered by David Barry, the reader sees
Smaragdus explain difficult Latin terms, often with the help of Isidore of
Seville's *Etymologies* or his *De ecclesiasticis officiis*. Cenobites, he thus
explains, are those monks who live in community, the term deriving from
Greek and Latin (p. 116). The gyrovagues are those who rove and wander
around the houses and cells of others (p. 122). Often Smaragdus offers a spiritual interpretation of the Rule's precepts. When commenting upon
Benedict's list of the instruments of good works (chap. 4), he moves, for example, the emphasis from the literal killing of others to a monk murdering his
own soul through entertaining feelings of hatred toward another person. The
term *adultery* is redefined so as to include sins like fornication, worship of
idols, and greed for worldly things (p. 167). Benedict's incorporation of an
obligation to bury the dead was also in need of a spiritual interpretation, since
a literal interpretation would, as Smaragdus notices, either mean that Benedict
was stating the obvious, as monks could not, of course, leave their deceased
fellow brethren unburied, or he was prescribing behavior that was deemed
unseemly for a ninth-century monk—that is, to "go about through villages and
estates to bury the dead" (pp. 182–83). The dead must therefore mean "sins"
here, so that monks need to bury their sins. Smaragdus is well aware of the
fact that inaccurate versions of Benedict's text were used in his time. When
discussing the possibility of arguing with the abbot, some versions of the rule
read "inside or outside the monastery," but Benedict wrote only "outside the
monastery" here, so Smaragdus maintains. He probably consulted the copy of
Benedict's Rule that had been sent to Charlemagne's court, since he refers to
a manuscript that Benedict would have written with his own hand (p. 159).

Smaragdus's commentary not only shows us how Benedict's Rule was
read and interpreted in the early-ninth century but also informs us about
other texts that were regarded as authoritative in this period of reform. Apart

from the almost ubiquitous Isidore, Smaragdus refers continually to Gregory the Great, John Cassian, and the Venerable Bede as the great experts of monastic life. Next to these authorities, he frequently used the *Concordia Regularum*, the compendium of monastic rules that Benedict of Aniane had assembled in the ninth century as a preliminary to his reform ideas. Since Smaragdus regularly confronts his readers with long citations from these sources, a translator is faced with the difficulty of presenting a readable text while at the same time making it clear that we are reading, for instance, Gregory the Great and not Smaragdus himself. This problem has been solved elegantly in the present edition by using different typefaces to distinguish the text of Benedict from those of Smaragdus and his sources. Marginal annotations offer additional help with identifying biblical citations, providing Latin equivalents (particularly helpful where Smaragdus follows Isidore in advancing etymological explanations), and referring to the edition used for this translation (the text prepared by Alfredus Spannagel and Pius Engelbert for the series Corpus Consuetudinum Monasticarum edited by Kassius Hallinger). The three introductory essays to Barry's translation stress the significance of the commentary for modern monks as well as for Cistercian monks in the twelfth century. While this is defensible on the basis of the series in which this translation appears, a bit more information on the author and his times would have been welcome.

University of Utrecht ROB MEENS

Die Touler Vita Leos IX. Edited and translated (into German) by Hans-Georg Krause, Detlev Jasper, and Veronika Lukas. [Monumenta Germaniae Historica, Scriptores rerum Germanicarum in usum scholarum separatim editi, Vol. 70]. (Hannover: Verlag Hahnsche Buchhandlung. 2007. Pp. viii, 314. €35,00. ISBN 978-3-775-25391-8.)

The elevation of Bishop Bruno von Egisheim-Dagsburg of Toul as Pope Leo IX in 1049 has long been seen as a decisive moment in the fortunes both of the movement for ecclesiastical reform in the eleventh century and in the revitalization of the papacy in general. By most contemporary accounts, Leo was the reformer *par excellence*. As bishop of Toul, he was a champion of monastic reform, placing the abbeys of St. Evroul, St. Mansuy, and Moyenmoutier under the authority of the renowned reformer William of Volpiano. He also founded a priory at Deuilly and was a strong advocate of the female house at Poussay, founded by his predecessor, Berthold. When designated by Emperor Henry III as successor to Pope Damasus II in 1048, Leo reportedly declared that he would not ascend the papal throne unless the clergy and people of Rome unanimously elected him as pope. Even his subsequent journey to Rome was said to have been marked by miraculous events; Leo apparently heard angels singing. His pontificate has been seen by contemporaries and modern historians alike as an auspicious one and, in many ways, Leo was a model for how the Roman papacy could assume tangible leadership over the universal Church, whilst simultaneously becoming a focal point of reform.

Although historians have had access to a much better version of the *Vita Leonis IX. papae* than was previously available in the *Patrologia Latina* (thanks to the edition by Michel Parisse in 1997 for *Les classiques de l'histoire de France au moyen âge*) the text there—albeit based on the two oldest manuscripts (Bern, Burgerbibliothek 22 [B₁] from Upper Lotharingia [Toul?] and 292 [B₂] from St. Arnulf, Metz)—did not seek to engage with the wider manuscript transmission and especially the later additions to the text in the main manuscript families. This new and much-anticipated critical edition of the *Vita Leonis IX. papae*, by clarifying the manuscript tradition, enables historians to appreciate the expansion of the original text that is believed to be close to that transmitted in the Bern manuscripts.

As is to be expected from Krause's own previous editorial work and from the Monumenta Germaniae Historica, the edition is a magisterial one. The volume includes an introduction with discussion of the ongoing debate about the *Vita*'s compiler, its date and provenance, its value as a historical source for Bruno/Leo's career, and its literary sources and style. Most important, as previously noted, is the attention paid to the manuscript transmission in the Toul (and later Reims version) and Metz branches of the *Vita* and the other subsequent versions deriving from the Metz tradition; this is clearly set out both in the stemma and in the apparatus. A bibliography of primary and secondary literature is also included. The edition of the *Vita Leonis IX. papae* itself is meticulous with a full scholarly apparatus with variants and explanatory notes. In the end, this is an excellent critical edition of an extremely important source that will not only set a high standard for other editions but also will be a vital part of medieval scholarship on the early reform papacy for many years to come.

Keele University   KATHLEEN G. CUSHING

The Children's Crusade: Medieval History and Modern Mythistory. By Gary Dickson. (New York: Palgrave Macmillan. 2008. Pp. xviii, 246. $35.00. ISBN 978-1-403-99989-4.)

The Children's Crusade has long deserved a treatment in depth. Sometimes rejected as pure myth, other times taken as a real event, it has always been surrounded with an impenetrable quality that challenged all who tried to sort reality from myth or just storytelling. Gary Dickson has given us a work that is entirely worthy of its subject. In doing so, he has placed the history of the Children's Crusade in a context that will make his work one that all historians will find intellectually enriching. Indeed, this is a case in which the vessel may be more important than its contents. This is a book about mythistory that also happens to be history of the Children's Crusade. The author provides an understanding of mythistory that adheres to and enriches the historical narrative, which he views as a hybrid that cannot exist without history. In doing so, he recognizes a valid point about medieval sources, namely that myth provides a source for explaining alongside of and even within the factual schema. Therefore, the historian must deal with it as an important part of the history. The author takes up this daunting task and helps us to better understand the complex story of the Children's Crusade.

But he goes further, recognizing that the Children's Crusade must be placed in the context of those movements that spring up throughout history and reflect the emotional depths of human reactions. He has himself written extensively about crowd psychology and religious enthusiasm, including studies of the Shepherds' Crusades in the thirteenth and fourteenth centuries. His approach is not from the perspective of psychology, although he is obviously well informed, but as an historian. For him, the meticulous piecing together of the story of the Children's Crusade is the key to making those events understandable. He situates the beginnings of the movement in the Chartrain region, a rich agricultural region in Western Europe. Although he notes the discussion of overpopulation in his search for a cause of the popular movement, he focuses chiefly on the charismatic leadership of Stephen of Cloyes, whom he sees as the leader of the French contingent that made its way northward to St. Denis and the court of Philip Augustus. He traces some ties between the French group and a group that formed in the areas around Aachen and Cologne. This group, probably larger than that under Stephen, who disappears from the scene, is led by a youth named Nicholas, about whom there is better evidence than for Stephen. It made its way southward through one of the Alpine passes to Piacenza, and Dickson traces its path westward to Genoa. This change in direction is interesting in light of the anti-Venetian sentiment found in some circles after the Fourth Crusade. He deals with the various accounts in medieval chronicles, providing a valuable, step-by-step picture of the development of mythistory in such authors as Alberic of Trois-Fontaines. He explores in depth the horror stories of the bad end met by the French crusaders at Marseilles and the Germans in Genoa as well as the stories of enslavement by Muslims, but he strongly advocates for the view that many either returned home or settled where they ended up. He spends considerable space on the issue that has long produced the most romantic image of the crusade, the picture of children caught up in a rapture of enthusiasm marching toward Jerusalem, expecting the sea to part so that they might cross it in the way of the Israelites under Moses passing through the Red Sea. Recent scholarship has presented a picture that argues against the idea of children in favor of a movement of urban and rural young people, with some elders, as the core of the crusade. The view that contemporaries were not misled in labeling the Children's Crusade seems plausible, although the term may have been derisive more than descriptive. One point seems definite: There were no notable members of the aristocracy associated with it. No contemporary would have missed out on the opportunity to mention any nobles who were present.

Dickson has done a remarkable job of sorting out the Children's Crusade and tracing its afterlife to the present. There is no question that mythistory will continue to trump *histoire éventuelle* in the popular market, but Dickson has provided an original and profound work that deserves serious study by all historians and wide use in the historiography classes of history majors as well as graduate students.

Syracuse University (Emeritus)   JAMES M. POWELL

The Crusades and the Christian World of the East: Rough Tolerance. By Christopher MacEvitt. [The Middle Ages Series.] (Philadelphia: University of Pennsylvania Press. 2008. Pp. viii, 272. $49.95. ISBN 978-0-812-24050-4.)

As in the Arab-Israeli wars of modern times, so in the confrontation of Islam and the Crusades, we tend to forget the third party, the eastern Christians. They barely figure in most histories of the crusades. Yet when Pope Urban II launched his expedition in 1095, they were in the forefront of his mind, for he wanted to aid them against their Islamic oppressors. Since then, they have been written out of the story. In this book MacEvitt explains why the sources appear to underpin this silence and shows that in reality they were much more important than we have come to believe. To some extent he is following the work of Roni Ellenblum, who has suggested, on the basis of archaeological and written evidence, that crusader relations with the native Christians were good and, indeed, important to the survival of the kingdom.[1] Ellenblum's focus, however, was the western settlers, while here MacEvitt is directly concerned with the eastern Christians. His subtitle, "Rough Tolerance," does not refer to *convivencia*, the grudging tolerance, so often laced with random violence, conceded to conquered Muslims in Spain. MacEvitt's central thesis is that Latin sources say so little about the various sects of eastern Christians because the Latin Kingdom in the twelfth century, by and large, treated them like anybody else and was uninterested in the theological niceties that distinguished Jacobites from Armenians and even Latins. Moreover, this tolerance extended to treating with native Christian elites and ecclesiastical leaders, and accepting them into positions of power, notably the Arrabi family in Jerusalem. This is startling rereading of our sources and a complete revision of the view, essentially devised by Joshua Prawer but followed by many others, that after 1099 the Latins simply took over the confessional system from their Islamic predecessors, but inverted it so that Muslims communities had the lowest status, and native Christians enjoyed a servile and bare tolerance.[2] A good deal of the book is concerned with Edessa, for which his conclusions are less surprising, because there Latins

---

[1] Roni Ellenblum, *Frankish Rural Settlement in the Latin Kingdom of Jerusalem* (Cambridge, UK, 1998).
[2] See especially Joshua Prawer, *The Crusaders' Kingdom: European Colonialism in the Middle Ages* (New York, 1972).

were few and the Armenian lords were so important that both the first two counts, Baldwin I and Baldwin II, married Armenian women. When it comes to the Latin Kingdom itself, where, as he says, we have more evidence, MacEvitt convincingly demolishes the notion that only Latins were free and all others were servile. His emphasis is on ecclesiastical relations, and here he produces a very convincing argument for Latin recognition of the importance of native Christians by stressing their role in the Holy Sepulchre and Latin recognition of their hierarchy. Moreover, Latins took communion from native priests of all denominations. The analysis of the Council of Jerusalem of 1141 is particularly impressive, and the idea that the Byzantines used their influence to emphasize their differences from Jacobites and others is interesting. MacEvitt argues that the Latins became exclusive only in the thirteenth century, as a result of European ecclesiastical development and the radically changed nature of their settlement. The only application of the term *heretic* to eastern Christians before Jacques de Vitry in the thirteenth century occurs in the Letter of the Crusader Leaders dated September 11, 1098 (p. 1): it would have strengthened MacEvitt's case if he had recognized that this denunciation was rooted in political events that also led to what he curiously describes as the crusaders "having chosen not to return the city [Antioch] to Byzantine control" (p. 100). These are, however, very minor blemishes. This is an excellent and exciting book that states a novel case succinctly and clearly.

Swansea University JOHN FRANCE

Letters of Peter Abelard: Beyond the Personal. Translated by Jan M. Ziolkowski. [Medieval Texts in Translation.] (Washington, DC: The Catholic University of America Press. 2008. Pp. lii, 232. $29.95 paperback. ISBN 978-0-813-21505-1.)

With this new translation of Peter Abelard's lesser known letters, Jan M. Ziolkowski encourages readers to look "beyond the personal" as they consider a man who, more than any other, embodied the spiritual, cultural, and intellectual currents of the twelfth-century renaissance. Philosopher, theologian, and logician, Abelard earned fame as a young man in the schools of northern France, establishing himself not only as a creative thinker but also as a controversial and even divisive figure, whose intellectual battles reflected the military ethos of the knightly class. Early disputes with his teachers—Roscelin of Compiègne, William of Champeaux, and Anselm of Laon—presaged Abelard's later quarrels with the monks at St. Denis, with whom he took refuge following his disastrous affair with Heloise, and with Bernard of Clairvaux, his chief opponent at the Council of Sens. Appropriately, an entire section of Ziolkowski's translation is devoted to letters relating to Abelard's stormy relationship with Bernard (Epp. 10, 15 and his *Apologia*) and another to "Other Controversies," among them Abelard's missive to the abbot of St. Denis (Ep. 11); a letter celebrating the superiority of the monastic versus the canonical life (Ep. 12); a sophisticated defense of Dialectic addressed to an "Ignoramus" (Ep. 13); and a letter to the bishop of Paris, written during the course of Abelard's conflicts with Roscelin (Ep. 14).

Ziolkowski's subtitle, *Beyond the Personal*, takes issue with the fame of the so-called "personal" letters of Abelard and Heloise (Epp. 1–5). Although written in the early 1130s, some years after the two had entered the religious life, these tell the poignant story of their love affair, marriage, and monastic profession, a dramatic tale that has gripped readers since the fourteenth century. Dogged by questions concerning their authenticity, however, these letters have attracted their own share of controversy. Moreover, the traditional division between the "Personal Letters" and the "Letters of Direction" (Epp. 6–8), as they appear in the Penguin translation, has served to solidify Abelard's reputation as a romantic antihero, whose callous seduction of Heloise plays badly against her own protestations of selfless love. That Abelard continued to care for Heloise after she entered the monastery, composing for her and for the nuns of the Paraclete ("our oratory," as he writes to her [p. 70]) a corpus of liturgical, exegetical, and exhortatory texts, has often been overlooked. Ziolkowski remedies this state of affairs, including in the first section translations of Abelard's letters to the nuns of the Paraclete, among them Ep. 9, encouraging the study of Hebrew, Greek, and Latin; Ep. 16, his prologue to the sermon collection he compiled for the women; his prefaces to the 133 hymns of the Paraclete Hymnal; and his dedication to the *Expositio in Hexameron*. As Ziolkowski notes, many of these works were written at Heloise's explicit request, making her Abelard's active collaborator and intellectual partner, even after the end of their affair.

This helpful and appropriately revisionist collection will be warmly welcomed by scholars, teachers, and students. Ziolkowski's translation is elegant and readable while remaining faithful to Abelard's characteristic style. The letters themselves, spanning some twenty years of Abelard's career, provide important insights into the spiritual and intellectual context of northern France in the early-twelfth century. All are authentic. Together with the Penguin translation, Ziolkowski's volume now presents Abelard's letters in their entirety, affording a new appreciation of a man, who, in his own life, richly reflected the tensions and contradictions of his age.

New York University					Fiona J. Griffiths

Simone da Collazzone Francescano e il processo per la sua canonizzazione (1252). By Ernesto Menestò. [Uomini e mondi medievali, Vol. 11.] (Spoleto: Centro italiano di studi sull'alto medioevo. 2007. Pp. x, 192. €35,00 paperback. ISBN 978-8-879-88067-1.)

Franciscan studies, especially in Italy, have been experiencing a golden period. The focus of the scholarship has been mainly on the founding moment, the origin of the rule of life developed by St. Francis and his companions—presently celebrating the 800th anniversary of its approval by Pope Honorius III—and efforts toward the resolution of the "Franciscan question": Which one of the dozen or so hagiographical accounts of Francis's life presented the real Francis? Current research has also focused on the "heredità difficile": the multifaceted evolution of the early Franciscan movement often referred to as the quarrel between the Spirituals (those who fought for an unmitigated observance of the Franciscan rule) and the Community (those who felt that relaxations and accommodations were needed).

Simone da Collazzone belongs to the third generation of Franciscans and on the cusp of the burgeoning battle about who were the "legitimate sons" of Francis and how to interpret his rule. Unfortunately, very little is known about Simone's life; most of it is culled from the Acts of his canonization trial (1252), which never reached a successful conclusion. In the opening chapter, Ernesto Menestò, who has been at the forefront of current Franciscan scholarship, sketches the framework for Simone's life: he entered the Franciscan Order when he was fourteen years old (he knew Francis personally); was quickly sent on a three-year missionary venture to Germany; was elected, upon his return to Italy, provincial minister of the Marches and later Umbria; and died (1250) in Spoleto where he had the reputation for holiness and as a miracle maker. Menestò qualifies him as a "prospiritual" because he shared and lived the ideals of the primitive Franciscan community: observing the Gospel life and the *sequela Christi* by sharing the social condition of the poor, refusing money and power, serving the sick and the lepers; also, his life included periods spent in hermitages, which was also part of his protest against the nascent adaptations of the more conventual-minded Community.

Most of Menestò's excellent monograph consists of a collection of the relevant available documentation concerning Simone's life: the *negotium* for his canonization trial; its manuscript tradition and the criteria for a new critical edition; the Acts of the trial itself; the list of witnesses (seventy-four) and miracles; the numerous and sometimes lengthy references to him in the early chronicles of the Order; and selected illustrations.

Catholic Theological Union, Chicago   PAUL LACHANCE, O.F.M.

Il divorzio imperfetto: I giuristi medievali e la separazione dei coniugi. By Giuliano Marchetto. [Annali dell'Istituto storico italo-germanico in Trento, Monografie, Vol. 48.] (Bologna: Il Mulino. 2008. Pp. 500. €32,50 paperback. ISBN 978-8-815-12500-2.)

The formation and dissolution of marriage is vitally important, not only to the parties involved but also to historians who study medieval society. Marchetto's investigation of the canon law dealing with *divortium a mense et thoro*, or "incomplete divorce," as he calls it, is a magisterial treatment of the development of a central, if sometimes puzzling, element in the matrimonial law of the medieval church.

Separation from bed and board was a creation of medieval Western canon law and had no direct parallels in Roman, Jewish, Byzantine, or Germanic law. As Marchetto demonstrates, the concept originated among teachers of canon law and theology in medieval universities, was subsequently incorporated into ecclesiastical law, and still survives in one form or another as an alternative to "complete" divorce, which in modern Western legal systems carries the right of remarriage.

Marchetto divides his book into three parts. The first and longest of them (pp. 21–231) deals with the development of doctrine concerning marriage and divorce among medieval canonists, civilians, and theologians. Part 2 (pp. 235–324) outlines the gradual crystallization of a procedural system for handling separation cases, while part 3 (pp. 327–426) analyzes the grounds on which a separation might be granted. A concluding section (pp. 427–41) summarizes Marchetto's arguments and is followed by an impressively comprehensive bibliography (pp. 443–91). The author limited the index at the end to personal names and hence excludes subject entries. This is a pity, especially in a work of this size and complexity, although the detailed table of contents at the beginning of the book provides at least a modicum of help for those who wish to locate his treatment of a particular matter.

One especially fascinating topic among the many that Marchetto treats is his investigation of the emergence of cruelty (*saevitia*) as a ground for marital separation. What makes this so unusual is that it first appeared in the writing of Bulgarus, a teacher of civil law, was then adopted and developed by later twelfth- and thirteenth-century canonists and theologians, and was widely accepted by church courts as a legitimate basis for granting separations long before it was formally approved and incorporated into the official texts of canon law.

Marchetto's book centers almost exclusively on the development of academic doctrines concerning marital separation and pays scant attention to the actual practice of courts and judges. Although it seems true that judges usually did follow the formal prescriptions found in the texts of the *Corpus iuris canonici* and the interpretations of those texts current among university teachers of canon law, it has become increasingly clear that regional variations from the doctrinal norms were not entirely uncommon. To understand how the law concerning marital separation was actually implemented in practice, therefore, requires investigation of the surviving case records of ecclesiastical courts. Those records are widely scattered and often difficult to access, and scholars have begun to study them systematically only in recent years. A realistic understanding of the workings of marital separation law thus requires that Marchetto's treatment be supplemented by consultation of case record studies such as *Coniugi nemici: la separazione in Italia dal XII al*

XVIII secolo, ed. Silvana Seidel Menchi and Diego Quaglioni (Bologna, 2000) or Charles Donahue, Jr.'s *Law, Marriage, and Society in the Later Middle Ages: Arguments about Marriage in Five Courts* (New York, 2007).

University of Kansas (Emeritus)   JAMES A. BRUNDAGE

The Court Book of Mende and the Secular Lordship of the Bishop: Recollecting the Past in Thirteenth-Century Gévaudan. By Jan K. Bulman. (Toronto: University of Toronto Press. 2008. Pp. xiv, 179. $50.00. ISBN 978-0-802-09337-0.)

The oldest register of an "ecclesiastical court" yet found in France is the register of the episcopal court of Mende housed in the departmental archives in the remote, mountainous city of the same name (1268-72, A[rchives] d[épartementales de la] L[ozère] G963). The quotation marks are necessary because the exact nature of the jurisdiction reflected in the book is the subject of Bulman's study. To place the register in context, she tells the story of the jurisdictional claims of the bishops of Mende from the earlier Middle Ages with particular focus of Aldebert III (bishop of Mende, 1151-87) and later to Guillaume Durand (nephew of the famous canonist and bishop of Mende, 1296-1330). Early in Guillaume's pontificate (1307) and in settlement of litigation in the *parlement* of Paris that began in 1269, Guillaume and Philip (IV) the Fair agreed to a *paréage* whereby at least the secular jurisdiction in the county of Gévaudan, which was coterminous with the diocese of Mende, was to be exercised by a single court controlled jointly and roughly equally by the bishop and the king. This arrangement seems to have continued, not without tensions, at least into the fifteenth century.

At their strongest Bulman's theses are that ADL G963 and the following series of now-lost court registers was begun by Odilon de Mercoeur (bishop of Mende, 1247-74) to bolster his claim in the *parlement*, that the registers were used by Guillaume Durand in what has come to known as the *Mémoire relatif au paréage*, and that as a result of the *Mémoire* Guillaume's *paréage* with Philip was more favorable to Mende than was that concluded by the bishop of nearby Le Puy at approximately the same time. Bulman connects the development in Mende with the slow and painstaking transition from orality to literacy, from memory to written record, that was taking place in this period. In her view, Guillaume used the new tools of literacy to construct a memory of what had happened at Mende, a memory that was quite different from what had actually happened.

The use that Guillaume made of the court registers in his *Mémoire* is solidly grounded. Bulman has documented the use of the surviving register, and there is no reason to doubt that the others she cites existed at the time. That the creation of these registers in the first place is to be connected quite as directly as Bulman does with the appeal to the *parlement* is somewhat more problematic. The surviving register begins in the year preceding that of Odilon's appeal and that such records should be kept had been the law of the western Church since the Fourth Lateran Council of 1215 (c. 38). Perhaps, as seems to be the case with the thirteenth-century ecclesiastical court records that survive at Canterbury, the jurisdictional dispute helps to explain not the making of the records in the first place but their preservation. The comparison with Le Puy invites skepticism. Bulman offers (pp. 75–76) institutional explanations for why the bishop of Le Puy was not in as a good a position as that of Mende to settle favorably with the crown, and how the bishop of Le Puy or his lawyers supported their claims is difficult to determine. That Guillaume used the new tools of literacy to construct a memory of what had happened is the most problematical claim. Tendentious documents were not an invention of the early-fourteenth century, and I think it unlikely that the sophisticated lawyers of Philip the Fair expected anything more than a selection of the truth from another sophisticated lawyer in what was, after all, a *plaidoyer*.

The theses of the book are, however, of some interest. The narrative, too, is interesting and useful, and seems correct in its main outlines. The analysis of the types of cases in ADL G963, while not as detailed as one would like, is a considerable advance in the study of this important and quite intractable record.

Nonetheless, this book should not have been published in its present condition. Seeming contradictions cry out for an explanation. For example, on page 30 we learn that a notary named Guillaume Traversier testified in the *enquête* of 1270, but on page 55, we learn that the first evidence of notarial activity in Mende dates from 1283. The form of ADL G963 could have usefully been compared with other early efforts to create running records of judicial business. Editions of the roughly contemporary "court of Canterbury rolls" (Adams and Donahue, eds., London, 1981) and the somewhat earlier *Imbreviaturbuch* of the court of Archbishop Hubaldus of Pisa (Dolezalek, ed., Köln, 1969) are in print. Although this was not the place to offer an edition of ADL G963—given its size, condition, and difficulty of the script—a full transcription of a few of the cases would have been helpful. The transcriptions that are offered would have benefited from more care and analysis. For example, *Scribens die lune post Festem Omnium sanctorum ad difinitivum* (p. 64) has to be *post Festum*, and *difinitivum* is probably *difinitivam* (scilicet, *sentenciam audiendam*)—that is, the day set down for rendering the final or definitive sentence. The use of this piece of standard diplomatic in court records could then have been connected with the known presence of a notary in Mende in 1270. Typographical and other errors abound, such as "Capetain" for "Capetian" (p. 3), "Privatii" for "Privati" (p. 20), "Chronicron" for "Chronicon" (p. 21), "Chatueau" for "Chateau" (p. 35), "epsicopatu" for "episcopate" (p. 40), "criminal" for "mostly civil" (p. 50), and "small surprise" for "no small surprise" (p. 66).

Harvard Law School   CHARLES DONAHUE, JR.

Thomas Aquinas on the Jews: Insights into His Commentary on Romans 9-11. By Steven C. Boguslawski, O.P. (Mahwah, NJ: Paulist Press. 2008. Pp. xviii, 145. $18.95 paperback. ISBN 978-0-809-14233-0.)

In the compelling dialogue today between Jews and Christians, the long and devastating tradition of contempt for Jews within Christianity is a persistent preoccupation. In recent decades, this has prompted historical reexaminations to understand more fully this onerous tradition, with special interest in those who challenged it. Commonly, such treatments have integrated social and theological analyses, but this has often meant modest theological analysis at best.

Boguslawski seeks to correct this problem in reference to the leading theological voice in the matter in the medieval period, St. Thomas Aquinas, and to do so on the basis of the central theological source for this relationship, St. Paul's Letter to the Romans. Through a close scrutiny of Aquinas's seldom examined *Commentary on Romans (Super epistolam ad romanos)*, Boguslawski develops a thesis against the grain—namely, that Aquinas did not in fact perpetuate the dominant *adversos Judaeos* tradition in presumed continuity with Augustine, but rather substantially corrected that tradition in a positive soteriological assessment of the covenantal role of Judaism and, even more remarkably, a theological basis for a continuing one.

In recent decades, there has been no dearth of scholarship on Aquinas and his understanding of Jews and Judaism, portraying consistency with the Augustinian tradition to which he was so indebted. But Boguslawski has two particular scholars in mind here, arguably the two most important recent interpreters in this area: Jeremy Cohen (*The Friars and the Jews: The Evolution of Medieval Anti-Judaism,* Ithaca, NY, 1982) and especially John Y. B. Hood (*Aquinas and the Jews,* Philadelphia, 1995). Both Cohen and Hood focus on the social-historical context in assessing Aquinas's view of the Jews as thoroughly consistent with Augustinian supersessionism and depreciative of Judaism and Jewish status. This is the traditional view that sets up Boguslawski's counterassessment in a theological reinterpretation through Aquinas's exegesis of Romans.

Boguslawski's thesis is precise and provocative in a threefold sequence. First, he exposits the traditional assessment of Aquinas's view on the Jews in his own social context and in the *Summa Theologiae.* Second, he asserts that this analysis needs to be reframed on the basis of Aquinas's *Commentary on the Romans,* which presents not only a substantial agreement between the two contemporaneous textual treatments but also posits the stronger influence of the biblical text. Third, from such an exegetical analysis, he claims that Aquinas clearly has a central and positive understanding of the role of the Jews that has not previously been adequately understood.

The key interpretive basis for Boguslawski is a reframing of Aquinas's perspective in terms of the concept of God's providence as the key in Romans 9–11, placing the essential focus in an emphasis on election and predestination. Aquinas, in this *Commentary* and reflectively in the *Summa*, asserts a foundational understanding of the Jews as a permanently valued element in divine design and continually essential for Christianity. This thesis runs counter to later Reformation views and much of modern interpretation on the Pauline focus in Romans 9–11 as grounded in the sequential history of salvation and issues of justification rather than providential design. Boguslawski extends his discussion into the area of contemporary traditional and revisionist Romans interpretation but complicates the analysis of the primacy of providence by his citation of a supplemental soteriological key in Aquinas's focal use of John 4:22 (". . . for salvation is from the Jews"). Nonetheless, the reframing here in Aquinas's providential understanding of covenant asserts a most valuable broader biblical agenda.

Boguslawski has provided an important and necessary corrective from a historical-theological perspective. He presents a valuable shift from a social-historical perspective that sees Aquinas as a traditional Augustinian in his view of the Jews, hence a passive voice in the rising hostility of the Church and society against Jews in the thirteenth century, to a historical-theological perspective of Aquinas as an advocate of a positive view of Judaism and Jews, one that offers a constructive theology that revises the Augustinian tradition. This contribution now suggests the continuing place for Aquinas's understanding of Jews and Judaism in correlation with the ongoing debate in Pauline studies on Romans, one that promises to become an essential ingredient both in the discussion of medieval views of Judaism and in the contemporary Jewish-Christian dialogue. Additionally, this is a work valuable for those who are well grounded in the historical-theological discussion as well as those new to these issues, and, for both, the footnotes are comprehensive and extraordinarily helpful.

St. Norbert College (Emeritus)					MICHAEL B. LUKENS

Living Together, Living Apart: Rethinking Jewish-Christian Relations in the Middle Ages. By Jonathan Elukin. [Jews, Christians, and Muslims: From the Ancient to the Modern World.] (Princeton: Princeton University Press. 2007. Pp. xii, 193. $25.95. ISBN 978-0-691-11487-3.)

According to the dust jacket, this book is to "challenge the standard conception of the Middle Ages as a time of persecution for the Jews." In the author's own words, "Instead of persecution and suffering, it is more important to understand how and why Jews survived in societies whose dominant theology increasingly cast them in the role of deicides" (pp. 6–7, as also the following quotations). The book intends to show "that Jews in the Early and High Middle Ages were deeply integrated into the rhythms of their local worlds." Thus, they "could analyze, contextualize, and hope to manage the violence that did erupt." Such skills "would help them to survive or at least to take actions that they thought would protect them." More than that, "Jews were not singled out in medieval societies as the preferred target of violence. The level of violence against Jews—either oppressive laws, outright attacks, paranoid accusations, or expulsions—were essentially transitory and contingent events that did not fundamentally destroy the modus vivendi between most Christians and Jews of the time. The transient nature of the violence gave Jews a sense of fundamental stability and security."

How did the author arrive at such a far-reaching thesis? Much of the road traveled is just verbal hedging—"could, might, hope, at least, essentially, not fundamentally, most," as in the quotations above, and many more that fill the book. The evidence and scholarship to the contrary of the thesis is relentlessly downplayed, belittled, explained away, and denied. Without exception, sources are quoted solely from English translations or from secondary works, never from scholarly editions in the original language. The scholarship referred to is almost entirely in English and all of the last years, as if generations of scholars writing in German, French, Italian, Spanish, and—yes—Hebrew had nothing to contribute to such a grave problem. Throughout, the reading of sources is a literal one, as if historical scholarship had not developed over the last two hundred years sophisticated tools of source criticism.

Unencumbered by the confines of the historical craft, Elukin reads not "against the grain" but as he wishes. To present one example, on page 39, when downplaying the seriousness of the Visigothic persecutions, Elukin argues that such "actions did not reflect a pan-Visigothic consensus," as shown by "the opposition of count Froga in Toledo to attempted forced baptisms by Bishop Aurasius." The authority for this episode is Bernard Bachrach's *Early Medieval Jewish Policy in Western Europe* (Minneapolis, 1977). Had Elukin checked Bachrach's source, he would have found a nonevent: it begins with a short contemporary (early-seventh century) letter of excommunication directed by this bishop against a Count Froga for the latter's alleged judaizing tendencies and derision of the Church, to which he had given voice *in the presence of the elders, the whole palace, the Catholic people and also the Jews* (*Epistolae Merovingici et Karolini aevi*, Munich, 1892, I:689–90). To this episode Julian, an otherwise unknown priest of mid-twelfth-century Toledo, appended an explanatory comment, by which the pontiff had *converted to the faith by his unceasing exhortations Ioseph, Rabbi Isaac, Nephtalim and others highly placed. Levi Samuel, archisynagogus of the synagogue of Toledo, complained to Frogo, count and prefect of Toledo*, who protected them against the bishop, for which the count was excommunicated (*Luitprandi, subdiaconi toletani, ... opera quae extant*. R. Hieronimi de la Higuera societatis Jesu presbiteri et D. Laurenti Ramirez de Prado consiliarii regii notis illustrata, Antwerpen 1640, p. 524). The story was further enhanced by Bachrach, to read: "In Toledo, where Bishop Aurasius actually carried out forced baptisms, Froga, the count of the city, opposed him. This oppo-

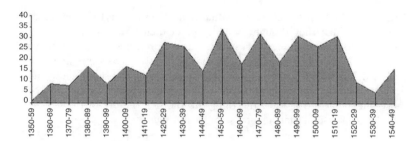

FIGURE 1. Number of violent anti-Jewish events, Germany, by decades, 1350–1550. Source: Michael Toch, "Die Verfolgungen des Spätmittelalters (1350-1550)," *Germania Judaica*, Band III, Teilband 3, ed. Arye Maimon, Mordechai Breuer, and Yacov Guggenheim (Tübingen, 2003), p. 2309.

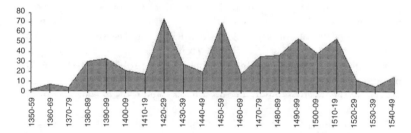

FIGURE 2. Number of places in Germany where Jews were expelled from, by decades, 1350–1550. Source: Michael Toch, "Die Verfolgungen des Spätmittelalters (1350-1550)," *Germania Judaica*, Band III, Teilband 3, ed. Arye Maimon, Mordechai Breuer, and Yacov Guggenheim (Tübingen: 2003), p. 2311.

sition led to violence, and the bishop's letter excommunicating the count still survives" (Bachrach, p. 10). The earliest version has Jews solely in a passive capacity as part of the public setting. The more concrete details and active stance, including such a central component as the voluntary or involuntary baptism, are additions of the twelfth, seventeenth, and twentieth centuries. Of the four emblematic names Joseph, Isaac, Naphtali, and Levi, the two latter make their first appearance in Spain only in the eleventh century. This tale with its embellishments is not credible evidence.

Elukin makes much of developments in late-medieval Germany, where the wholesale expulsions are interpreted not so much as an end to Jewish existence than as a prelude to readmittance (from the seventeenth century onward). In the course of the research project Germania Judaica III (1963–2003) a large number of European and Israeli scholars, including this reviewer, combed the archives of Europe for manuscript sources. Do the fruits of their work bear out Elukin's soothing contention that violence was usually in the form of "unexpected outbursts" (p. 99) and expulsions resulted "from decisions of individual rulers at moments of crisis"? (p. 117). The labors of the Germania Judaica III scholars have been synthesized by this reviewer in two figures that appear above. One figure shows the sheer numbers and frequency of violent attacks; the other shows the number of expulsions. There is little to be added to the figures by way of commentary.

The Hebrew University of Jerusalem   MICHAEL TOCH
Herbert D. Katz Center for Advanced Judaic Studies,
Philadelphia

Den Irrtum liquidieren: Bücherverbrennungen im Mittelalter. By Thomas Werner. [Veröffentlichungen des Max-Planck-Instituts für Geschichte, Band 225.] (Göttingen: Vandenhoeck & Ruprecht. 2007. Pp. 813. €118,00. ISBN 978-3-525-35880-1.)

"What a day, what a day for an auto da fé." The macabre lyrics to a song from Bernstein's *Candide* typify a widespread impression that an "auto da fé" was a public ceremony of burning at the stake. ("What a day, what a treat, did you save me a seat?") But one of the several arguments of the tome under review is that incriminated books were burned at such ceremonies but not people. Thus Marguerite Porete's *Mirror of Simple Souls* (c. 1296–1306) was burned as part of the ceremony of her condemnation in what Henry Charles Lea accurately called "the first formal *auto de fé* of which we have cognizance at Paris,"[1] but the author herself was given to the flames by a secular officer on the following day. The Church burned books but "recommended mercy" for their authors.

I refer to Werner's "tome" advisedly. To offer one measure of its Brobdignagian extent, it includes 2,828 footnotes. In mentioning this I do not mean to be disparaging, for Werner is a veritably awe-inspiring scholar. His concept of studying the rituals of medieval book-burnings (with "books" here broadly understood) and probing the logic that lay behind them is fully original, and his pursuit of this concept is studded with fascinating information. Werner is also enormously thorough and unblinkingly critical; over and over again he demonstrates how previous historians of heresy trials have misread evidence because they were not alert to the right questions. Finally, he offers a large (sic) bonus: a meticulously documented hundred-page appendix cataloguing every ascertainable book-burning (or so it seems) from 492 to 1515. Students of instances of attempted medieval thought control are certain to find new data or corrections of what presumed experts have previously said; if such students cannot read German, they ought to seek help.

Here it is possible to mention only a sample of Werner's many findings. Even if an otherwise orthodox writing contained a single error, it was still

---

[1] Henry Charles Lea, *A History of the Inquisition of the Middle Ages* (New York, 1888), 2:122–23.

meant to be burned because one part spoils the whole. If a condemned heretic recanted, his lot was to throw his incriminated writings into the flames with his own hands as part of a public shaming. If errors were expressed from the pulpit without their having been written down, it was still appropriate to have the reported error list publicly burned. Unrepentant heretics were never burned with their books even if some surviving contemporary images give that impression. (Unfortunately the cover illustration, perhaps chosen by the publisher for its luridness, displays one of these misleading images.)

Werner's all-inclusiveness extends to coverage of visual imagery, apparently as exhaustive as that of his written records, and equally full of fresh insights. The author often seems to be saying, "let's look again": for example, in Berruguete's frequently reproduced painting of St. Dominic's miracle of the leaping book, it has never been noticed that two events are displayed in the same image—a miracle and an energetic book-burning. A twenty-five-page excursus considers "burnings of the vanities," largely to see whether books were among such vanities. One is surprised ever to catch Werner off guard, but it does happen. He gives a mistaken date for the opening of the Parisian trial of Marguerite Porete; he ignores the presence of a dreamer in Harley MS 3487 (which was probably not made in Oxford, but Paris); and he is unaware of evidence that Olivi's exhumed remains very likely were taken to Avignon and secretly thrown into the Rhône. But I probably should apologize for this desperate attempt at one-upmanship given that I have been working assiduously in much of Werner's area for forty years and this is all I have to correct.

Northwestern University   ROBERT E. LERNER

Memory and Community in Medieval Southern Italy. The History, Chapter Book, and Necrology of Santa Maria del Gualdo Mazzocca. By Charles Hilken. [Studies and Texts, 157, Monumenta Liturgica Beneventana IV.] (Toronto: Pontifical Institute of Mediaeval Studies. 2008. Pp. xii, 320. $79.95. ISBN 978-0-888-44157-7.)

St. Maria del Gualdo Mazzocca is a Benedictine monastery in the Fortore valley not far from Benevento. Founded by John the Hermit (d. 1170) in the mid-eleventh century it grew by donations and acquisitions in the region and by incorporations of other churches and monasteries. Not long after its institutional zenith, when it was declared an abbey in 1294–98, it attempted to take over the abbey of St. Maria de Crypta, an ambition it had to relinquish because of a papal sentence in 1326. Its decline began in 1362–63 with great losses from the plague, followed by litigations among the monks; Arnold (O. Cist.), their reformist abbot; and Elizarius, their first commendatory abbot. The monastery never recovered from the great earthquake in 1456 and finished its monastic history with the conversion into a community of canons regular in 1506.

Charles Hilken provides a concise report on the economic and spiritual history of the monastery, although his book started as an edition of the necrology of the monastery as conserved in the codex Vat. lat. 5949. The full codex was used by the monks at the daily readings in the chapter room; thus besides the necrology it contains a martyrology and the chapter book itself. Hilken's book shows the possibilities of a thorough analysis of a medieval manuscript: the edition does not stop at the transcription, nor with a codicological and paleographical analysis, but considers every textual and practical aspect. Hilken reports his findings on the relationship of the necrology with different martyrologies, the similarities in the *punctorium* between Vat. lat. 5949 and several other manuscripts of Benevento provenance. He establishes a catalog of the priors and maps the distribution of the monastery's possessions. Hilken wishes to understand the monastic ideas of the community, even if only suggested by the layout and the formulae of the necrology. The reader might ask what Hilken's book adds to the knowledge about the necrology already published by the Italian scholars in the past sixty years,[1] but in its concise compilation of the literature and primary sources, the book could become the first reference for the history of St. Maria del Gualdo for scholars. It remains the first critical edition of the necrology, an edition connecting the manuscript and its text to almost any related documentation.

Università del Salento (Lecce)   GEORG VOGELER

Nicholas of Cusa's Didactic Sermons: A Selection. Translated and introduced by Jasper Hopkins. (Loveland, CO: Arthur J. Banning Press. 2008. Pp. xxx, 474. $40.00. ISBN 978-0-938-06053-8.)

In an accomplishment spanning over three decades and ten volumes, Jasper Hopkins has made Cardinal Nicholas of Cusa (1401-64) available to an English-speaking readership. This volume concludes what Hopkins has called his "major scholarly activity." (p. iv) Intended as a companion to *Nicholas of Cusa's Early Sermons: 1430-1441* (Loveland, CO, 2003), the sermons in the present volume range more widely in time, between 1431 and 1459, with most from the years 1455-57. Most of them, therefore, were preached in Brixen. The texts are in greatly disparate lengths, since they are in different forms: sermon sketches, complete sermons, and transcriptions by hearers.

---

[1]See especially Emma Condello, "'Scriptor est Eustasius....' Nuove osservazioni sul-l'orgine del codice Vaticano latino 5949," *Scrittura e Civiltà,* 18 (1994), 53-75; Jean-Marie Martin, *Le cartulaire de S[an] Matteo di Sculgola en Capitanate,* 2 vols., [Codice Diplomatico Pugliese, 30], (Bari, 1987); Enrico D. Putrella, "La Proprietà della badia di p. Maria del Gualdo," *Samnium,* 20 (1947), 20-27, 146-61, *Samnium,* 21 (1948), 15-126, and *Samnium,* 22 (1949), 1-27; Fiorangelo Morrone, La "Legenda" del Beato Giovanni Eremita di Tufara (Naples, 1992); Fiorangelo Morrone, *Monastero di Sancta Maria de Gualdo Mazocca. Badia Baronia di p. Bartolomeo in Galdo* (Naples, 1998); and Antonio Vuolo, "Il 'Chartularium' del monastero di p. Maria del Gualdo e di p. Matteo di Sculcula (1177-1239). (Indicazioni di storia monastica, sociale ed economica della media valle del Fortore)," *Benedictina,* 25 (1978), 327-63.

Some were in fact small treatises that must have expanded the original sermon considerably. All were written in Latin, even though most would have delivered in German. There are few references to the localities in which they were delivered; so Cusa likely excised them when he revised or reviewed the sermons for wider circulation. Hopkins admits that his own principles of selection and arrangement were "purely subjective." He chose "the sermons that most appealed" to him and arranged them according to his "degree of interest" (p. iii). As a result, the sermons are presented neither chronologically nor thematically. The latter would have been very difficult in any event, since there could be several themes within a single sermon.

Although Cusa's sermons are not scholastic thematic ones in format, the content and argumentation would strain the abilities of all but the most educated. In fact, Hopkins warns modern scholars that they dare not ignore them. *Didactic* does not quite capture the style; as Hopkins concedes, all of Cusa's sermons were, after all, didactic. Perhaps *academic* would be a good description; *exegetical* even better. The sermons are highly intellectual with little appeal to the emotions, so the fact that St. Thomas Aquinas was an important source comes as no surprise. But Cusa was quite capable of trimming his sails to his audience. The remarkable little treatise on "Fides autem Catholica" (pp. 95-114) places faith above or even against intellect, something one would not expect from Cusa. While Hopkins argues that if one thinks very carefully about what Cusa said, one could actually place intellect at the pinnacle. That may be, but the sermon is clearly written to suggest the opposite. Cusa affirms the faith taught by the Church as a reliable standard, especially for those who had neither the time nor the talent for intellectual pursuits. The bishop had trumped the scholar.

As always, Hopkins's translations are clear and reliable. He has also provided a helpful list of corrigenda to the Latin texts in the *Opera Omnia,* currently being published by the Heidelberg Akademie der Wissenschaften.[1] Hopkins also includes a useful bibliography, although the volume lacks an index. Given the variety of topics found in the sermons, the latter would have been greatly appreciated.

Villanova University   R. EMMET MCLAUGHLIN

Early Modern European

Reform and Expansion 1500-1560. Edited by R. Po-Chia Hsia. [The Cambridge History of Christianity, Vol. 6.] (New York: Cambridge University Press. 2007. Pp. xxii, 749. $205.00. ISBN 978-0-521-81162-0.)

This is a history of what most scholars call the Protestant and Catholic Reformations, plus a small section about the reception of Christianity in

[1]*Nicolai de Cusa opera omnia* (Hamburg, 1959-).

parts of the non-European world. The editor announces that the work has three goals. The first is to "provide an exposition of the . . . classic common places of the history of the Reformation and confessional conflicts" (p. xv), in other words, the Lutheran, Calvinist, and radical Reformations, plus Catholicism. The second goal is to include "themes that transcend the Protestant-Catholic divide, themes of social and cultural history that have animated a generation of recent historical scholarship" (*ibid.*). The third goal is to study the history of Christianity in the larger world, meaning Christianity's relations with Judaism and Orthodoxy, plus how a few non-Europeans looked at Christianity. The book does not provide accounts of the introduction of Christianity into Latin America, North America, or Asia. Thirty-one authors, many quite distinguished, have written twenty-nine short chapters (seventeen to twenty-five pages) and one longer chapter on the topics assigned them. In most cases they are established authorities on their subjects. All the articles are balanced; they treat Protestantism of various kinds and Catholicism without confessional prejudices. All the articles are competent, and some are excellent.

The book begins with a short chapter on Martin Luther, which summarizes the basic points that scholars have debated about him but does not capture his dominating and exciting impact. Thomas A. Brady follows with an excellent account of the consolidation of Protestantism in the Holy Roman Empire to 1600. Other fine articles include, but are not limited to, Robert Kingdon on the Calvinist Reformation in Geneva, Philip Benedict on the second wave of the Reformation, Robert Bireley's survey of Catholicism, Brad Gregory on persecution and martyrdom, Alexander J. Fisher on music and religious change, and Miriam Bodiam on Christianity and Judaism.

All of this is good. However, the organizational and interpretive choices made by the editor and authors limit the usefulness of the volume. Much of the book consists of chapters that deal with topics dear to social and anthropologically-oriented historians. The chapters are competently done and interesting. But assuming that the editor did not have unlimited pages at his disposal, they come at the expense of ignoring major aspects of the Reformation era. The papacy only flits in and out, while the Italian Reformation is completely ignored. The English Reformation gets a handful of pages here and there. Separate chapters on Italy and England would have served readers better. The only material on Christianity in Latin America is an anthropological study (nearly twice as long as the Luther article) discussing how Andeans negotiated an understanding of Christian saints. The book as a whole marginalizes ideas. For example, historians have debated how much influence humanism had on the Protestant Reformation since George Voigt's book of 1859. Bernd Moeller wrote "Ohne Humanismus keine Reformation" in 1959. This book ignores humanism except for about three pages on Erasmus, mostly about his notion of toleration. There is no discussion of such theological topics as casuistry, probabilism, and Calvinist and Jesuit resistance theories. Christian biblical scholarship is barely mentioned.

There are several factual errors. On page 427 it is asserted that the University of Padua did not have a faculty of theology. Although they were organized differently from faculties of theology in northern Europe, all Italian universities had faculties of theology; they taught and awarded thousands of degrees. On page 431 it is asserted that "the Jesuits in particular took an explicit oath of allegiance to Aristotle." Despite extensive study of Jesuit education in archival, primary, and secondary sources, I have never encountered this. Even the Jesuit *Ratio studiorum* did not endorse Aristotle unequivocally. On page 297 it is stated that Tridentine bishops approved an Index of Prohibited Books in 1564. Rather, the Council of Trent charged the papacy with preparing the Index. The papacy did so and promulgated it after Trent had concluded. In addition, the Clementine Index appeared in 1596, not 1597 (*ibid.*).

The book has not been carefully edited or proofread, thus producing some garbled names and confusion. For example, "Carione de Crema" on page 166 should be "Battista Carioni" or "Battista da Crema." Little or no attempt has been made to standardize names. Catherine de' Medici is presented three ways in four occurrences, and only the index entry uses a generally accepted form of her name. Some authors give life dates for historical figures while others do not, and some obscure figures are not identified at all. This could have been handled with a biographical appendix or by giving life dates in the index entries. Some footnote and bibliographical references are garbled; for example, "Ottavia" on page 180, note 1 should be "Niccoli." Twenty-eight chapters are clearly written in the third person. Thus, it is jarring to encounter two chapters written in the first person singular. Since the publisher is charging a very high price for the book, it should have devoted more resources to editing.

There are some unresolved historiographical issues. Although the terminus is 1660 rather than the traditional 1648, the editor gives no explanation. Only two contributors address the issue; they defend 1660 as the terminus but give equally strong or stronger reasons for 1648. "Early modern" is used relentlessly, but never with a chronological definition. Although the survey article on Catholicism uses "early modern Catholicism," other authors make a point of employing and sometimes defending Catholic Reformation, Counter-Reformation, or Catholic renewal. More discussion of these historiographical differences might have been helpful.

The volume has much good historical information that readers can and should appreciate. But if the aim was to present an authoritative, comprehensive, and reliable study of Christianity over a century and a half of revolutionary changes, admittedly a difficult goal, the book could have come closer.

University of Toronto (Emeritus) and Chapel Hill, NC   PAUL F. GRENDLER

Tomb Destruction and Scholarship: Medieval Monuments in Early Modern England. By Phillip Lindley. (Donington, UK: Shaun Tyas Publishing. 2007. Pp. x, 257. £35.00. ISBN 978-1-900-28987-0.)

In *Tomb Destruction and Scholarship*, Phillip Lindley, reader in the history of art department of the University of Leicester, deals with the destruction of medieval tomb monuments in England during the sixteenth and seventeenth centuries. The study, which resulted from Lindley's 2007 Leverhulme Research Fellowship, offers new insight into the mechanisms of early-modern iconoclasm in England. At the same time, Lindley points to the side effects of destruction—that is, the increasing number of cultural tourists visiting tomb monuments as well as the growing historical scholarship.

In his first chapter, Lindley recounts the fate of funerary monuments during the sixteenth century. Often parts of tombs were sold for the sake of the material. However, Lindley is able to show that tomb defacement was nothing more than "collateral damage" under King Henry VIII and that active defacement of tombs started only under King Edward VI. Now, images of saints as well as phrases requesting prayers for the dead or—for the most zealous reformers—representations of clergy in their traditional vestments were regarded as offensive. These attacks also influenced the design of new monuments. We might think of the ensuing concentration on the virtues of the deceased and the celebration of his bloodline through the display of heraldry.

Lindley is convinced that it was the sixteenth-century experience of the fragility of material heritage that created a particularly strong desire to study and document tomb monuments. Chapter 2 thus analyzes the genesis and development of Tudor antiquarianism, which differs from late-medieval antiquarian attempts in various aspects: the introduction of formalized networks (Society of Antiquaries), a more critical evaluation of historical sources, and the wider dissemination through printed records. Many quotations from the works of authors such as John Leland, Sampson Erdeswick, or Ralph Brooke give a sense of the discussed antiquarian writings and point to the scholarly debates going on at the time. A good example of such debates is the argument between Camden and Brooke, which demonstrated that the knowledge of heraldry had to be supplemented by a knowledge of the stylistic development of tomb monuments as well as by archival research. Consequently, the preservation of medieval texts and the inclusion of illustrations in antiquarian works was afforded more and more importance. Significant examples such as Sir Robert Cotton's library and John Weever's *Ancient Funerall Monuments* (1631) are discussed in chapter 3. Weever's publication was the first nationwide collection of epitaphs. The inclusion of illustrations in this work shows an awareness of the fact that images possess an authority distinct from that of texts. Chapter 3 further deals with the fate of tomb monuments during the Civil War, when Parliament actively encouraged iconoclasm. The Puritan iconoclast William Dowsing even kept a journal of the destructions he carried out in various churches between 1643 and 1644.

The first three chapters, which offer a broad overview of the attacks from the time of Henry VIII to the 1640s, are followed by three chapters with detailed case studies: Lindley employs antiquarian accounts to reconstruct the appearance of King Arthur's tomb at Glastonbury (chapter 4), to draw conclusions about the original functions of the Percy tomb in Beverley Minster (chapter 5), and to analyze the attacks and reconstructions of the Herbert monuments at Abergavenny (chapter 6).

However, considering that this is a book dealing with the development of research into tomb monuments, it is disappointing that the book does not include an overall bibliography of the large number of primary and secondary sources consulted.

In his conclusion, Lindley concedes that he might have exaggerated the extent of tomb destruction in the sixteenth and seventeenth centuries. Indeed, many scholars have already shown that a lot of damage was inflicted only in the eighteenth and nineteenth centuries. Still, Lindley has achieved his aim—namely, to show that early-modern attacks were endorsed by national authorities on a scale unprecedented in Western Europe.

This is a fine piece of research, which contributes to our understanding of early-modern tomb destructions and the antiquarian study of funerary monuments.

Heinrich Heine Universität Düsseldorf   STEFANIE KNÖLL

The Vestry Records of the United Parishes of Finglas, St. Margaret's, Artane and the Ward, 1657-1758. Edited by Maighréad Ní Mhurchadha. (Dublin: Four Courts Press, distrib. ISBS, Portland, OR. 2007. Pp 240. $65.00. ISBN 978-1-846-82052-6.)

This is the third volume in the Texts and Calendars series published by Four Courts Press in association with Ireland's Representative Church Body Library. Focusing as it does on a largely rural Church of Ireland community in north Dublin, it complements the first two volumes that are editions of the Dublin city parishes of St. John (1595-1658) and Ss. Catherine & James (1657-92), edited by Raymond Gillespie. As Raymond Refaussé, the series editor, explains in his preface, this series aims to provide critical editions of important Church of Ireland archives and manuscripts with substantial interpretative and explanatory apparatus. Combining vestry minutes, parish accounts, and fragmentary lists of baptisms, marriages, and burials, this meticulously presented edition of the Representative Church Body Library Manuscript (P 307/1/1) brings to light a largely neglected, vibrant Church of Ireland worshiping community with a viable local administration.

The value of this edited manuscript for researchers is significantly enhanced by Ní Mhurchadha's scholarly introduction in which she provides a concise, contextualized overview of the structures and operation of the vestry as well as tantalizing glimpses into the world of clerics and parish-ioners living in this rural community. Drawing upon her extensive knowledge of the region—Ní Mhurchadha is the author of *Fingal, 1603-60: Contending Neighbours in North Dublin* (Dublin, 2005)—she provides a useful com-mentary on the evolution of the united parishes from the thirteenth century onward and also profiles this Protestant community that, in the mid-1630s, was reportedly termed the "Irish Geneva" (p. 11) by its inhabitants. Ní Mhurchadha draws upon an impressive range of contemporary printed and manuscript sources to construct a finely nuanced and well-structured inter-pretative framework within which researchers may trace the evolution of this community and explore the wide range of issues addressed in this rare archival source. Her commentary deftly intertwines evidence extracted from the vestry records with material garnered from such diverse sources as Archbishop Launcelot Bulkeley's visitation report (1630), the Convert rolls, the 1659 census, the travel narratives of writers such as John Dunton (1698) and Richard Pococke (1753), *Pue's Occurrences,* and *The Dublin Journal.*

The editor offers a clear exposition of the structure, chronological devel-opment, and operation of this vestry in its three key areas of responsibility—namely, the church, local government, and finance. In highlighting major issues such as structural repairs and additions to the church, cess collection, appointment of personnel, and founding schools, as well as colorful vignettes including the vestry's ruling in 1682 that only persons wearing blue coats and badges given them by the churchwardens could beg in the area, Ní Mhurchadha accurately reflects the mixed composition of this archival source, much of which is inevitably composed of lists of names, expenses, indentures, and minutes of meetings. By its very nature, this edition will be of particular interest to scholars with a specialist interest in religious, family, and local history, and readers will find the accessibility of the text is greatly enhanced by extensive annotation and an excellent index.

Refaussé, Ní Mhurchadha, and Four Courts Press are to be commended on publishing this handsome volume that adds significantly to the growing corpus of archival material made available in print, thus enabling historians to reach a fuller understanding of Church of Ireland parish community life and the mechanics of poor relief and local government in early-modern Ireland.

St. Patrick's College, Dublin City University MARY ANN LYONS

Mícheál Ó Cléirigh, His Associates and St Anthony's College Louvain. By Brendan Jennings, O.F.M., Paul Walsh, Felim O'Brien, O.F.M., and Canice Mooney, O.F.M.; edited and revised by Nollaig Ó Muraíle. (Dublin: Four Courts Press; distrib. ISBS, Portland, OR. 2008. Pp. 251. $75.00. ISBN 978-1-846-82082-3.)

As a Louvain-trained historical theologian and now a resident of Louvain (Leuven) for close to three decades, I read this book with great fascination.

The Irish Franciscan College of St. Anthony at Louvain, established in 1607, was an intellectual powerhouse for an attempt to save and promote the religion, culture, and language of Gaelic Ireland.

For the Irish in 1607, Louvain was a natural choice and close to Ireland. Founded in 1425, the Louvain University could boast of association with such famous scholars as Juan Vives, Erasmus, and Justus Lipsius. The Irish Franciscan College became one of the forty-four colleges that constituted the university. Philip III of Spain became its patron, and Archduke Albert of Austria and his wife, Isabella, laid the foundation stone.

The Irish print alphabet and the first Irish dictionary were created at St. Anthony's. During the seventeenth century, St. Anthony's was the site of a key Irish-language printing press. Distinguished individuals at St. Anthony's included Franciscans (and future Irish archbishops) Flaithrí Ó Maoil Chonaire and Aodh Mac Cathmhaoil, as well as Fathers Hugh Ward, Patrick Fleming, Robert Chamberlain (or Mac Artúir), John Colgan, and Thomas O Sheerin. Brother Mícheál Ó Cléirigh led a team of academics that produced the Annals of the Four Masters, among other works. For more than two hundred years the college fostered Irish literary activity and served as a major missionary training school for the Church in Ireland and elsewhere.

This volume—which includes a revised short work by historian Brendan Jennings, O.F.M. (originally published in 1936), and eight academic articles by Paul Walsh, Felim O'Brien, O.F.M., and Canice Mooney, O.F.M.—is the first book to tell the nearly complete story of St. Anthony's. The one missing element is its neglect of the story of today's St. Anthony's. No longer a Franciscan house, it is an international conference center—the Louvain Institute for Ireland in Europe—that focuses on the preservation and promotion of Irish culture. The book is very well documented and solidly anchored in abundant primary sources. This book is recommended for anyone interested in Irish Catholic history.

Université Catholique de Louvain and the   JOHN A. DICK
Katholieke Universiteit Leuven

Christ in Our Midst: Incarnation, Church and Discipleship in the Theology of Pilgram Marpeck. By Neal Blough. [Anabaptist and Mennonite Studies, Vol. 8.] (Kitchener, Canada: Pandora Press, 2007. Pp. 275. $30.00. ISBN 978-1-894-71077-0.)

This fine book is a reworking of the French publication *Christologie anabaptiste. Pilgram Marpeck et l'humanité du Christ* (Geneva, 1984) of Neal Blough's dissertation. The author contributes to a "renaissance" of research on the Anabaptist leader Pilgram Marpeck (c. 1495–1556). A layman who trained as an engineer, Marpeck served in civil office and, after his expulsion from the Tirol as an Anabaptist leader, sought employment in public works projects for much of his adult life. He was, then, an unusual progenitor of the Hutterite and Mennonite traditions that advocated a strict separation from the civil communities around them.

The author examines four themes that demonstrate Marpeck's creative contributions to his sixteenth-century communities and to theology more generally—authority within the church, the link between internal and external dynamics of faith, the connection between justification and sanctification, and the relationship of church and state. Consistent with other reformers, Marpeck insists on an Christological reading of Scripture; however, his Christology—focused as it was on an increasingly persecuted gathered community of believers—led to a reading more critical of the use and abuse of power by ecclesiastical and civil authorities. Combining what Blough calls a "Lutheran sacramental logic" that emphasized the external, physical media of grace with "an almost Calvinist understanding of the 'real' (though) spiritual presence," Marpeck affirms "the visibility of the church and a communal Spirit-filled presence that reflected the humanity of Christ in the world" (p. 22). By refusing to separate justification from sanctification, Marpeck, according to Blough, was truer to the positions of St. Augustine of Hippo and much of the medieval Church than was Luther. However, his insistence on justification by faith and his belief that "infused grace" comes through the direct gift of the Holy Spirit, rather than the institutional sacraments *ex opera operato* places him closer to Protestant views in that regard. The inherent link between justification and sanctification led him to criticize the social and political quietism of many under the sway of Luther's justification by faith alone. According to Blough, Marpeck believed that the "victory of resurrection over the forces of evil and the subsequent sending of the Holy Spirit" brings not only "forgiveness and reconciliation" but also empowers disciples in the present to such things as feeding the hungry and the "confrontation of false theological, political or ethical options" (pp. 220, 226). The gathered community of believers is Christ's humanity continuing to act in history. Due to his emphasis on the cross of Christ and the noncoercive nature of the Holy Spirit, Marpeck rejected the role of the sword in matters of faith, whether wielded by the Anabaptists at Münster, the princes of the Schmalkaldic League, or Charles V. Believers are empowered to follow Christ and are "transformed collectively in his image," thereby constituting the "unglorified" body of Christ, which is sent "into the world to take on the same form as Jesus of Nazareth, the form of self-giving and nonviolent love" (p. 220).

Believing "only an internationally embodied Gospel can combat the disparities of wealth and privilege" in the world, Blough calls on Mennonites to engage "other traditions and theologies" in a "catholic" effort to address them (p. 244). His explication of Marpeck's use of "traditional theological categories of Incarnation and Trinity" (p. 244) offers entry points for dialogue and exchange for Roman Catholic and Protestant scholars from other traditions. With these goals and conversation partners in mind, readers can benefit greatly from Blough's careful exposition of this passionate, sixteenth-century advocate of peace and justice.

Wake Forest University   STEPHEN BOYD

The Rosary Cantoral: Ritual and Social Design in a Chantbook from Early Renaissance Toledo. By Lorenzo Candelaria. [Eastman Studies in Music, 51.] (Rochester, NY: University of Rochester Press. 2008. Pp. x, 212. $55.00. ISBN 978-1-580-46205-1.)

Lorenzo Candelaria's study of MS 710, acquired by the Yale University's Beinecke Rare Book and Manuscript Library in 1989, reads like a detective story—which it is, in actuality. The author's fascinating account of searching out the provenance, context, and significance of this extraordinary chantbook highlights perfectly what mesmerizes medievalists. Looking for clues and tracking leads (including false ones), the researcher tries to unlock the mystery of a manuscript. Only by reconstructing the scene of the event—applying the tools of various disciplines—can one come close to understanding "whodunit" and why.

The Beineke's MS 710 is a monumental artifact. Measuring approximately 3 feet by 2 feet (each leaf requiring an entire calf skin), the manuscript's exact provenance and history were little understood at the time of its acquisition in 1989. Claims that it was from Switzerland and Franciscan turned out to be false. By carefully comparing contents and purchase records of eight single-leaf fragments in other public and private collections, the author traced the chantbook to the monastery of San Pedro Mártir in Toledo, Spain, where it was first used *c.*1498 in the ritual and for services of a rosary confraternity of silk weavers.

The second stage of the investigation stitches together the background of the work: the history of Toledo's San Pedro Mártir Dominican community, the Inquisition, early printers of *buleta* (for a crusade against the Moors), and the religious lay brotherhood of silk weavers who owned the manuscript. In chapter 3, evidence is gathered from an illustration—common to most of the eight related manuscript fragments—of the legend of "The Gentleman of Cologne," a tale that had particular significance for this brotherhood. The legend can be traced back through versions in Germany, France, and Portugal, as far as *"Las Cantigas de Santa María"* of Alfonso X (1221–84), king of Castile.

Other clues in chapters 4 and 5 deal with the history of the rosary confraternity, the make-up of its membership, the emblem of the Five Wounds of Christ, and—rather surprisingly—the manuscript's images of two of the Labors of Hercules (one copied from an engraving *c.* 1498 by Albrecht Dürer). Chapter 6 turns to musical clues found in the manuscript's unusual tropes, its incorporation of polyphony at particular points, its contrafacture of the famous tune "L'homme armé," and an excerpt from Josquin Desprez's (c. 1455-1521) work, the "Missa sine nomine."

Yet it is the last chapter that brings the payoff, surprising the reader and unlocking the significance of this manuscript as a witness to a pivotal period in Spanish history. It illustrates not only a culture at an intellectual and religious crossroad, the contradictory intersection of medieval and Renaissance ideas, but also is witness to a fateful intercultural conflict, tragically intertwined with the religious one, that marks the darkest chapter of Spanish history. The rituals, images, and meanings embodied in this book represent conflicts surprisingly relevant in our own day. Candelaria's sensitive multidisciplinary reading of the work constitutes a fine example of how a cultural artifact from 500 years ago speaks to our own time.

Southern Illinois University-Carbondale   Anne Winston-Allen

San Francisco Javier entre dos continentes. Edited by Ignacio Arellano, Alejandro González Acosta, and Arnulfo Herrera. [Biblioteca Indiana, Publicaciones del Centro de Estudios Indianos, 7.] (Madrid: Iberoamericana. 2007. Pp. 269. €28,00 paperback. ISBN 978-8-484-89290-8.)

The editors of *San Francisco Javier entre dos continentes* have put together a very interesting collection of largely descriptive essays that provide details about the events, paintings, prayers, poems, relics, comedies, and songs that celebrated St. Francis Xavier in the early-modern Iberian world. Taken together, the collection offers impressive detail about devotion to the saint that specialists of the period can mine for indications as to how religious material culture sustained early-modern Catholicism. Scholars working on the early-modern Jesuits will also appreciate what can be construed as a multifaceted approach to understanding Jesuit influence via the spread of material culture. Readers will come away with a more comprehensive notion of the place that Xavier occupied in the early-modern Catholic imagination. The essays also implicitly contribute to scholarship on the Jesuit desire for a universal Christian empire, for although the title makes clear that the contributors are telling a transatlantic story ("between two continents"), it is important to note that almost all essays deal with materials that illuminate how Francis Xavier, as "the Apostle of the Indies," opened a window in the mind's eye to Asia, animating the imaginations and the vocations of Jesuits like the German Eusebio Kino (who wanted to go to Asia but ended up in northern New Spain), as well as the devotional desires of laity who belonged to religious congregations dedicated to Xavier. The terms *implicitly* and *can be construed* signal the shortcomings of the collection. The individual essays vary in quality. Most lamentable is that, although the work is full of rich description, there is no sustained analysis either within the essays or in an introductory essay that could have tied together the various threads that beg for deeper scrutiny.

Northwestern University   J. Michelle Molina

Päpste und Kardinäle in der Mitte des 18. Jahrhunderts (1730-1777). Das biographische Werk des Patriziers von Lucca Bartolomeo Antonio Talenti. Edited by Sabrina M. Seidler and Christoph Weber. [Beiträge zur Kirchen- und Kulturgeschichte, Band 18.] (Frankfurt am Main: Peter Lang. 2007. Pp. 690. $145.95. ISBN 978-3-631-56436-3.)

This volume publishes for the first time the lives of eighteenth-century cardinals and popes composed by the Lucchese patrician Bartolomeo Antonio Talenti, silk merchant, patron, man of learning, and collector. This edition, based on manuscripts in the Biblioteca Angelica, Rome, is complemented by an extended historical introduction by the editors. Here a full account of the Talenti family is offered, including their commercial activities that were still flourishing in eighteenth-century Lucca, a city linked closely to the republican tradition that had sustained its independence, successively, from the Medici and then from the Habsburg-Lorraine grand dukes of Tuscany. The editors have succeeded in recovering the cultural climate of the Republic, which was influenced by currents of Enlightenment thought; from Febronianism to anti-Jesuit polemics, which spread, not only in Italy, over the course of the eighteenth century. Due attention is also paid to the state of the Church, and that of the Lucchese Church in particular, which was racked by tensions caused by the spread of anti-Roman attitudes. Bartolomeo Antonio Talenti was distinguished for his rich and varied cultural and learned interests. His extensive library, examined in detail by the editors, demonstrates the extent of his interest in contemporary works; if Talenti might be considered anti-Jesuit, he was certainly no Jansenist (there are no works by French Jansenists listed in his library). Author of other learned works that reflected his wide interests, Talenti probably wrote these lives of popes and cardinals between 1763 and 1777. According to a tradition widespread since the middle of the fifteenth century, collections of the lives of popes and cardinals circulated widely in manuscript and then in print throughout of Europe. They were frequently the work of clerics, some of whom were also members of the Roman Curia itself. Their purpose was to inform the diplomats of Europe about the Court of Rome and its principal actors and factions, particularly when there was a conclave for the election of a new pope imminent. However, there also circulated biographies of leading figures of the Roman Court that had an explicitly satirical purpose. Talenti's collection does not share any of these characteristics, and in this we see its originality. To begin with, it was written by a layman. Neither did it have as its purpose the desire to inform the diplomats of Europe about its subject nor to entertain them by means of satire. Instead, one can consider it a richly erudite study that becomes fuller of details of curiosity and interest as the biographies close in on the author's own lifetime. The fulcrum of this collection is the life of Pope Clement XIV (pp. 572–622), which is full of information not only about the pope's life and political standpoint but also about the extensive polemics and tensions that marked his pontificate.

The biographies of the cardinals take different forms and are of varied length. Most are brief, but some are particularly lengthy, as in the case of Cardinals Silvio Valenti (pp. 333–66) and Domenico Passionei (pp. 412–22). Frequently, Talenti inserts into his texts contemporary sources, such as passages from other works, poetry, or eulogies. This collective biography is therefore a primary source of particular significance that enriches our understanding of the Roman Curia and its protagonists over a period that was particularly difficult for the papacy. At the same time, it shows how in the eighteenth century the Roman Court and its leading members were still the object of erudite attention for circulation throughout Europe.

Università "G. d'Annunzio," Chieti-Pescara, Italy   Irene Fosi

"Giansenisti," ebrei e "giacobini" a Siena: Dall'Accademia ecclesiastica all'Impero napoleonico (1780-1814). Con un'appendice di documenti inediti. By Francesca Piselli. [Biblioteca della *Rivista di storia e letteratura religiosa*, Studi XX.] (Florence: Leo S. Olschki Editore. 2007. Pp. xiv, 219. €24,00 paperback. ISBN 978-8-822-25711-6.)

This slender work presents an interesting snapshot of what happens when a peaceful effort of church reform collides with the much larger events of the French Revolutionary movement.

In 1783, Archbishop Tiberio Borghesi of Siena authorized the formation of an ecclesiastical academy for his diocese and the six others nearby. His action coincided with the hoped-for ecclesiastical reforms envisioned by Tuscany's grand duke, Pietro Leopoldo (who would succeed his brother Joseph II in 1790 as Emperor Leopold II). The academy was to serve as a major vehicle of clergy formation and discipline, in harmony with the grand duke's vision of the enhanced position of pastors. Like his brother, Pietro Leopoldo wanted to diminish the influence of religious orders, chapters, lay confraternities, and other nonparochial institutions. He saw the local pastor as the ultimate agent of local culture and well-being, with a chain of accountability that certainly favored an absolutist regime.

One other person who favored the new reforms and the academy was Bishop Scipione de' Ricci of Pistoia, the same one who would preside over the troublesome Synod of Pistoia in 1786. Ricci favored the tendencies of late Italian Jansenism as the most efficient way to foster a return to what he saw as the values of primitive Christianity. In addition to rigorist discipline, moral studies, liturgy, and social control, Ricci favored a reduction in the influence of the Roman Curia, as well as the Jesuits and other religious orders. Whatever the motivation, the reforms of the grand duke were highly unpopular with the ordinary citizens and in any case were swept up in the revolutionary tide, as French forces overran northern Italy just a few years later.

In the minds of the more traditional Catholics, all those promoting significant changes in both Church and society were considered to be elements of
one grand *massa damnata* of "Jansenists, Jews, and Jacobins" as the book's
title reminds us. The heart and soul of the academy was Fabio de' Vecchi, a
serious and energetic cleric who quickly locked horns with others who felt
that the filo-Jansenists were a seditious force within the body politic and who
would eventually upset the balance between Church and state in favor of the
latter. Borghesi had second thoughts about his new creation almost immediately, but it was left to his successor Alfonso Marsili finally to suppress it in
1793. Perhaps the most horrific episode of the reaction was the "Viva Maria"
violence in 1799, when the French troops were temporarily withdrawn.
Armed mobs from Arezzo, including many priests and monks, invaded the district around Siena, beating and killing Jews and other perceived enemies.

Piselli has given us an interesting and extensively documented account of
this little-known vignette of Tuscan history. The much-neglected Jewish community of Siena comes in for a very well-documented examination. She has
taken advantage of newly uncovered documents and records. The highlight
of the papers that she provides in the appendix is a carefully prepared "enemies list" cataloguing personal data on "Jacobins, rogues, and irreligious" from
Siena and its surrounding diocese. This is the only surviving document of its
type that remains in the archives of the Archdiocese of Siena. Students of this
period will be very pleased with Piselli's careful analysis.

Washington Theological Union   LEOPOLD GLUECKERT, O.CARM.

Late Modern European

Newman et le mouvement d'Oxford: Un réexamen critique. By Paul Vaiss.
    (Bern: Paul Lang, 2006. Pp. viii, 204. $59.95 paperback. ISBN 978-3-039-
    10881-7.)

Paul Vaiss is the most significant recent French commentator on Cardinal
John Henry Newman and the Oxford Movement. His previous publications
include a major monograph on Newman's intellectual and spiritual development up to the beginning of the movement and an edited volume of articles
by several historians on topics related to Newman's Anglican career. The present book consists of eleven relatively brief essays written by Vaiss between
1992 and 2006, seven of which are republished here with little or no revision.
The topics include Newman's first conversion, his ecclesiology prior to the
Oxford Movement, analyses of his sermons, the Tractarian debate over the
identity of the Anglican church, Newman's understanding of the origins of
Arianism, his view of the Anglican via media, and his position in later Roman
Catholic thought. Vaiss also includes a helpful, happily even-handed, biblio-
graphic essay on Newman studies just past the turn of the century.

Vaiss has read more widely than many Newman scholars, but his essays make little or no use of manuscript sources. Several of the essays will seem dated to English readers in that they draw upon older monographs and with little bibliographic updating since the date of the original composition and publication of the essays. Vaiss has a real gift of criticizing Newman while still conveying his considerable admiration of the cardinal. He also challenges in the kindest fashion many of Newman's earlier interpreters. For example, Vaiss insists persuasively that Newman's first conversion was a genuinely evangelical conversion. Vaiss's essay on Newman and the church Fathers is a model of succinct historical analysis pointing to the manner in which the influence of Edward Hawkins, provost of Oriel, and R. H. Froude provided the template to Newman's reading of patristic sources. Vaiss's most interesting essay relates to Newman's return to evangelical positions in his sermons between 1829 and 1832, a period of particular personal and academic stress in his life. Throughout his essays Vaiss has also paid important attention to Newman's learned contemporary evangelical critics, such as William Goode, whom most scholars ignore. Unlike many Newman scholars, Vaiss understands and appreciates both the learning of such evangelical critics and the validity of much of their criticism. What characterizes all of Vaiss's analysis is his appreciation of the problematic character of Newman's intellectual and theological development. Vaiss has a clear eye of the role of contingency in Newman's thought as well as much of its idiosyncratic character. Vaiss continues the mode of analysis that sees Newman as essentially opposed to erastianism and liberal theologians, while the evidence displays a steady and ever-growing challenge to evangelical religion that informed many supporters of church establishment and of ecumenical relations between Anglican and Protestant nonconformists. Readers will need to assess the evidence here for themselves.

More of Vaiss's own voice would have been welcome here. He is a far more interesting and sensitive historian than most of the scholars he quotes. To see him challenge more of the works he cites would have been ideal, because his comments would have been invariably interesting. Whenever Vaiss introduces his own opinions and outlook, his views are fresh and present Newman in a light far removed from the all-too-frequent hagiographic treatments that are endlessly repetitive. Vaiss's essays are well worth reading, less as examples of cutting-edge historical analysis than as thoughtful, well-informed meditations on the most interesting and difficult of all the voices of Victorian religion, theology, and devotion. For those meditations he deserves our thanks.

Yale University   FRANK M. TURNER

Católicos, devociones y sociedad durante la Dictadura de Primo de Rivera y la Segunda República: La Obra del Amor Misericordioso en España (1922-1936). By Federico M. Requena. [Colección Historia Biblioteca Nueva.] (Madrid: Editorial Biblioteca Nueva. 2008. Pp. 359. €24,00 paperback. ISBN 978-8-497-42877-4.)

Spain's devotional magazines and diocesan bulletins from the 1920s and 1930s have many references to *Amor Misericordioso* (Merciful Love), and in Spain's secondhand bookshops one still finds the little Merciful Love pamphlets and books once printed in the hundreds of thousands. Yet until now there has been no well-documented history of this devotional movement. From 1922 to 1942 an international and somewhat unruly coalition of middle- and upper-class enthusiasts—well-heeled laywomen, aristocrats, diplomats, and Dominican specialists in mysticism—propagated and strove to gain papal approval for the anonymous writings of a French Salesian sister, Marie Thérèse Desandais, which largely took the form of first-person messages seemingly dictated by Christ. This thorough and revealing study by Federico M. Requena is based on the unpublished correspondence among many of the chief protagonists, including Desandais; her chief Madrid enthusiast, Juana Lacasa; the Dominicans of Salamanca, Atocha, and Rome; several Jesuits including José María Rubio; three active and influential Chileans; a group in Lyons around the wealthy Emilie Blanck; and, most surprisingly, the nuncio in Spain, Federico Tedeschini. In it, we see a Catholicism that is a changing field of decisions and inspirations, in which strategy, enthusiasm, and critical judgment come into play and in which the prestige and saintliness of individual actors give them special influence.

Requena shows how Desandais's writings built on the cult of the Sacred Heart and the enthusiasm for St. Thérèse of Lisieux and how they were in synchrony with and adapted to successive papal encyclicals. His valuable description of the evolving content of the divine messages goes hand in hand with the evolving process, with many false starts, of the movement's attempt to gain approval. It shows something that readers who have depended on *Vida Sobrenatural*, the most accessible source for the movement's history, and on the biographies of its director, Juan González Arintero, would never know—that the height of Merciful Love's popularity was the last two years before the Spanish Civil War. Requena's work is based on unexamined sources and reveals an unexamined side of Spanish devotional history, far from the theocratic tendencies of the Integrists or the more militantly patriotic side of the cult of the Sacred Heart. Tedeschini, working for accommodation with the Republic, had a hand in this, convincing Desandais, for instance, to modify her paintings of the Christ of Merciful Love by de-emphasizing the crown. The popularity of the devotion, Requena asserts, "questions purely political interpretations of Catholic devotion" and points to "a spiritual and pacific interpretation of the reign of Christ," along with "the existence of true ferments of renovation in Spain's Catholic panorama involving religious, secular clergy, and laity" (p. 317).

The author distinguishes between a sociological approach and a doctrinal-theological one, and seems to lean more toward the latter, but his account is rich in sociological insight, as he follows the arresting tale of enthusiasts jostling for control (the desire to be known as a founder, the spiritual direction of Desandais, and the editing and framing of the messages) and Desandais's attempt to maintain the integrity of her writings and keep the devotion noninstitutional.

The reader notes the author's sympathy for Desandais's messages, and the book has a discreetly apologetic slant, as if seeking to rehabilitate the devotion. Be that as it may, one might take a step back and consider the wider matrix of competing doctrines, messages, and devotions in this period that may have affected Merciful Love's success and demise. Its chief proponent in Spain, González Arintero, had a strike against him because of fierce criticism of his book on evolution, denounced to the Holy Office as modernist. Later, in addition to the dubious and increasingly apocalyptic messages flooding in from Ezkioga, there were retrospective prophecies of Mother Rafols being invented by a nun in Zaragoza, initially to achieve Rafols's canonization, but then with the onset of the Republic (a clear parallel with Desandais, who wrote an extremely popular message to the Spanish Catholics) directly addressing Spain's political predicament. If, as Requena shows, by the mid-1930s many Spanish theologians were on guard against "new devotions," there were local reasons why: they had been burned by "revelations" too often. Whereas during the Spanish Republic popular demand for divine news and guidance was at a peak, this demand was no longer so urgent after the Civil War was won, which is when the devotion was snuffed out after doubts arose about its approval in Rome.

Requena shows, in any case, that devotion to Jesus of merciful love lives on, in institutional form in the religious order of Esperanza of Jesus, in the devotional writings of Faustina Kowalska, and, one might add, in the hearts of Christians of mercy everywhere.

Las Palmas de Gran Canaria   WILLIAM A. CHRISTIAN, JR.

Gunpowder and Incense: The Catholic Church and the Spanish Civil War. By Hilari Raguer. (New York: Routledge. 2007. Pp. xix, 418. $170.00. ISBN 978-0-415-31889-1.)

This important book by the Catalan Benedictine scholar Hilari Raguer begins (after a short prologue by Paul Preston) with an introduction that summarizes previous studies. It is an excellent précis. Chapter 1 outlines the Church's response to the coming of the Spanish Republic in 1931, setting firmly in parliamentary context the oft-quoted statement of Manuel Azaña in October 1931, "Spain has ceased to be Catholic" (p. 28). Chapter 2 reviews the reasons behind the military uprising of 1936, noting that a war in defense of Catholicism was not at the forefront of initial reasonings for the military uprising. Chapter 3 sketches the development of a self-justifying ideology of "crusade" that would sustain many on the Nationalist side. Chapter 4 examines the initial attitudes of the Spanish bishops in the face of such events as the bombing of the great basilica of El Pilar in Zaragoza (p. 68). Chapter 5 presents some thoughts on the stance of the Vatican press during the Civil War, in particular *L'Osservatore Romano,* which refused to print unedited Francoist propaganda despite general sympathy for the Nationalist position. Chapter 6 provides a scholarly analysis of the famous Collective Letter of the Spanish bishops of July 1, 1937, addressed to the Catholic world, and examines the cases of the bishops whose signatures did not appear on the letter: Bishop Juan Torres Ribas (Menorca), Cardinal Pedro Segura y Sáenz (exiled in Rome), Bishop Francisco Javier de Irastorza Loinaz (Orihuela-Alicante), Bishop Mateo Múgica y Urrestarazu (Vitoria), and Cardinal Francisco de Asís Vidal i Barraquer (Tarragona). Chapters 7 and 8 tackle objectively the still simmering issue of religious persecutions. Chapter 9 deals with the impact of the arrival in Spain of Archbishop Ildebrando Antoniutti as papal representative in the Nationalist zone. Chapters 10 and 11 analyze respectively the attitudes of Catholics outside Spain (not all of whom fell into line with the Francoist cause) and those of Catholics in Spain itself who supported the Republic. Influential foreign figures like Jacques Maritain urged caution among coreligionists before offering unconditional support to the Nationalist cause. Chapter 12 relates the tragic final years of Vidal i Barraquer and the means by which some of his supporters were able to return to Spain to influence events to some degree. Finally, Chapter 13 on "The Church of Victory" allows Raguer to outline the consequences of Francisco Franco's victory. The reader can sense the author's indignation with the entire concept of "National-Catholicism," and, while remaining scholarly in its composition, his depiction of the ceremony of May 20, 1939, in the Madrid church of Santa Bárbara, when Franco laid his sword at the feet of the *Cristo* of Lepanto in the presence of Cardinal Isidro Gomá, is positively disdainful. Benedictine liturgists from Silos drafted a ceremony fit for a medieval monarch of the *Reconquista.* The conscious choice of ritual and ceremony on this occasion illustrated how Spanish history under the victorious Francoists—and the perceived contribution of the Church to "national history"—had already become infected by myth and myopia.

That Raguer should wish to distance himself from an "integrist" Catholic stance throughout this book is not to say that the reader is presented with an overcompensating attempt at providing balance when discussing the Republican position or argument. The crudities of Left/Right, Republican/Nationalist polemics are not for Raguer, for he presents a reality of the Civil War that never conforms to the stereotypes of some past treatments. What Raguer does betray sensitivity about are, first, the aspirations for autonomy of peoples within Spain, particularly his fellow Catalans, and, second, the revealing gestures of key individuals. With regard to the first, the *leitmotiv* that runs through the book is the heroism of Vidal i Barraquer, exiled by the Civil War and never allowed to return to Spain by the Francoist authorities for his rejection, in essence, of their narrow definition of "Spanishness" and his unease at the reduction of the Church to effectively an arm of the state. With regard to the second, there is Raguer's depiction of a broken Múgica—himself also an exile and sickened by the Francoist persecution of Basque priests—acknowledging that he also had finally been abandoned by the Vatican in being forced to stand down from his see. His scratching out of the words *Bishop of Vitoria* from the letterhead in a missive of October 7, 1937, to Vidal i Barraquer is touchingly symbolic of events that do not fit any "Catholic-versus-Communist" template of this period's history (p. 291). Raguer's book is full of such telling vignettes. Scholars of modern Spain and, indeed, the Church in twentieth-century Europe more generally must not hesitate to refer to this engrossing, thoroughly researched, and perspective-changing work.

University of Glasgow   RAYMOND MCCLUSKEY

Ireland's Magdalen Laundries and the Nation's Architecture of Containment. By James M. Smith. (Notre Dame: University of Notre Dame Press. 2007. Pp. xx, 275. $28.00 paperback. ISBN 978-0-268-04127-4.)

James Smith's *Ireland's Magdalen Laundries and the Nation's Architecture of Containment* is divided into two distinct parts: a history of the magdalen asylum in twentieth-century Ireland and a critical reading of a wide array of cultural representations of the magdalen asylum (including films, documentaries, memorials, plays, and artwork). In part 1 Smith, a professor of English at Boston College, places the magdalen asylum in the framework of a so-called "architecture of containment." Smith's book makes a valuable contribution to what has become a controversial episode in Irish history, but his conclusions are not unproblematic. Smith alleges that the magdalen asylum was part of an institutional network used by the Irish state to "contain" sexual immorality; those who did not conform to narrowly defined codes of sexual morality that formed the cornerstone of the newly independent Irish state (including unmarried mothers and women convicted of infanticide) were locked away and essentially forgotten. In reality, the vast majority of unmarried mothers raised their children, sometimes with the help of family and friends, or made private arrangements for their children's care and carried on with their lives. In addition, far more women convicted of infanticide were freed than were sent to magdalen asylums. If there was an architecture of containment in postindependence society (and Smith has not convincingly shown there was), it was more rhetorical than real.

Historians reading this book may be disturbed by Smith's tendency to make substantial allegations based on scant evidence. He accepts at face value the testimony of the nine women whose stories of confinement in magdalen asylums have been chronicled in the media in recent years, without considering the extent to which these nine accounts should be regarded as representative. His analysis of the links between infanticide and the magdalen laundry further highlights his sparse use of evidence. Smith argues, based on an examination of Central Criminal Court trial record books, that the state relied on magdalen asylums as a means of punishing women convicted of infanticide and related crimes (concealment of birth or manslaughter). He excuses this selective use of sources by stating that the majority of cases were heard in district courts and therefore are lost to the historical record. Smith is patently incorrect on this latter count, and this serious oversight cannot help but raise questions about the overall validity of his historical narrative. Most cases of infanticide, manslaughter, and concealment of birth were heard in the circuit courts that met on a quarterly basis around the country, and these records are readily available at the National Archives of Ireland. The picture that emerges from a reading of all available sources is one not of containment, but of leniency. Many of the women convicted of infanticide and related crimes essentially were freed, often with no strings attached. The fact that so many women killed their babies and essentially "got away with it" further undermines Smith's "architecture of containment" argument.

In part 2 Smith deconstructs the various media and artistic representations of the magdalen asylum, and herein lies the strength of the book. On the surface some of these cultural artifacts, like Peter Mullan's film *The Magdalene Sisters,* appear to be little more than knee-jerk, thoughtless condemnations of the Catholic Church. However, Smith's astute analysis reveals their complexity, deftly showing how they attempt to reveal the culpability and complicity of all segments of Irish society in consigning some women to a lifetime of "imprisonment" in magdalen asylums. He also rightly argues that women confined to magdalen asylums were victimized twice: first when they were tossed away and forgotten by family, friends, and society, and again in their exclusion from recent soul-searching public discussions of the treatment of individuals in state-funded institutions. While the Irish government has established commissions and issued apologies to child victims of abuse and exploitation, it has ignored women who were confined, sometimes against their will, in magdalen asylums. Smith suggests that the page cannot be turned on this dark episode in Irish history until Irish society as a whole acknowledges its complicity in helping to perpetuate the magdalen system, and he hopes this book will help bring about that acknowledgment.

University of Arkansas, Little Rock   MOIRA J. MAGUIRE

Vatican II: Renewal within Tradition. Edited by Matthew L. Lamb and Matthew Levering. (New York: Oxford University Press. 2008. Pp. xxvi, 462. $29.95 paperback. ISBN 978-0-195-33267-4.)

Pope Benedict XVI's address to the Roman Curia on December 22, 2005, represents a major contribution to the debate about Vatican II, despite the fact that some journalists offered it to the public as the pope espousing an Italian-based polemic against the five-volume *History of Council Vatican II* directed by Giuseppe Alberigo, of which Joseph Komonchak edited the English version (Maryknoll, NY, 1995–2006). It is no surprise that the volume edited by Matthew L. Lamb and Matthew Levering opens with the text of Benedict XVI's address. The editors claim to be interpreting the Vatican II documents in "continuity," as "renewal within tradition" of the Catholic Church, while they accuse the highly respected international historiography about Vatican II of producing a "distorting impact of the hermeneutics of discontinuity and rupture" (p. 7). In brief, "the volume seeks to make a modest contribution to what Benedict XVI calls a hermeneutics of reform in continuity with the two millennial traditions of Catholic thought and wisdom" (p. 7).

But the twenty-two articles of the volume, in fact, present a much more diverse set of interpretations of the documents of Vatican II. The commentaries on the Constitutions stress more than those on the Decrees and Declarations the continuity between the nineteenth and early twentieth-century magisterial tradition and the texts of Vatican II. Cardinal Avery Dulles, S.J., for example, correctly describes as "false" a list of views that he incorrectly attributes to some of the most appreciated interpretations of the Council's impact on ecclesiology (quoting John O'Malley, Gregory Baum, Richard P. McBrien, and George Lindbeck, "together with many others who might be named," p. 25). Pamela E. Jackson, in her article about *Sacrosanctum Concilium*, stresses the continuity with the magisterium, lining up Augustine, the Council of Trent, Leo XIII, Pius X, the liturgical movement, Pius XI, and Pius XII. Romanus Cessario, in his essay about the liturgical constitution and the sacraments, dismisses the achievement of the liturgical movement, noting that it was moved by a "preferential option for the primitive" (p. 133).

But the landscape offered by other commentaries looks less polemical, more sound, and open to "renewal" as "development," such as the articles by Cardinal Francis George on *Ad gentes*, Guy Mansini and Lawrence J. Welch on *Presbyterorum Ordinis,* M. Prudence Allen and M. Judith O'Brien on *Perfectae caritatis,* and Khaled Anatolios on *Orientalium Ecclesiarum.* Even the closing article by Geoffrey Wainwright, a Methodist, on criteria for an interpretation of Vatican II emphasizes renewal more than tradition.

The volume provides a contribution, but not fully in the direction of a hermeneutics of "reform in continuity" as declared by its editors. It is difficult to initiate a new interpretation of Vatican II while leaving unaddressed the main issues raised by the best contemporary, international, and scholarly study of the Council, and it does not help when one draws inspiration from self-appointed *defensores concilii* who have not published anything scholarly about Vatican II. It is no surprise that some critics shows a woefully inadequate connection with the huge number of studies published every year on five continents (editions of new sources, historical studies, commentaries, books, and articles based on work in the recently opened, huge collection of unpublished papers on Vatican II in the Vatican Secret Archives).

The Jesuit Institute, Boston College   MASSIMO FAGGIOLI

The Belgian Contribution to the Second Vatican Council: International Research Conference at Mechelen, Leuven and Louvain-la-Neuve (September 12-16, 2005). Edited by Doris Donnelly, Joseph Famerée, Mathijs Lamberigts, and Karim Schelkens. [Bibliotheca Ephemeridum Theologicarum Lovaniensium, Vol. CCXVI.] (Leuven: Uitgeverij Peeters. 2008. Pp. xii, 716. €85,00 paperback. ISBN 978-9-042-92101-6.)

No one paid the Belgians at Vatican II a higher tribute than Father Yves Marie Joseph Congar, the important French Dominican *peritus* at the council, who observed in his diary that in large measure it was at the Belgian College in Rome that the council got its theological shape. Monsignor Gérard Philips, Bishop Émile-Joseph De Smedt, and, of course, Cardinal Léon-Joseph Suenens are familiar to even casual students of Vatican II, but they are only the most prominent members of a remarkably well-trained group of prelates and theologians that, as Congar suggests, had a collective impact on the council unlike that of any other national group. This volume provides both a panoramic overview of the Belgian contribution and careful analyses of key figures in their relationship to the council and to other participants in it.

With over half the papers in English, it is especially welcome in the North American context, where few scholars have followed the remarkable outpouring on the continent in the past twenty years of studies that have moved our understanding of the dynamics of the council far beyond the tired categories of progressives and conservatives that still largely hold sway here. The volume is also welcome as a corrective to the still commonly held opinion, à la Father Francis X. Murphy, C.Ss.R. (aka Xavier Rynne), that the council, despite what may have happened afterward, was an unmitigated triumph for "the progressives." In that regard it provides good case studies of the conflicts over theology and strategy that after the historic votes on collegiality on October 30, 1963, weakened the united front of those who had opposed, successfully, the original drafts of the council documents.

The volume is divided into three parts. The first, "Methodological Issues," is relatively short and opens with John A. Coleman's analysis of the council from a sociological viewpoint. In this section Leo Kenis's apologia for the importance of "private sources" for an understanding of the council is convincing and is an explicit and effective rebuttal of Agostino Marchetto's dismissal of such sources, part of his campaign to belittle the five-volume *History of Vatican II* edited by Giuseppe Alberigo (Maryknoll, NY, 1995–2006).

The second part is dedicated to Suenens and opens with the long, sober, and extremely well-informed piece by Mathijs Lamberigts and Leo Declerck on Suenens's role at the council. This piece provides the framework for the five that follow, each of which deals with Suenens's relationship with other prelates at the council—with Cardinals Julius Döpfner, Giacomo Lercaro, Paul-Émile Léger, and Giovanni Battista Montini/Paul VI. While they are all revealing, the pivotal contribution among the five is by Declerck and Toon Osaer on Suenens and Montini. Organized chronologically, it is a model of clarity and editorial reserve. Not surprisingly, it throws as much light on Montini/Paul VI as it does on Suenens.

The final, and longest, section looks at other members of "the Belgian team"—*Squadra Belga*, the Italian moniker the Belgians were given during the council. Under the rubric of the *squadra* is included a contribution by Eddy Louchez on the Belgian missionary bishops, an often neglected aspect of the story of Vatican II. Jared Wicks's piece is especially helpful for two reasons. First, he provides a list of the ten tasks the *periti* performed before and during the council, and then, by using Charles Moeller as an example, he illustrates how the *periti* contributed to the important and tricky task of revising the schemata in light of the *modi* received from the bishops.

In his article contrasting the strategies Philips and Giuseppe Dossetti espoused for dealing with the demands of the bishops of the minority, Jan Grootaers throws light on the "compromises" in the formulation of the final documents that after the council could be used to contravene what the majority wanted and intended. His *Postface* on the "theological background" of the polarities that came to mark the majority is particularly important. He here distinguishes between an "Augustinian or patristic" orientation (Joseph Ratzinger, Henri de Lubac, and Hans Urs von Balthasar) and a "Thomistic" orientation (Congar, Marie-Dominique Chenu, Edward Schillebeeckx, and Karl Rahner).

Silvia Scatena's article on the opposing views of De Smedt and John Courtenay Murray on the document on religious freedom will prove especially interesting for American readers. Other authors deal with the contributions of Belgian theologians such as Gustave Thils and Lucien Cerfaux. Philippe Bordeyne shows how Pierre Haubtmann, the French coordinator of the many subcommissions responsible for *Gaudium et Spes*, made use of Belgian theologians to help shore up the document's theological foundations in face of the severe criticisms launched against it by the "German armada" (p. 586).

As Michael Fahey mentions in his helpful comments concluding the volume, the topic of "the Belgian contribution" is not new. It has been explored in a number of studies over the past decades. Nonetheless, this volume moves us forward not only with the new information and insights it provides but also as a compendium of the most important results scholars earlier achieved. I recommend it very highly indeed.

Georgetown University   JOHN W. O'MALLEY, S.J.

American

The Faithful: A History of Catholics in America. By James M. O'Toole.
(Cambridge, MA: Belknap Press of Harvard University Press. 2008. Pp. viii,
376. $27.95. ISBN 978-0-674-02818-0.)

With the publication of *The Faithful*, James M. O'Toole has added a very
accessible, elegantly written, scholarly overview to the growing number of
works addressing the history of the laity in the American Catholic Church.
The author divides the material into six thematic and roughly chronological
ages: "The Priestless Church Dealing with the Time of John Carroll"; "The
Church in the Democratic Republic Focusing on the Constitutional
Ecclesiology of John England"; "The Immigrant Church Addressing
Developments from the Mid-Nineteenth Century to the Close of Immigration
in 1924"; "The Church of Catholic Action Covering the Period from
1930–1960"; "The Church of Vatican II"; and "The Church in the Twenty-first
Century, from the Mid-1980s to the Present." Each chapter has a common outline, beginning with a biographical profile of a representative Catholic of the
period and continuing in synthetic fashion to address the size and structure
of the community, its religious and devotional life, the real or imagined relationship with the papacy, the situation of the Church in the American context, and the public perception of the Church. Throughout the pages, O'Toole
focuses as much as possible on the life of laypeople, their agency in building
the Church and its institutions, and their expression of the faith in prayer life
and apostolic works. Fifty-six pages of notes ground the conclusions in original archival work and in a thorough coverage of the secondary literature on
specific topics. The whole is concluded with a very useful six-page index.

The Faithful does not claim to be a history of American Catholicism in the
classic vein of John Tracy Ellis, James Hennesey, S.J., and Jay P. Dolan; nor does
it try to supplement the more contemporary shorter accounts by James T.
Fisher and Patrick Carey. Instead, O'Toole incorporates particularly the historiographical advances of the last twenty years in the field of religious practice
and movements. He breaks from standard narrations focused on the growth
of institutions and ideas and from the periodization associated with immigrant history and Americanization. There is little if any detailed discussion of
anti-Catholicism as a shaping force for the community. The book might be
considered rather as a series of internally focused snapshots, even historical
meditations, on the Church, "a story of its people—the Faithful, the laity—
rather than its leaders and institutions"(p. 3). O'Toole's pages contain insight-
ful personal profiles (see the fine historical summary on pages 305–08);
subtle attention to regional examples and ethnic variations (see references to
Boston, New York, Milwaukee, New Orleans, St. Louis, San Francisco, and Los
Angeles, as well as Hispanic, African American, Polish, Italian, Irish, German,
and Asian Catholics); an analysis of the progressive emergence of a "church
going people" (p. 83); imaginative parallels between the changing architec-

ture of the churches and social and liturgical developments in the community (pp. 19, 112, 212); and solid presentations in each era of the mutations in devotional practices, ascetical disciplines, liturgical forms, and sacramental participation that have carried the faith commitments and expressions of the people. The chapters dealing with the last seventy-five years of the community's development are some of the finest general views available. If the five themes of each chapter are taken as emblematic, almost genetic components of Catholic Identity, then the book as a whole describes both the continuities and discontinuities of a religious community in motion.

When the snapshots of the various periods are juxtaposed, and they can be juxtaposed because of the common structure to each chapter, some fine insights and significant comparisons emerge. Our picture of the Catholic community as it exists in history changes. The weak infrastructure of the priestless parishes and the praying practices of the laity in the Carroll period parallel to some extent the collapsing infrastructure, the priestless parishes, and agency of the laity in the post-Vatican II period. The balanced discussion of lay trusteeism unveils a structural tension between lay and clerical concerns as central to understanding long-term developments in the community (compare pp. 72-73, 174-75, 252). The focused treatment of the community's relationship with the papacy in each era unveils a movement from an essentially "popeless Church" (p. 48) and the pope as "universal administrator" (p. 88) to an "emergent papalism" during the immigrant period (pp. 131$f\!f$.), new modes of affiliation with the papacy in radio, air travel, and popular pilgrimages (pp. 190-92), and finally, the current and more complex, in some ways ambivalent, relationship with the papacy (pp. 292-301). The popular "personalizing" (p. 190) of the vision and practices of Catholic Action—so well described in terms of its promotion of a changed profile for the laity in community building, public participation, and spiritual expression—sets the scene for the emergence of the changes of the 1960s. The thick descriptions of the "lived religion" of the immigrant Church (pp. 111-29) and that of the Church of Vatican II (pp. 202-21) would merit comparison in any classroom.

In conclusion, one may question the advisability of focusing solely on the laity when in fact the clergy and religious (men and women) were actively involved and provide many of the descriptions for almost all of the movements and trends mentioned. Certainly the vision of a certain class of laity is the one most articulated. The whole could be complemented a great deal by attention to the philanthropic and administrative role of the laity in the formation, organization, and perdurance of schools, hospitals, and charitable institutions. There is little attention to gender analysis as complementary to simple narration (see the treatments on pp. 103-06, 211-12) and slight reference given to the thorny questions of the "public" Church as those touched the life of the laity (for examples, arguments over participation in unions, dominantly Protestant organizations, and the Community Chest). Still, the whole narration captures the American Catholic past in an imaginative and stimulating way. Clergy and laity, students in college classrooms, parishioners in the local church, and professional historians can all profit from this rich, diversified, engaging, and scholarly presentation. In many areas, but above all in its structure and its mainstreaming of lay expressions of piety throughout the book, *The Faithful* makes a significant contribution to understanding and grappling with Catholic Identity through the lens of an accomplished historian.

Franciscan School of Theology   JOSEPH P. CHINNICI, O.F.M.
Berkeley, CA

Catholic Moral Theology in the United States: A History. By Charles E. Curran. [Moral Traditions Series.] (Washington, DC: Georgetown University Press. 2008. Pp. xiv, 353. $59.95 clothbound, ISBN 978-1-589-01195-3; $26.95 paperback, ISBN 978-1-589-01196-0.)

This work is a valuable contribution to the study of moral theology; it is the first comprehensive narrative of the origins and development of the discipline in the United States. The author does not claim to write as a neutral observer, but presents his work as that of a participant-observer. He acknowledges the difficulties that such an undertaking involves; he must record the opinions of moral theologians, including his own, while at the same time explaining his own personal views. The solution he has adopted is to present the positions he has taken in the third person, as the views of Charles E. Curran, while elucidating his own views in the first person. He frankly admits the tensions that this entails, while leaving the judgment on the success of the approach to the reader. This method had the advantage of enabling the author to state clearly both what he said and what he meant. Since his writings have been the subject of much debate and perhaps also misunderstanding, this provides useful clarification. Nevertheless, the other authors whose positions he records do not have a similar opportunity to explain and clarify what they meant, and this creates an imbalance. For example, it may be anticipated that the account of the moral theory of Germain Grisez would not be considered adequate by that author. However, Curran takes care to present the ideas of others clearly and objectively, including those with which he disagrees. This makes the book both a useful record and, at the same time, a kind of compendium of moral theologians; one can look up the different authors so as to find a succinct statement of their positions.

Physicalism is treated at length, but the term remains ambiguous. It is sometimes taken to mean that the moral law is derived directly from or even identified with the physical structure of the act, or with the biological law. The centrality of the person is, as Curran shows, generally accepted, but the history of the concept is unclear. My research suggests that "the person 'integrally and adequately considered'" (p. 105) has its roots in Suarezian ethics. The author notes correctly that Grisez adopted "Hume's law," according to which *ought* cannot be derived from *is*. However, there is no mention of the historical background to this theory nor of its rejection by some notable contemporary philosophers. Theologians need to study more philosophy. However, with its comprehensive account of the contributions of twentieth-century moralists, this work provides a place to start. It is necessary reading for all moralists.

The Catholic University of America   BRIAN JOHNSTONE, C.Ss.R.

Religious Liberty in America: The First Amendment in Historical and Contemporary Perspective. By Bruce T. Murray. (Amherst: University of Massachusetts Press, in association with the Foundation for American Communications. 2008. Pp. xvi, 213. $19.95 paperback. ISBN 978-1-558-49638-5.)

Authored by journalist Bruce T. Murray, this concise and readable book discusses topics relating to the religion clauses of the First Amendment and, more generally, to the interaction of religion and politics in the United States. It is the outgrowth of a series of seminars on journalism, religion, and public life, sponsored by the Foundation for American Communications (FACS) and the Pew Charitable Trusts. As an editor for FACS, Murray covered the seminars, and he draws heavily upon the scholarly lectures that they featured, but he incorporates and relies upon a range of additional sources as well. In line with its origins, the book is designed especially for journalists, to assist them in their reporting, but it also is written for undergraduate students and general readers. Murray intends the book to be "an easy read on a tough topic," a book that "boil[s] the issues down to the journalist's proverbial 'nut graph'" (p. xv). As such, the book is not so much an original contribution as a primer on the topics it discusses. Even so, the book is not simplistic, and it backs its assertions with references and footnotes to primary sources and scholarly materials.

In the course of the book, Murray addresses the character and diversity of religion in the United States, the historical underpinnings of the First Amendment's religion clauses, and the Supreme Court's evolving interpretations of these provisions. He gives special attention to the views of the current justices, including the court's most recent appointees, Chief Justice John Roberts and Justice Samuel Alito. He highlights debates concerning the role of religion in the public schools, public displays of the Ten Commandments, and the "faith-based initiative" of President George W. Bush. In addition, the book includes an especially engaging and in-depth chapter on American civil religion. This chapter relies upon the scholarly work of Robert Bellah, among others, even as it traces American civil religion from John Winthrop's (and Ronald Reagan's) "city upon a hill" to contemporary disputes over immigration, the "culture wars," and the religious rhetoric of Bush and other political leaders.

Throughout, the book cites historical antecedents and parallels as it considers contemporary issues. In discussing civil religion, for example, Murray addresses the roots of public virtue and economic self-interest as competing strands of the American dream, and he explains how current debates over immigration are similar to earlier episodes, albeit with significant differences as well. Likewise, in discussing the First Amendment and church-state relations, Murray argues (drawing upon lectures by Charles Haynes) that today's competing positions trace their origins to colonial times and, in particular, to the views of Winthrop of Massachusetts and Roger Williams of Rhode Island. Winthrop's "city upon a hill" demanded a tightly knit community featuring collaboration between church and state. Williams, by contrast, advocated freedom of conscience, free exercise of religion, and the separation of church and state. As Murray suggests, echoes of this debate have reverberated ever since. He also notes the historical antecedents of specific contemporary issues, including, for example, debates concerning the Ten Commandments and governmental funding of religious social-service providers.

This is a useful book for its intended purpose. It is a highly accessible introduction to the topics it addresses, complete with references for documentation or further reading. It is largely descriptive, as opposed to analytical or theoretical. The book is well written, engaging, and balanced in its presentations of competing views.

Maurer School of Law, Indiana University Bloomington   DANIEL O. CONKLE

Frontiers of Faith: Bringing Catholicism to the West in the Early Republic. By John R. Dichtl. (Lexington: University Press of Kentucky. 2008. Pp. x, 240. $50.00. ISBN 978-0-813-12486-5.)

Relying on documents from Catholic priests and bishops, John Dichtl argues that in the backwoods of Pennsylvania and Maryland to the far edge of Indiana, and especially in Kentucky from the 1780s through the 1820s, Catholics initially lived in harmony with their non-Catholic neighbors. As explored in the first two chapters, Catholic leaders, such as Archbishop John Carroll of Baltimore, encouraged such cordial relations. As a result, frontier priests not only performed sacramental duties but also bought and sold land, fostered businesses, engaged in politics, and started schools, all the while attempting to interact with non-Catholics as pleasantly as possible. Although the Catholic laity did not always see eye to eye with their priests, especially when priestly salaries were at stake, Catholics in general soon came to rely on priests for demonstrating how to survive as a religious minority.

At the same time some priests proved to be inept, misguided, and/or combative, as discussed in chapter 3. Since priest misbehavior threatened to stir latent anti-Catholic sentiment, Catholic authorities learned to downplay internal dissension and to handle public embarrassments as quickly and quietly as possible. Suppressing scandals in this fashion ultimately led to the implementation of European forms of church governance, which ironically alienated the previously appeased non-Catholic community.

While priests served as the focal point for Catholic-Protestant relations, Catholic churches and Catholic goods also provided another means of contact, as explored in chapter 4. Non-Catholics in fact often contributed to the construction of Catholic churches (although Catholics did not return the favor, as Catholics had deemed such contact to be too dangerous). Religious clothing, candles, books, paintings, and statues consequently proved to be a means to display to curious outsiders what Catholics believed. Such displays pointed, in part, toward Europe, which was where most of these religious objects were produced.

Chapter 5 illustrates how priests often feared interaction of Catholics with non-Catholics. What specifically concerned many priests was the fact that the frontier generated numerous opportunities for conversion both to and from the Catholic faith. The actual number of converts was small, even though a myriad of questions, including inquiries about money lending to non-Catholics, serving meat to non-Catholics, baptizing slaves of non-Catholics, and mixed marriages were routinely raised by frontier priests seeking answers from Rome.

Catholics eventually dared to express the distinctiveness of their faith, as is illustrated in chapter 6. By the second decade of the nineteenth century, Catholic schools proliferated, public processions increased, and priests took to the podium both to preach the word of God in the Roman Catholic fashion and to defend the faith when under assault. Sometimes these priests were warmly received. On other occasions they were not. Regardless, Dichtl concludes that by the close of the frontier period cautious optimism had given way to a more a confident declaration of what it meant to be Catholic. In other words, the frontier may have initially allied Catholics with non-Catholics, but a number of factors necessitated traditional European responses, which ultimately alienated Catholics from their neighbors, as was graphically illustrated in the resurgence of anti-Catholicism in the 1830s.

Had Dichtl's material been better arranged (more consistently following chronological order within each chapter, for example), his arguments would have been more clear and convincing, especially with regard to his contention that the congeniality of the American Catholic frontier was eventually supplanted by the imposition of European standards. Dichtl nonetheless certainly does provide some sterling insight into the frontier Church, especially concerning the impact of aberrant priests and the power of Catholic goods.

Xavier University C. WALKER GOLLAR

Sincerely, Seelos: The Collected Letters of Blessed Francis Xavier Seelos. Translated, edited, annotated, and introduced by Carl Hoegerl, C.Ss.R. (New Orleans: Seelos Center. 2008. Pp. 511. $29.50. ISBN 978-0-972-71693-2.)

The collected letters of Francis Xavier Seelos (1819–67), the Redemptorist missionary priest and Bavarian immigrant to the United States who was beatified in 2000, are an astonishingly rich resource. This new annotated edition of Seelos's letters, expertly compiled by the Redemptorist historian and archivist Carl Hoegerl, is an elegantly produced volume that, although clearly designed with scholars in mind, will be quite appealing to devotional readers as well. The editor has wisely chosen to provide all of the 201 extant letters in their entirety, including fragments where these are all that exist, as well as reproductions of hand-drawn sketches from Seelos's original letters. Summaries of the contents of each letter, which are arranged chronologically in the book, are also given with headings that make for easy browsing. Each section features introductory commentary and background by the editor.

Seelos, often referred to as the "cheerful ascetic," sacrificed much to come to the United States in response to the American bishops' calls for missionaries to the burgeoning immigrant communities whose demand for priests far outpaced the available supply. Seelos served immigrant parishes across Pennsylvania and New York in addition to making visits to churches as far away as Michigan, Illinois, and Ohio. His final station was in New Orleans, where he died of yellow fever in 1867. His cult quickly took off after his death, since his fame for sanctity had begun to spread even during his lifetime. Seelos, who would have been appointed bishop of Pittsburgh by Pope Pius IX but for his desperate pleading to be passed over for the honor, was a popular confessor and parish mission preacher who despite the rigors and penances of his own private spiritual life, enjoyed a reputation for gentleness, compassion, and humor, often "acting out" the parts of characters in the Gospels in his preaching.

This collection of Seelos's letters is remarkable for the rare glimpses it offers into several aspects of nineteenth-century religious life spanning about twenty-five years. It records not only the author's own experiences and perceptions but also provides place descriptions and accounts of meetings with prominent individuals, insight into formation experiences in religious orders of women and men, spiritual advice, and poetry. Abundant and detailed information can also be gleaned about early American Catholic education, challenges to immigrant Catholics from both nativists and the harshness of frontier life, the author's experiences ministering to Civil War soldiers, and his often strongly voiced opinions about the war, among much else.

One of the most interesting passages in these letters is Seelos's account of his personal meeting with Abraham Lincoln in July 1863, when he sought and gained an audience with the president to ask that Redemptorist seminarians be exempted from the draft: "I and another father went to Father Abraham. He treated me kindly but [Secretary of War Edwin] Stanton—! If the feast of rough characters should ever be celebrated in the Church, Stanton will get an octave added to it" (p. 362). Seelos also writes how he "could never see how the poor Irishmen rushed with such an eagerness into that bloody war" since the northern abolitionists, whom he saw as ultimately responsible for what was in his view a preventable war, "will reward them by persecuting their religion and faith. . ." (p. 358).

Hoegerl notes in his introduction his choice to leave misspellings as they are found in Seelos's originals, which "presents him as he spoke English: with a noticeable German accent" (p. 11). This book is indeed a most valuable contribution to American Catholic history and a commendable achievement by its producers.

University of Dayton Michael S. Carter

Worthy of the Gospel of Christ: A History of the Catholic Diocese of Fort Wayne-South Bend. Commemorating the 150th Anniversary of the Diocese and Catholic Life in Northern Indiana. By Joseph M. White. (Fort Wayne, IN: Diocese of Fort Wayne–South Bend. 2007. Pp. xiv, 609. $29.95 paperback. ISBN 978-1-59276-229-3.)

Many times, a diocesan history recounts the history of the bishops, the ecclesiastical superiors, the diocesan building development, and the major issues of the clergy and the important historical figures. Fortunately, this is not the type of history given to us here. Joseph White, noted historian and author of many works regarding American Catholic history, has written the story of the Catholic Church in northern Indiana from the seventeenth century to the beginning of the twenty-first century. Between 1830 to 2007, we have the foundation of the Diocese of Fort Wayne in 1857 and the redesignation of the see to Fort Wayne–South Bend in 1960. White has placed the Church in the broad context of north Indiana history: its people, its culture, its social relations, and its economic and political structures.

The historical account begins with the evangelization of the Native Americans, particularly the Pottowatami Indians through the efforts of Louis Deseille, Benjamin Petit, and the lay woman catechist Angelique Campeau. The beginning of the Church began with the tragedy of the Native American people and their forcible removal from their homes. People are the center in White's panoramic view of the Church, men and women, laypersons and missionaries, saints and the less saintly, among them St. Mother Theodore Guérin and the Sisters of Providence and Célestin de la Hailandière, the irascible bishop of Vincennes. The Church of northern Indiana began with the migration of various Europeans into that area, especially after Indiana became a state in 1816. At first came the Germans and then the Irish, followed by the Poles, the Slovaks, the Italians, and the Hungarians at the beginning of the last century. The author weaves together the diversity of the Church, the culture of the peoples, and the economic situation of the dioceses and of the ordinary people in the sections "Building a Catholic Culture, 1872-1900" and "Dimensions of Catholic Culture, 1900-1924."

White avoids restricting the history to the bishops, but his portrait of John Luers, the first bishop of Fort Wayne—1857-71—is one of the best sections of the book. His portrait of Archbishop John Noll reveals the man with his achievements and his mistakes. Noll's support of Father Charles E. Coughlin, his support of the America First Committee, his naive sympathy for Hitler in the early thirties, and his opposition to labor movements are treated objectively in the section that also recounts the bishop's remarkable life and work. In his preface White points out that "recent Catholic historical scholarship" now seeks "an honesty that makes inevitable the disclosure of the negative along with the positive aspects of the past." White has done so without bias or judgment.

At the very beginning of this work, the author reveals the paucity of archival resources. It seems that the archival records from the time of Bruté to the administration of Noll have disappeared or have not been processed. Despite this, however, White "launched [into] the . . . task of reading Catholic newspapers for articles that reveal the range of issues in diocesan life." He availed himself of the archives of religious congregations, especially the archives of the University of Notre Dame. The sheer size of this study is daunting, but the details are handled very well. The number of ethnic groups in an area where so many Catholics from diverse countries are represented could not be exhaustive. For instance, details regarding the establishment of black parishes in South Bend and Gary during the Noll administration are not passed over. Nevertheless, it would have been interesting to point out more clearly the determination and faith of black Catholic laypersons who fought for a parish of their own. St. Augustine in South Bend was founded by African Americans who were barely welcomed in the white parish church. Finally, this panoramic view of Catholicity in the northern part of Indiana should have been aided with a few maps and a bibliography besides the notes. No matter the suggestions, the historical work that White has given us is truly a work "worthy of the Gospel of Christ."

St. Meinrad School of Theology   CYPRIAN DAVIS, O.S.B.

More than Neighbors: Catholic Settlements and Day Nurseries in Chicago, 1893-1930. By Deborah A. Skok. (DeKalb: Northern Illinois University Press. 2007. Pp. x, 241. $38.00. ISBN 978-0-875-80374-6.)

The work of well-known Chicago social settlements such as Hull-House has been written about extensively, but, as Deborah Skok notes in her introduction to *More than Neighbors: Catholic Settlements and Day Nurseries in*

Chicago, 1893–1930, ". . . the work of Catholic women's settlements has until fairly recently been largely invisible" (p. 3). Although these institutions have received little attention from historians, the establishment of Catholic settlements was one way (among many) in which the Church attempted to meet the many material and spiritual needs of Catholic immigrants during the late-nineteenth and early-twentieth centuries. According to Skok, Chicago lay-women founded nine settlements and day nurseries between 1892 and 1939. *More than Neighbors* is the story of these settlements and the women (lay and religious) who labored in them. In the course of recounting their history, Skok also reminds readers that any examination of Catholic settlement houses should not neglect issues of class and gender.

Catholic social settlements were not always modeled on their secular counterparts. Not only were these institutions unabashedly religious; they were often smaller and had fewer residents. In addition, Catholic settlements, at least in Chicago, often began as day nurseries to provide working mothers with a safe place to leave their children. Many of these day nurseries eventually implemented programs (e.g., mothers' clubs) that not only offered educational and social activities for working mothers but also allowed them to perform charity work designed to help poorer women.

Rather than conforming to one model, Chicago Catholic settlements followed one of three patterns. Club-model settlements were established by Catholic women's clubs, such as the Catholic Women's League (CWL). The CWL established a "network" of settlement houses and day nurseries throughout Chicago that not only offered material assistance to needy families but also provided jobs for women of the lower and middle classes (p. 38). Proprietary-model settlements "were run by individual women of means, who used their families' money to bankroll" them (p. 66). Chicago's best-known example of a proprietary settlement was the Guardian Angel Mission (later Madonna Center), founded by Agnes Amberg. Parish-model settlements, such as the De Paul Settlement Club, were founded within parishes.

Skok's attempt to place the work and mission of these institutions within a larger discussion of class and gender is intriguing. Poor women were able to benefit from the programs offered by the settlements; middle-class women (e.g., white-collar working girls) were able to take advantage of settlement classes designed to help them develop skills employers would find valuable. Women from the upper classes were given the chance to help those in need, while honing skills that would allow them to become involved—if they chose—in city politics.

Although Skok's work sheds important new light on Catholic social settlements, readers should keep in mind that Catholic settlements in other cities (e.g., New York) did not always follow the three models detailed in the book. Some Catholic settlement workers, for instance, created a fourth model by consciously imitating the work and programs of secular settlements such as Hull-House. Nevertheless, *More than Neighbors* is an extensively researched and well-written book, and will be of interest to scholars working in a number of areas, including women's history, American Catholicism, the Progressive Era, immigration, and the history of social work in the United States.

La Salle University   MARGARET M. McGUINNESS

Latin American

Christian Texts for Aztecs: Art and Liturgy in Colonial Mexico. By Jaime Lara. (Notre Dame: University of Notre Dame Press. 2008. Pp. xii, 372. $75.00. ISBN 978-0-268-03379-8.)

This book provides ideas and materials for thinking in a more comprehensive way about the processes of conversion of Amerindians to Christianity. As the author explains, he wants to take a stand not in black and white, but in gray. That is, his ideological position is where a great many scholars are today: trying to understand more than one side of situations in which different cultures come together and how the dissimilarities and similarities evolve into something that is unlike, although rooted in, both. Although well expressed and exemplified here, this aspect of the book is no longer unusual. The particular interest of this study, however, is its emphasis on liturgical practices in the history of the establishment of Christianity in New Spain.

After laying out these premises, the author then affirms in the first chapter the crucial role of liturgy for understanding religious and cultural change, and introduces important conflicts that emerged out of liturgical disagreements in European history. These provide the background for chapter 2, which presents European liturgical reforms of the period immediately before the conquest of Mexico in 1521 and their impact during the early years of evangelization, including comments on the role of the newly invented printed book. The third chapter deals with preaching, which depended not only on skill in speaking but also on performance and the use of certain object-images, such as the monogram of Jesus, which friars in Europe used to work on the emotions of their hearers. In the New World, the study of metaphor and its representation in visual images is crucial. Lara discusses several examples as well as strategies for translating particular concepts.

Chapter 4, the longest one, provides very valuable information about the administration of the sacraments in New Spain. Besides dealing with analogous practices in pre-Hispanic rituals, Lara reports on how the friars spoke of the sacraments, reviews the texts that gave shape to the ceremonies (the most important are translated in the appendices), and examines the objects that were used, such as baptismal fonts. He presents visual evidence to discuss certain ideas taught by the friars, like wall paintings that show what was to be considered sinful with regard to the sacrament of penance and how the character of the sacred was materialized in images made of feathers. In the next two chapters he deals with the liturgical calendar, theater, music, and processions. Lara then devotes a full chapter to the celebration of Corpus Christi, a feast in which many of the previously mentioned elements play major roles. Central to his presentation is the metaphor of Christ as the sun. Although not invented in the sixteenth century, the sun metaphor, he maintains, was first fully exploited in the New World in what he calls "a unique conflation of solar imagery and Christ's eucharistic presence" (p. 199). Next is a chapter that examines the sounds and the objects that accompanied and participated in ceremonies, with discussions of Old and New World variations on similar themes. The last chapter, based on both verbal and visual images, engages in "informed conjecture" on the topic of "holy blood." A brief closing chapter acknowledges problems and the questions that remain, but insists on celebrating the creativity of friars and natives.

Although the book is centered on the sixteenth century in Mexico, its arguments and the materials presented have direct implications for the study of later periods, as well as for other Latin American contexts. Indeed, the author makes frequent references to contemporary Mexican religious expressions. Finally, the book's usefulness is considerably enhanced by excellent illustrations.

Universidad Nacional Autónoma de México CLARA BARGELLINI

Pastoral Quechua: The History of Christian Translation in Colonial Peru, 1550–1650. By Alan Durston. [History, Languages, and Cultures of the Spanish and Portuguese Worlds.] (Notre Dame: University of Notre Dame Press. 2008. Pp. xvi, 395. $42.00 paperback. ISBN 978-0-268-02591-5.)

Sixteenth-century missionaries to Latin America evangelized through music, ritual, and the spoken and written languages. Music and ritual were rather noncontroversial because they awakened sentiments that in a vague way communicated a sense of the sacred and transcendental. But language proved much more difficult, among other reasons because the missionaries were forced to be specific and precise. For this reason also the Church was especially concerned about the Indian languages: could they be proper vehicles to transmit Christian truths, particularly abstract concepts such as the Trinity, the Incarnation, and grace? As Alan Durston argues in a clear and convincing way, the decision to use Quechua to evangelize the area once conquered by the Incas was not made lightly. In fact, not any Quechua was chosen, but rather the Quechua of Cuzco became "standard colonial Quechua" and the prime instrument for evangelization. The author points out that there were several other important dialects of Quechua spoken throughout colonial Peru and even to this day. But the missionaries needed a uniform language with which to work. In the background there lurked an ideological factor: control over the language required uniformity, and uniformity enhanced control over a huge geographical area. The Council of Trent was decisive in this decision-making process. Before Trent, the missionaries were less concerned about precision. But after Trent, even in America, so far removed from the great battles of the Reformation, churchmen feared that the Indians had not really been evangelized, even though they went to Mass and participated in processions.

The culminating moment in this process was the Third Council of Lima (1582–83), during which Archbishop Toribio de Mogrovejo and all the bishops of Spanish South America, assisted by the Jesuit theologian José de Acosta and several linguists, carefully composed a universal catechism and other books on ritual for the entire Andean region. From that point on, all other catechisms and texts not approved at the Lima council were disavowed. But the story did not end there. By the seventeenth century the regional dialects began to reassert themselves. Tight control over the use of language and correct translation fueled resistance among mestizo authors such as Garcilaso de la Vega and the mendicants, like the Franciscan Luis Jerónimo de Oré, who had been largely excluded from the decision-making process. At the same time newly arrived Spanish clergy, backed by the crown, pushed to Hispanicize the Indians. As Durston convincingly demonstrates, language and the control of translations were perceived as a key to ideological control. Even the process of converting Quechua or Aymara sounds to Spanish letters was a way of subordinating a people and their language to the new rulers.

This is a fascinating, and for historians who are not linguists, an eye-opening, story of how language reflects and shapes history. The author analyzes Quechua texts and compares them to the original Latin or Spanish and with other, variant forms of Quechua. Durston also discusses how sixteenth- and seventeenth-century authors attempted to present God, Christ, and the Virgin Mary in the new standard Quechua to the Andean world. But the author also raises many issues that he admits have not been resolved satisfactorily. Even though the missionaries used Quechua, they still thought in European categories. But this raises a more fundamental question: was the new standard Quechua really Quechua, or simply a new language created from above and imposed upon the population? As the author readily acknowledges, two chapters require a basic knowledge of Quechua to fully appreciate the main arguments. Nevertheless, the essential message is clear: language, especially in the context of conquest and domination, is not and never was a neutral issue. For specialists in Andean languages, *Pastoral Quechua* is obligatory reading. For the nonspecialist, this is a fresh and enlightening way of looking at history. In most colonial church histories language appears as a subtopic under evangelization. In this case, language itself, and the background battles over language, become the lens through which the reader views and relives colonial Andean history.

Pontifical Catholic University of Peru   JEFFREY KLAIBER, S.J.

Australian and Far Eastern

Rome in Australia: The Papacy and Conflict in the Australian Catholic Missions, 1834-1884. By Christopher Dowd, O.P. 2 vols. (Boston: Brill. 2008. Pp. xxvi, 300 (vol. 1); viii, 301-658 (vol. 2). $252.00. ISBN 978-9-004-16529-8.)

As one of the last outposts of white civilization laid down forcefully among an indigenous people, the early development of Australia deserves to be treated with gravity. In the growth of a specifically Australian society, the Catholic Church played a significant role and, although others have studied its development in early colonial Australia, none has done so on such a wide canvass as Christopher Dowd.

His work is eminently scholarly in that the sources, both primary and secondary, are extensive and rich, and a thorough use has been made of them in English, Italian, and Latin. The writing stands up for clarity and precision. The author remains balanced and astute in his judgments, despite the justifiable temptation to scorn some of the actors. There is nothing narrow or pedantic about the theme and the treatment given to it.

One figure—John Bede Polding, the Benedictine first bishop of Sydney—rightly tends to dominate the early story. With his dignity and integrity intact, he stands amidst a goodly company of popes, high-ranking Roman bureaucrats, prelates (both Irish and English), drunkards, liars, opportunists, sycophants, and scoundrels (some wearing mitres), as well as devoted missionaries and saintly nonentities. At times vacillating, slipshod, and sentimental, Polding was not mean and petty, and he never hated. His greatest weakness, which almost brought him down, was his stubborn loyalty to the Benedictine Order.

Polding dreamt a noble dream in which Benedict's sons would be the founders and custodians of a high civilization in Australia, as they had been in the shadowed centuries after Rome fell and Europe was born. They were the midwives of that renewed civilization, and Polding dreamt that they would be so again in Australia. Thus he petitioned Rome, fruitlessly, to ensure that Benedictine monks would always be chosen as archbishops of Sydney. In the end, but rapidly, a lack of Benedictines caused the dream church to fail. No one could rightly grieve that the Australian church failed to be become a Benedictine church. The fading of a Benedictine presence with all the treasures it could have woven into the fabric of a young nation was the true sorrow.

This work has a universal value because it deals with an important theme, which is played out on an international stage. Rome, London, Dublin, Melbourne, and Sydney mingle, and meddle with, the Church in Australia, even with obscure hamlets out in the bush such as Bungendore. The

Australian hierarchy was the first to be erected in any part of the British Empire since the Reformation, and it suffered abundant birth pangs. Dowd's is a rich and important study of the development of that hierarchy. By extension, the work is also a study of the workings of the papacy in its period and of that singularly influential arm of the Church, the Congregation de Propaganda Fide. Its influence was felt throughout all those countries in which the hierarchy remained subject to Roman tutelage.

Dowd examines the Congregation in detail by dwelling at length on its methods and its officials. Together with good decisions, others were tainted by procrastination, by sowing confusion, by playing double games, by listening to calumny and detraction, but always protecting their sources no matter how venal, insignificant, and unreliable they were. Thus Pio Nono, and Propaganda, rather than listening to the bishops, often turned to obscure sources such as the mysterious English convert, Monsignor George Talbot, to the detriment of the Church in Australia. Curiously, Dowd has an almost inordinate fascination with assorted Roman layabouts, often of minor aristocratic origin, who wander through his pages. That he treats them with respect is to his credit, especially given that their knowledge of Australia was miniscule.

In this story there are many curiosities. Can it be that the assumption of a mitre sometimes tended to send men half-mad, or was the Australian climate at fault? John Brady in Perth was thus afflicted, and James Quinn of Brisbane matched him, which perhaps explains why they were the only bishops who refused to cringe to Rome. Yet many others frequently veered toward extremities in their lack of balance. It is difficult to write kindly of Bishop James Murray, but Dowd manages to do so, as he does of Roger Vaughan, O.S.B., of Sydney, an English upper-class racist snob. Vaughan sailed close to idolatry when he told the Prefect of Propaganda, on learning he was to become archbishop of Sydney, that he saw his principal task was that of glorifying Pio Nono's blessed name in Australia. In Rome, Cardinal Alessandro Barnabò lied and cheated constantly, but Dowd remains unfazed by this behavior, while Polding almost fretted his heart out at the extent of Roman perfidy.

The author saw fit to regard my own modest work of long ago, *The Roman Mould*, as worthy of notice even to the degree that he felt the need to give another view of the period treated. I rejoice now that I gave little emphasis to the kind of "Hibernianism" outlined by Dowd. Frail vessels that those Irish bishops were, they nonetheless left behind them a rich legacy of faith. They had been reared in that faith at the knees of their Irish mothers, but it came to them from Rome.

While it is clear that Dowd's text is consistently lively and rarely flags to hold one's attention, some critics may say that the Aborigines should have been considered at greater length. The answer is that they have their own story, and it is better to wait for their telling of it.

A wide readership and an acceptance by other English-speaking countries that Australia was not unique in the way in which a hierarchy developed there will be the best outcome for this valuable book and its author.

Australian National University (Emeritus)   JOHN NEYLON MOLONY
Australian Catholic University

Mandarins and Martyrs: The Church and the Nguyen Dynasty in Early Nineteenth-Century Vietnam. By Jacob Ramsay. (Stanford: Stanford University Press. 2008. Pp. xii, 212. $50.00. ISBN 978-0-804-75651-8.)

Ramsay's monograph analyzes the relationships among Vietnam's Nguyen Dynasty, missionary Catholicism represented by the Paris-based Foreign Missions Society, and the Catholic communities of southern Vietnam between 1802—the founding of the Nguyen Dynasty—and 1867—France's annexation of southern Vietnam's "Six Provinces." Exploiting dynastic annals and other primary Vietnamese sources as well as newly available missionary sources, Ramsey aims to reshape scholarly understanding in three ways. First, he tries to present preconquest Vietnamese Catholicism as a "popular religion" that had blended into local society. Second, he seeks to refine generally accepted motivations for Nguyen repression of Catholicism by stressing the dynasty's "restoration" ideology and centralizing agenda rather than inculcation of "Confucianism" per se. Third, he attempts to demonstrate that the separation of Catholic and nonconvert Vietnamese into hostile communities dates from the conquest—not before.

Regarding the first theme, Ramsey asserts that preconquest Catholic villagers were integrated into Vietnamese society by showing that, throughout southern Vietnam, they often lived among nonconvert co-villagers, although no scholarly monograph maintains that Catholics always lived apart. However, he does not address arguments by Nicole-Dominique Lê in *Les Missions-Étrangères et la pénétration française au Viet-Nam* (Paris, 1975) and Ta-Chi Dai-Truong in *Lich su noi chien Viet Nam* [*History of the Vietnamese Civil War*] (Saigon, 1973) that Catholic villagers often provoked the ire of nonconvert neighbors by refusing to pay taxes to support village-level rituals that Catholics considered "superstitious" and withdrawing to form new hamlets or villages, thus increasing the charges levied on nonconvert inhabitants. Ramsey does, however, demonstrate variety in Nguyen officials' views: some were less than ardent in their anti-Catholicism and primarily interested in preserving peace in their bailiwicks.

As to the second theme, motivations for Nguyen-era anti-Catholic repression, Ramsey criticizes previous scholars for emphasizing ideological antagonisms between Confucianism and Catholicism. He stresses instead the dynasty's need to assert legitimacy via the dissemination of a "restoration" thesis that represented the events of 1802 as continuity, its centralization programs launched in the 1830s, and its beliefs that Catholicism "intoxicated" Vietnamese subjects, causing them to reject imperial authority. Ramsey underestimates the complexity of existing interpretations such as those of Lê, in the work previously cited, or of Vo Duc Hanh, in *La Place du Catholicisme dans les relations entre la France et le Viet-nam* (Leiden, 1969), which are multicausational and nuanced. In addition to considering the causes Ramsey propounds, these scholars take seriously the dynasty's reactions to the facts that some missionaries called for French intervention (which Ramsey admits) and some Vietnamese Catholics facilitated the mid-century invasions (which he denies). Yet both points have been documented in existing works with reference to French archival sources in which the officers who commanded the 1858 attacks recorded their debts to the Catholic Vietnamese who had come to their aid. These facts may be inconvenient, but they cannot be wished away as "largely unsubstantiated by primary evidence" (p. 140). Dismissing these events as significant causes of the Nguyen Dynasty's mid-century anti-Catholic edicts and declining to examine relevant French archival records, Ramsey offers a very narrow view of the motivations for repression. Ramsey nonetheless expands our understanding of the repression's impact, showing how accounts of "persecution" were published in France, stimulating public support for missionary activity, which brought to Vietnam more missionaries with more resources to protect Catholic communities via the bribing of local officials. However, these protections collapsed with France's 1858 invasion, as pressures from above proved too strong for local officials to resist, leading to massacres, for example, at Bien-hoa.

The third theme, that Vietnamese followers of Catholicism, an integrated popular religion, were transformed into an isolated community antagonistically related to nonconvert Vietnamese by France's conquest and colonization, is problematic since the other themes remain unproven. Since Ramsey has not refuted existing scholarship that has established some precolonial alienation between the communities and because he has declined to engage evidence that some Catholic Vietnamese aided French forces from 1858 onward—itself proof of alienation from Nguyen society and state—he can hardly argue that colonialists were the prime movers. Nonetheless, the point is well taken, if hardly novel, that the opportunities available to Vietnamese Catholics who served in the shadow of French power increasingly distinguished them from their nonconvert compatriots, a gap that would expand, as Charles Fourniau has demonstrated in *Vietnam: Domination coloniale et résistance nationale, 1858-1914* (Paris, 2002), with the conquest of northern and central Vietnam.

Mandarins and Martyrs is a major contribution to research on Vietnamese history, the missionary enterprise, colonialism, identity formation, and religious conversion; it will be read with interest by scholars in diverse fields.

University of Delaware MARK W. McLEOD

NOTES AND COMMENTS

Research Tools and Archives

The cultural association Reti Medievali, an online initiative for medieval studies begun in 1998 and composed of scholars from various universities and institutes of learning from within and outside of Italy, makes available reliable scholarly information free of charge. Among its offerings are 1,500 texts by more than 800 authors, teaching materials, and a schedule of conferences on medieval topics from around the world. To maintain this network, the Reti seeks financial contributions. For more information, visit its Web site, http://www.retimedievali.it, or email redazione@retimedievali.it.

The Press and Information Office of the Society of Jesus in Rome has announced that incorrect information has been disseminated regarding the papers (more than 25,000 documents related to Pope Pius XII and World War II) in the archive of Father Robert Graham, S.J. While Graham's papers are being catalogued, they will not be published until the archives of Pius XII are opened in the Secret Vatican Archives.

The American Catholic History Research Center and the University Archives of The Catholic University of America (CUA) has announced the creation of a finding aid, using Encoded Archival Description (EAD), for the papers of the "labor priest" Monsignor George Gilmary Higgins. Born in 1916 in Chicago, Higgins earned a Master's degree in Economics in 1942 and a PhD in 1944 from CUA. He served the American bishops' conference from 1944 to 2001 in various capacities relating to Catholic social thought, labor relations, and ecumenical affairs. He attended the Second Vatican Council and was a moving force in the Church's support for César Chávez and the farm workers' union movement. He also served as chairman of the Public Review Board of the United Auto Workers of America (AFL-CIO) and as a member of the Executive Committee of the Leadership Conference on Civil Rights. Higgins wrote numerous book reviews for *Commonweal* and *America*, penned the syndicated column "The Yardstick" (1945-2001), and, in his later years, returned to CUA as a lecturer. He was awarded the Presidential Medal of Freedom by Bill Clinton in 2000 and died on May Day, 2002. He was widely mourned as a tireless champion of the labor movement and a progressive voice in the Roman Catholic Church. The bulk of the collection consists of paper records including correspondence, subject files, and publications.

To use the finding aid, visit http://libraries.cua.edu/achrcua/higginsfa. html. For further information, contact University Archives, The Catholic University of America, 101 Aquinas Hall, 620 Michigan Avenue, NE, Washington, DC 20064, tel: (202) 319-5065, email: archives@mail.lib.cua.edu, WWW: http://libraries.cua.edu/archives.html.

The Huntington Library of San Marino, California, reports that its California Microfilm Project that will bring together microfilm or digital copies of the surviving documentation for the Alta California up to *c.* 1850 has acquired microfilm from the Archivio General de Indias in Seville, Spain, of sixteen complete and fifty-three selections from *legajos*, comprising 3,300 items that can be searched by author, addressee, and date. From the Archivio General de la Nación in Mexico City it has received the first installment of microfilms related to California and Marina. This will be enriched by further materials from the Museo Naval in Madrid of ship logs and other maritime materials related to Spanish explorations of the west coast of North America during the eighteenth century.

EBSCO Publishing, which offers a number of databases in religious history, has announced that three new historical digital archive collections will be available soon: (1) *American Antiquarian Society Historical Periodicals*, which covers more than 6,500 periodicals published during the period 1693-1877; (2) *American Theological Library Association (ATLA) Historical Collection*, which features, in a monograph series, more than 29,000 titles focused on religious thought and practice from the thirteenth to early-twentieth centuries and, in a serials collection, 5.4 million pages from more than 1,200 serials from the early-nineteenth to early-twentieth centuries; and (3) *Arte Público Press Digital Collection—Recovering U.S. Hispanic Literature and Culture,* which contains scholarly books, historical newspapers and photographs, and letters and diaries of which 80 percent are in Spanish and 20 percent in English.

Conferences, Lectures, and Workshops

On March 12, 2009, at the Lowenstein Center of Fordham University, John Morrill of Cambridge University presented the St. Robert Southwell, S.J., Lecture on "The Dilemmas of Religious Liberty in the English Revolution."

On March 28, 2009, an observance of Maryland's 375th anniversary was held at Saint Mary's Hall in Historic Saint Mary's City. Among the presentations were talks by John Krugler on "Why Maryland? The Lords Baltimore and Their Colonial Enterprises," Joseph M. Greeley on "The Ark and the Dove: The Ships That Founded Maryland and Their Crews," Henry Miller on "A Relation of Maryland's Founding Voyage," Gabriella Tayac on "The Piscataway and Yaocomico Peoples of Maryland," Garry Wheeler Stone on "Manorial Maryland: Establishing the Colony," and Edward Papenfuse on "Maryland at the Beginning: Significance and Legacy."

On April 2-4, 2009, the Cushwa Center for the Study of American Catholicism hosted a conference on "Catholics in the Movies." The starting point for the conference was the outstanding volume *Catholics in the Movies* (Oxford, 2008), to which the conference speakers contributed essays. Cinema is arguably the most understudied and potentially enlightening lens through which to examine the historical trajectories of Catholics in the United States over the previous century. This conference explored how American Catholics produced, acted, viewed, boycotted, and were depicted in film.

Participants included Colleen McDannell, University of Utah; James T. Fisher, Fordham University; Tracy Fessenden, Arizona State University; Carlo Rotella, Boston College; Judith Weisenfeld, Princeton University; Anthony Burke Smith, University of Dayton; Thomas J. Ferraro, Duke University; Timothy Meagher, CUA; Amy Frykholm, correspondent for *The Christian Century*; María Amparo Escandón, novelist and screenwriter; Paula Kane, University of Pittsburgh; and Darryl Caterine, LeMoyne College.

On May 7-9, 2009, the XXXVIII Incontro di Studiosi dell'antichità cristiana was held in Rome with over sixty papers being presented on the theme "Διακονία, *diaconiae*, diaconato: Semantica e storia." They were organized under eleven sections: Agostino e Girolamo; Diaconato femminile; Oriente; Giovanni Crisostomo; Le più antiche testimonianze cristiane; Autori greci; Autori latini; Temi vari; Archeologia, epigrafia e iconografia; Febe; and Sessione plenaria. For more information, please email the Segreteria "Incontri" at incontri@patristicum.org.

On May 25, 2009, the Canadian Catholic Historical Association held a conference at Carleton University in Ottawa that offered five sessions. I: "Ottawa Catholicism" with "From the Ottawa Valley to the Four Corners of the World: Reconceptualizing the Identity of the Grey Sisters of the Immaculate Conception" by Elizabeth Smyth; "J. J. O'Gorman, Ottawa and the Imperial Irish, 1914-1919" by Mark McGowan; and "Fr. Aeneas M. Dawson and Canadian Expansionism" by Fred McEvoy. II: "Women in the 20th Century Church" with "'Setting Up Shop'—The Arrival of the Sisters of Social Service in Hamilton, Ontario" by Christine Lei; "'For League Members and Their Friends': Gender, Ethnicity and Class in the St. Louis Catholic Women's League, 1924-1945" by Marilla McCarger; and "The Sisters of the Assumption Teaching Japanese Canadians during World War II—Nation, Homeland, Territory" by Jacqueline Gresko. III: "The Impact of the Laity" with "Nationalism in a Catholic Weekly? The Case Study of Gazeta Katolicka in Interwar Canada" by Gabriela Kasprzak; "Pitching, Pies, and Piety: Early 20th Century Saint Hedwig Parish Picnics" by Joshua Blank; and "Catholic Studies and the Study of Catholicism in Canadian Universities and Colleges: History and Prospects" by Ryan Topping. IV: "Developments in the Canadian Church Before and After the Second Vatican Council" with "Rooted in the Vision of Vatican II: Youth Corps and Its Efforts to Empower Young Catholics in Catholic Social Justice,

1966-1984" by Peter Baltutis; "'Going back to the Land' in the 1930s: Lived Religion and Living Otherwise in Toronto" by Robert Dennis; and "Public History? Motherhouse Museums in Canada, 1962-2008" by Heidi MacDonald. V: "Saints and the Faithful" with "Nationalist Saint: Jean de Brébeuf and the Politics of Canadian Identity" by Emma Anderson; "Gérard Raymond: The Making of a French Canadian Adolescent Saint" by Donald Boisvert; and "'Nearly all the back township have neglected their Lenten duty': Lay Initiative and Obstacles to Clerical Control in Nineteenth Century Rural Ontario" by Laura Smith.

The Cushwa Center for the Study of American Catholicism at the University of Notre Dame has announced several forthcoming events. On September 23, Michael E. Lee of Fordham University will deliver the annual Cushwa Center Lecture on "Ignacio Ellacuría, Martyred Professor: A Catholic University Confronts El Salvador's Reality." The Seminar in American Religion will be led by Curtis J. Evans of the Divinity School of the University of Chicago on the topic "*The Burden of Black Religion* (Oxford, 2008)" with Anthea Butler of the University of Rochester and Milton Sernet of Syracuse University as commentators; it will be held on September 12. The American Catholic Studies Seminar will be conducted on November 10 by Kelly Baker of Florida State University under the title "Rome's Reputation Is Stained with Protestant Blood: The Klan-Notre Dame Riot of May 1924." Finally, the Hibernian Lecture will be delivered on October 9 by Maurice Bric of the University College of Dublin on the topic "'Squaring Circles': Daniel O'Connell and Public Protest, 1823-1843."

.

On June 8-12, 2009, the Institut d'histoire de la Réformation at the Université de Genève has offered a summer course on "Challenges to Religion from the Renaissance to Deism" that investigated questions of tolerance, natural religion, and atheism. On June 15-19, 2009, it offered a summer course on "Mediating the Sacred in the Sixteenth Century: Anticlericalism and the Redefinition of Religious and Ecclesiastical Roles in the Reformation and Counter-Reformation" that studied the transformation and renewal of pastoral ministry and the controversies regarding the nature and scope of ecclesiastical authority and functions, the role of women as propagators of noninstitutional charismata, the training of ministers, missionary zeal, and religious propaganda.

On November 26-28, 2009, a *Dies Academicus* will be sponsored by the Biblioteca Ambrosiana and the Università Catholica di Milano on the theme "La Cultura della Rappresentazione nella Milano del Settecento: Discontinuità e Permanenze." Among the papers to be presented are "Il sistema della religione cittadina dei milanesi del Settecento e S. Maria presso S. Celso" by Paola Vismara; "Tommaso Ceva e i gesuiti del Settecento" by Emanuele Colombo; "La virtù rappresentata: Scudi ed emblemi di 'principes academiae' del Collegio gesuitico di Santa Maria degli Angeli di Monza (1738-1773)" by Angelo

Bianchi; "Giovan Battista Castiglioni e i *Sentimenti di San Carlo intorno agli spettacoli*: nuove ricerche sull'autore e la sua cultura" by Marzia Giuliani; "La scultura nei grandi cantieri lombardi del Settecento: i casi del Duomo di Milano e della Certosa di Pavia" by Maria Grazia Albertini Ottolenghi; "Il completamento del Duomo: la questione della facciata, terminale scenografico della città" by Alessandro Rovetta; "Un ciclo sconosciuto di quadri per la canonizzazione di Andrea Avellino del 1713" by Simonetta Coppa; "Momenti della ritualità civile e religiosa: il teatro. La fine del Carnevale e della quaresima" by Claudio Bernardi and Carla Bino; and "Liturgy and Music in Settecento Milan" by Robert Kendrick and Christoph Riedo.

Awards

The Cushwa Center for the Study of American Catholicism at the University of Notre Dame has conferred two Hibernian Research Awards, which are funded by the Ancient Order of Hibernians and provide travel funds for the support of scholarly study of the Irish in America. The recipients are Timothy Meagher of CUA, who is writing a book, *"The Lord Is Not Dead": A History of Irish Americans*, and Elizabeth Dilkes Mullins of the University of California at Santa Cruz, who will conduct research under the title "Making Girls, Women, Ladies, and Nuns: Sister Mary Philip Ryan, O.P., and the History of Femininity in American Colonial Spaces, 1923–2003."

Call for Papers

On the occasion of the publication of the *Historical Dictionary of the Inquisition* by the Edizioni della Normale, the next edition of the *Annali della Scuola Normale Superiore di Pisa: Classe di Lettere e Filosofia*, in a fully renovated format and under the new direction of Adriano Prosperi, will devote its monographic section to the history of those institutions that monitored and controlled religious orthodoxy, as well as to the people affected by those institutions, from the Middle Ages to the present. Articles are welcomed on the history of Catholic tribunals both in Europe and elsewhere, on theological and legal reflections about the activities of the inquisitors, on censorship, on literary and visual representations linked with the changing image of the Inquisition, and on comparative reviews of recent literature or historiographical debates. The articles must be sent electronically by July 31, 2009, to the following email address: segreteria. annali@sns.it. The guidelines and editing rules can be found on the Web page http://www.sns.it/en/edizioni/riviste/annalilettere. Decisions regarding publication of submissions will be made by internationally renowned referees and communicated to authors within a month. For further information, please contact Giuseppe Marcocci, Segretario Scientifico di Redazione, Annali della Classe di Lettere e Filosofia, Scuola Normale Superiore, Piazza dei Cavalieri 7, I-56126 Pisa, Italy; tel: (+39) 329-7460048; fax: (+39) 050-563513; email: segreteria.annali@sns.it.

Publications

The theme of the third number of *Erbe und Auftrag* for 2008 (vol. 84) is "Hildegard von Bingen," which is articulated threefold: "Gotteskräfte: Über die Tugenden bei Hildegard von Bingen," by Maura Zátonyi, O.S.B. (pp. 246-62); "Klosteralltag und Klausur: Die Regelauslegung Hildegards von Bingen," by Gisela Muschiol (pp. 263-72); and "Die Klause Hildegards von Bingen: Zu den Lebensumständen der Inklusin Hildegard auf dem Disibodenberg," by Gabriele Mergenthaler (pp. 273-84).

The centenary of the founding of the *Archivum Franciscanum Historicum* is celebrated in its issue for July–December, 2008 (vol. 101, fascicles 3-4), in which the following articles appear: Pacifico Sella, O.F.M., "Genesi di un periodico scientifico: l'*Archivum Franciscanum Historicum*" (pp. 343-62); Barbara Faes, "Il contributo dell'*Archivum Franciscanum Historicum* agli studi di teologia e filosofia medievali" (pp. 363-451); Francisco Víctor Sánchez Gil, O.F.M., "La importancia de *Archivum Franciscanum Historicum* para la historiografía franciscana moderna. Balance de un Centenario (1908-2007)" (pp. 453-89); Attilio Bartoli Langeli, "L'apporto dell'AFH alla pubblicazione delle fonti della storia francescana" (pp. 491-97); and Luca Dalvit and Pacifico Sella, O.F.M., "Index auctorum cum eorum commentariis quae exstant in AFH 1908-2007" (pp. 499-584).

With a colorful new cover, *The Sixteenth Century Journal* has published a special issue for spring, 2009 (vol. XL, no. 1) to commemorate the fortieth anniversary of the founding of the periodical and of the Sixteenth Century Society and Conference. Raymond Waddington, Merry Wiesner-Hanks, and David Whitford have contributed "A History of the Sixteenth Century Journal and Conference" (pp. 13-17), which is followed by a list of the presidents from 1969-70 to 2009. Instead of scholarly articles, the editors have presented forty-five brief reflections by recognized historians on "The Field and the Future" (pp. 173-278). Sandwiched between these two sections are evaluations by senior scholars of forty-two books published in the last four decades (pp. 23-165) that have notably influenced historiography of the period.

Volume 155 of the *Bulletin de la Société de l'Histoire du Protestantisme Français* for 2009 is devoted to the theme "Études historiques: Calvin et la France." Following an introduction by Bernard Cottret, the twenty-one articles are divided into three sections: I. "Calvin et la France à l'époque de Calvin," including a contribution by Robert Kingdon, "Calvin et la discipline ecclésiastique" (pp. 117-26); II. "Réception et images de Calvin (XVIe-XVIIIe siècles)," including a contribution by Irena Backus, "Un chapitre oublié de la réception de Calvin en France. La *Vita Calvini* de Jean-Papire Masson (1583)" (pp. 181-207); and III. "Calvin dans la culture française et l'historiographie moderne."

"800 Jahre franziskanische Mission" is the theme of *Heft* 3-4 for 2008 (vol. 92) of the *Zeitschrift für Missionswissenschaft und Religionswissenschaft.* The introduction by Lothar Billy, S.D.B. (pp 227-28), is followed by a dozen articles: Hermann Schalück, O.F.M., "Von der Expansion zur Relation: Zum Grundparadigma des franziskanischen Missionsverständnisses" (pp. 229-37); Leonhard Lehmann, O.F.M.Cap., "Franziskanishe Mission als Friedensmission: Ein Vergleich der frühen Quellen" (pp. 238-71); Anton Rotzetter, O.F.M.Cap., "Mystik und Mission bei Franz von Assisi" (pp. 272-79); Jan Hoeberichts, "Francis' Understanding of Mission: Living the Gospel, Going through the World, Bringing Peace" (pp. 280-97); Johannes Meier, "Die Franziskanermissionen der Frühen Neuzeit—ein Überblick" (pp. 298-308); Mariano Delgado, " «Den Fußspuren unseres Vaters Sankt Franziskus folgend»: Licht und Schatten der frühneuzeitlichen Franziskaner-Mission in Lateinamerika und auf den Philippinen" (pp. 309-29); Linda Báez-Rubí, "Die «Rhetorica Christiana» (Perugia 1579) des Fray Diego de Valadés als Ausdruck franziskanischer Missionstheologie" (pp. 330-49); Othmar Noggler, O.F.M.Cap., "Die Kapuziner—ihr Verhältnis zur Sklaverei in Amerika" (pp. 350-63); Claudia von Collani, "Die China-Mission der Franziskaner" (pp. 364-79); Benedict Vadakkekara, O.F.M.Cap., "Die Indienmission der Kapuziner" (pp. 380-92); Jan Bernd Elpert, O.F.M.Cap., "Die zeitgenössische Kapuzinermission in Afrika: Ein Einblick in drei unterschiedlichen Nahaufnahmen aus Tanzania, Zambia, Südafrika" (pp. 393-407); and Ute Jung-Kaiser, "«es wurde der Welt eine Sonne geboren . . .» Künstlerische Annäherungen an Franziskus und seinen «Sonnengesang»" (pp. 408-32).

Causes of Saints

On April 26, 2009, Pope Benedict XVI canonized five blesseds. St. Bernardo Tolomei (1272-1348) was the abbot and founder of the Benedictine Congregation of the Blessed Virgin of Monte Oliveto who died during the Plague of 1348 while assisting his fellow monks who had contracted the disease. St. Nuno de Santa Maria Àlvares Pereira (né Nuno) (1360-1431) was a noted Portuguese soldier (known as the "Father of the Nation" and the "Condestável" or constable/general) who stopped an invasion of Castilian soldiers at the Battle of Aljubarrota in 1385 and participated in the expedition to Ceuta in Africa in 1415. Made the third count of Ourém in 1383, he is considered the founder of the Bragança royal family that ruled Portugal from 1640 to 1910. He established the secular Confraternity of Our Lady of Mount Carmel in Lisbon to work with the poor, which eventually evolved into the present Carmelite Third Order. Following the death of his wife, he ended his life as a professed layman of the Order of Friars of the Blessed Virgin Mary of Monte Carmel (of the Ancient Observance), in a convent he had ordered to be built. St. Caterina Volpicelli (1839-94) was the foundress of the Institute of the Handmaidens of the Sacred Heart that ministered to the spiritual and social needs of late-nineteenth-century Naples. St. Gertrude Caterina Comensoli (1847-1903) was the Italian foundress in 1882 of the Congregation of the Sacramentine Sisters of Bergamo that was dedicated to care of the rural poor who came to cities to engage in the industrial revolution and fell into moral degradation due to excessive hours of work and spiritual neglect. She promoted the perpetual adoration of the Blessed Sacrament and service in education, social welfare, and the liturgy. St. Arcangelo Tadini (1846–1912), an Italian priest, evangelized the world of work by establishing the Catholic Workers' Mutual Assistance Association, building a textile mill and residence for female workers, and founding the Congregation of Worker Sisters of the Holy House of Nazareth in 1900.

Personals

The Most Reverend Timothy M. Dolan was installed on April 15, 2009, as the tenth archbishop of New York. He has been a member of the ACHA since 1979 and a life member since 1992.

Reverend Monsignor Francis R. Seymour has been appointed by the Most Reverend John J. Myers, archbishop of Newark, as chairman of the New Jersey Catholic Historical Commission.

Jo Ann McNamara, professor emerita of history at Hunter College, CUNY, and an ACHA member since 1986, died May 20, 2009, in New York City.

Reverend Robert F. McNamara died on May 22, 2009, in Rochester, New York. An ACHA member since 1941, Father McNamara served as second vice-president of the association in 1971.

Obituary notices for both Dr. McNamara and Father McNamara will appear in an upcoming issue of *The Catholic Historical Review*.

Addendum

In the list of contributors toward the expansion of *The Catholic Historical Review* that was published in the April issue (pp. 294–95), the name of Dr. Daniel F. Tanzone, editor of the *Slovak Catholic Sokol*, was inadvertently omitted. His support is hereby gratefully acknowledged. *The Catholic Historical Review* regrets this oversight.

PERIODICAL LITERATURE

General and Miscellaneous

La primauté du patriarche œcuménique dans l'Empire ottoman. Job Getcha. *Istina*, LIV (Jan.-Mar., 2009), 17-28.

The Origins of Modernity: An Alternate Interpretation of Western Cultural History. Owen C. Thomas. *Anglican Theological Review*, 91 (Spring, 2009), 235-54.

L'archivio dell' Inquisizione e gli studi storici: primi bilanci e prospettive a dieci anni dall'apertura. Elena Bonora. *Rivista Storica Italiana*, CXX (Dec., 2008), 968-1002.

Le rôle des laïcs dans la coopération missionnaire selon les documents de l'Église, de Grégoire XVI à Paul VI. Marek A. Rostkowski. *Theoforum*, 38 (3, 2007), 321-59.

L'Arcivescovo G.B. Montini ricorda Papa Giovanni XXIII. Annibale Zambarbieri. *Istituto Paolo VI*, No. 56 (Dec., 2008), 11-26.

Ein romanischer Tragaltar auf der Flucht. Provenienz und Werkgeschichte des Abdinghofer Tragaltars im 19. und 20. Jahrhundert. Jürgen Werinhard Einhorn, O.F.M. *Wissenschaft und Weisheit*, 71 (2, 2008), 163-86.

Una aproximación a la historia de una parroquia suburbana gallega: San Miguel de Marcón—Pontevedra. Jesús Niño Sánchez Guisande y Roberto Acuña Rey. *Compostellanum*, LIII (July-Dec., 2008), 603-29.

"Ili a Baluarte": Revisiting the Cradle of Aglipayanism. Ericson M. Josue. *Philippiniana Sacra*, XLIV (Jan.-Apr., 2009), 129-86.

Ancient

Chrèstianoi / Christianoi. Ce que *«chrétiens»* en ses débuts voulait dire. Cécile Faivre and Alexandre Faivre. *Revue d'histoire ecclésiastique*, 103 (July-Dec., 2008), 771-803.

La penitenza tra rigore e lassismo: Cipriano di Cartagine e la riconciliazione dei lapsi. Attilio Carpin. *Sacra Doctrina*, 53 (3, 2008), 7-174.

Distraction or Spiritual Discipline: The Role of Sleep in Early Egyptian Monasticism. Charles J. Metteer. *St Vladimir's Theological Quarterly*, 52 (1, 2008), 5-43.

The Evolution of Donatist Theology as Response to a Changing Late Antique Milieu. Matthew Allan Gaumer. *Augustiniana*, 58 (3-4, 2008), 201-33.

Constantin und Lactanz in Trier—Chronologisches. Eberhard Heck. *Historia*, 58 (1, 2009), 118-30.

La rhétorique au service de la critique du christianisme dans le *Contre les Galiléens* de l'empereur Julien. Fabrice Robert. *Revue d'Études Augustiniennes et Patristiques*, 54 (2, 2008), 221-56.

Church Properties and the Propertied Church: Donors, the Clergy and the Church in Medieval Western Europe from the Fourth Century to the Twelfth. Janet L. Nelson. *English Historical Review*, CXXIV (Apr., 2009), 355-74.

Los orígenes de los clérigos regulares de san Agustín: un monasterio en Hipona, hacia el año 391. José Antonio Calvo Gómez. *Religión y Cultura*, LIV (Oct.-Dec., 2008), 971-1005.

Augustine and Corruption. Peter Iver Kaufman. *History of Political Thought*, XXX (1, 2009), 46-59.

Saint Augustine's Milan vision reconstructed. John Paletta. *Augustiniana*, 58 (3-4, 2008), 151-80.

Jerome's Animosity against Augustine. Stuart Squires. *Augustiniana*, 58 (3-4, 2008), 181-99.

La carta 93 de san Agustín y el uso de la fuerza pública en materia religiosa. José Fortunato Álvarez Valdez. *Augustinus*, LIV (Jan.-June, 2009), 33-61.

'Imitatio Christi, imitatio Stephani'. El pensamiento de Agustín sobre el martirio, a partir de los sermones sobre el protomártir Esteban. Anthony Dupont. *Augustinus*, LIV (Jan.-June, 2009), 143-71.

The Trial of Eutyches: A new interpretation. George A. Bevan and Patrick T. R. Gray. *Byzantinische Zeitschrift*, 101 (2, 2008), 617-57.

Vicende postcalcedonesi. Il potere imperiale tra scismi e eresie. Enrico Dal Covolo. *Annuarium Historiae Conciliorum*, 38 (2, 2006), 255-64.

Acta Conciliorum e repetita praelectio giustinianea: la διάταξις di Marciano del marzo 452. Elio Dovere. *Annuarium Historiae Conciliorum*, 38 (2, 2006), 241-54.

The Revolt of Vitalianus and the "Scythian Controversy." Dan Ruscu. *Byzantinische Zeitschrijt*, 101 (2, 2008), 773-85.

Medieval

Motive und Strukturen des Schismas im monenergetisch-monotheletischen Streit. Heinz Ohme. *Annuarium Historiae Conciliorum*, 38 (2, 2006), 265-96.

The *Vita Columbani* in Merovingian Gaul. Alexander O'Hara. *Early Medieval Europe*, 17 (May, 2009), 126-53.

Bede on the Papacy. John Moorhead. *Journal of Ecclesiastical History*, 60 (Apr., 2009), 217-32.

Bede on the Britons. W. Trent Foley and Nicholas J. Higham. *Early Medieval Europe*, 17 (May, 2009), 154–85.

«Per intendere questi tempi bisogna essere un poco monsignore». I Longobardi e la Chiesa romana secondo Louis Duchesne (II parte). Francesco Mores. *Rivista di Storia della Chiesa in Italia*, LXII (July–Dec., 2008), 413–47.

The *Memoriale Qualiter*: An Eighth Century Monastic Customary. Matthew Mattingly, O.S.B. *American Benedictine Review*, 60 (Mar., 2009), 62–75.

Deux documents en relation avec l'enquête de Charlemagne sur le baptême. Jean-Paul Bouhot. *Revue d'Études Augustiniennes et Patristiques,* 54 (2, 2008), 295–314.

Les *liberi homines* dans le polyptyque de Saint-Germain-des-Prés. Alain Sigoillot. *Journal des Savants* (July–Dec., 2008), 261–71.

Das Papstprivileg für Cluny vom März 931. Übersetzung und kirchenhistorische Einordnung. Tobias Georges. *Zeitschrift für Kirchengeschichte*, 119 (3, 2008), 380–86.

A propos du millenaire de la naissance du pape Léon IX (1002–1054). Charles Munier. *Revue des Sciences Religieuses*, 83 (Apr., 2009), 239–55.

Regarding the spectators of the Bayeux Tapestry: Bishop Odo and his circle. T. A. Heslop. *Art History*, 32 (Apr., 2009), 223–49.

In the Wake of Mantzikert: The First Crusade and the Alexian Reconquest of Western Anatolia. Jason T. Roche. *History*, 94 (Apr., 2009), 135–53.

"Let Not a Remnant or a Residue Escape": Millenarian Enthusiasm in the First Crusade. Robert Chazan. *Speculum*, 84 (Apr., 2009), 289–313.

La «littérature des croisades» existe-t-elle? Alexandre Winkler. *Le Moyen Age*, CXIV (3–4, 2008), 603–18.

La proprietà fondiaria dei grandi enti ecclesiastici nella Tuscia dei secoli XI–XV. Spunti di riflessione, tentativi di interpretazione. Francesco Salvestrini. *Rivista di Storia della Chiesa in Italia*, LXII (July–Dec., 2008), 377–412.

Medieval Benedictines in Iceland: The Personal was Political. Micaela L. Kristin-Kali. *American Benedictine Review*, 60 (Mar., 2009), 3–26.

"Like a Boat Is Marriage": Aelred on Marriage as a Christian Way of Life. Marie Ann Mayeski. *Theological Studies*, 70 (Mar., 2009), 92–108.

John of Salisbury's Second Letter Collection in Later Medieval England: Unexamined Fragments from Huntington Library HM 128. Karen Bollermann and Cary J. Nederman. *Viator*, 40 (1, 2009), 71–91.

Children in the Monastic Liturgy of the Earlier Middle Ages. Mark Spurrell. *Downside Review*, 127 (Apr., 2009), 127–38.

'Canonici Albi et Moniales': Perceptions of the Twelfth-Century Double House. Katharine Sykes. *Journal of Ecclesiastical History*, 60 (Apr., 2009), 233–45.

Usura ed interesse dal XII al XV secolo. L'usura: forma degenerativa dell' interesse? Claudio Gallotti. *Antonianum*, LXXXIII (Oct.-Dec., 2008), 625-52.

Envisaging the Particular Judgment in Late-Medieval Italy. Virginia Brilliant. *Speculum*, 84 (Apr., 2009), 314-46.

The Problem of Religious Union and its Literature. Aristeides Papadakis. *Annuarium Historiae Conciliorum*, 38 (2, 2006), 297-312.

Zwei Häresien in einer Stadt. Die Anhänger von Waldensern und Katharern in Montauban (Quercy) im 13. Jahrhundert. Jörg Feuchter. *Zeitschrifi für Kirchengeschichte*, 119 (3, 2008), 297-326.

Nueva cronología de Clara de Asís. Niklaus Kuster. *Naturaleza y Gracia*, LV (Sept.-Dec., 2008), 563-628.

The White and Black Confraternities of Toulouse and the Albigensian Crusade, 1210-1211. Laurence W. Marvin. *Viator*, 40 (1, 2009), 133-50.

La représentation de l'islam dans l'*Historia orientalis*. Jacques de Vitry historien. Jean Donnadieu. *Le Moyen Age*, CXIV (3-4, 2008), 487-508.

Les acteurs du commerce des reliques à la fin des croisades. Pierre-Vincent Claverie. *Le Moyen Age*, CXIV (3-4, 2008), 589-602.

Spuren einer religiösen Bruderschaft in Epirus um 1225? Zur Deutung der Memorialtexte im Codex Cromwell 11. Günter Prinzing. *Byzantinische Zeitschrift*, 101 (2, 2008), 751-72.

Qualiter vita prelatorum conformari debet vite angelice: A Sermon (1244-46?). Attributed to Thomas Gallus. Declan Lawell. *Recherches de Théologie et Philosophie médiévales*, LXXV (2, 2008), 303-36.

The Language of the Market Place in the Sermons of Robert de Sorbon (1201-1274). F. N. M. Diekstra. *Recherches de Théologie et Philosophie médiévales*, LXXV (2, 2008), 337-94.

The Immaculate Kiss Beneath the Golden Gate: The Influence of John Duns Scotus on Florentine Painting of the 14th Century. Michelle A. Erhardt. *Franciscan Studies*, 66 (2008), 269-80, with 4 color plates.

Philippe de Mézière's *Life of Saint Pierre de Thomas* at the Crossroads of Late Medieval Hagiography and Crusading Ideology. Renate Blumenfeld-Kosinski. *Viator*, 40 (1, 2009), 223-48.

The Exequies of Edward III and the Royal Funeral Ceremony in Late Medieval England. Chris Given-Wilson. *English Historical Review*, CXXIV (Apr., 2009), 257-82.

Of Captains and Antichrists. The Papacy in Wycliffite Thought. J. Patrick Hornbeck II. *Revue d'histoire ecclésiastique*, 103 (July-Dec., 2008), 806-37.

William Swinderby and the Wycliffite Attitude to Excommunication. Ian Forrest. *Journal of Ecclesiastical History*, 60 (Apr., 2009), 246-69.

The Auffahrtabend Prophecy and Henry of Langenstein: German Adaptation and Transmission of the "Visio fratris Johannis." Jennifer Kolpacoff Deane. *Viator*, 40 (1, 2009), 355-86.

Puentes y hospitales en el Camino de Santiago en el Noroeste peninsular (siglos XIV-XV). Saturnino Ruiz de Loizaga. *Compostellanum*, LIII (July-Dec., 2008), 347-74.

Common Ground for Contrasting Ideologies: The Texts and Contexts of *A Schort Reule of Lif.* Mary Raschko. *Viator*, 40 (1, 2009), 387-410.

Der endgültige Bruch Kastiliens mit Benedikt XIII. und das Ende des großen abendländischen Schismas. Ein Beitrag zur Lösung einer offenen Forschungsfrage. Ansgar Frenken. *Zeitschrift für Kirchengeschichte*, 119 (3, 2008), 327-57.

Bernardus Baptizatus (Bernard de la Planche) and the sermon *Sedens docebat turbas* at the Council of Constance. Chris L. Nighman and Sophie Vallery-Radot. *Annuarium Historiae Conciliorum*, 38 (2, 2006), 313-20.

Resolving benefice disputes after the Great Schism: The survival of the council of Constance's 4 July 1415 decrees *omnia et singula* and *pro majori pace* in two disputes from Auch and Rieti brought before the rota auditor Gimignano Inghirami at the time of the council of Basle. Martin Cable. *Annuarium Historiae Conciliorum*, 38 (2, 2006), 321-424.

"Alors nous lui serons obéissants ... comme au Sauveur Lui-meme". Syméon de Thessalonique et la question de la primauté du pape de Rome. Assaad Elias Kattan. *Istina*, LIV (Jan.-Mar., 2009), 9-15.

Sermoni Mariani di Alessio da Seregno vescovo di Piacenza (1412-1448). Giuseppe Motta. *Aevum*, LXXXII (Sept.-Dec., 2008), 621-49.

Gabriel Biel: Brother of the Common Life and *Alter Augustinus?* Aim and meaning of his *Tractatus de communi vita clericorum*. Paul Van Geest. *Augustiniana*, 58 (3-4, 2008), 305-57.

Libri, guardaroba e suppellettili del veronese Giovanni Francesco Brusati, vescovo di Cassano. Elisabetta Lo Cascio. *Aevum*, LXXXII (Sept.-Dec., 2008), 659-81.

Une réforme de l'intérieur. . . : les constitutions pastorales du patriarche de Venise Tommaso Dona (1492-1504). Présentation, examen, et édition. Pascal Vuillemin. *Studi Veneziani*, LIV (2007), 65-87.

De Jure novo: Dealing with Adultery in the Fifteenth-Century Toulousain. Leah Otis-Cour. *Speculum*, 84 (Apr., 2009), 347-92.

The immaculate body in the Sistine ceiling. Kim E. Butler. *Art History*, 32 (Apr., 2009), 250-89.

Sixteenth Century

Documentos inéditos sobre la reforma de algunos monasterios benedictinos en Galicia, La Rioja, Carrión y Portugal (1497-1545). Ernesto Zaragoza Pascual. *Compostellanum*, LIII (July-Dec., 2008), 375-429.

Das Projekt eines *Sodalitium Episcoporum* im frühen 16. Jahrhundert und die heutige Bischofssynode. Reinhard Knittel. *Archiv für katholisches Kirchenrecht*, 176 (2, 2007), 361-93.

The Decree *Inter multiplices* of Lateran V on *Montes pietatis*. Nelson H. Minnich. *Annuarium Historiae Conciliorum*, 38 (2, 2006), 425-50.

Ius et potestas circa sacra. Le consulte teologiche in età post-tridentina (1564-1650). Alessia Ceccarelli. *Nuova Rivista Storica*, XCII (Sept.-Dec., 2008), 743-62.

La visita apostolica alla diocesi di Cagli del 1574. Stefano Orazi. *Rivista di Storia della Chiesa in Italia*, LXII (July-Dec., 2008), 507-67.

Dalla «perfezione» alla «sovranità»; da Paruta a Sarpi. Gino Benzoni. *Studi Veneziani*, LV (2008), 167-201.

Consolation on Golgotha: Comforters and Sustainers of Dying Priests in England, 1580-1625. Sarah Covington. *Journal of Ecclesiastical History*, 60 (Apr., 2009), 270-93.

L'istituzione dei vicariati foranei nelle diocesi di Concordia e Aquileia. Un aspetto della modernizzazione dei costumi della Chiesa nel Friuli storico tra Cinque e Seicento. Luigi Gervaso. *Studi Veneziani*, LV (2008), 283-347.

«Una materia gravissima, una enorme heresia»: Granada, Roma e la controversia sugli apocrifi del Sacromonte. Pierroberto Scaramella. *Rivista Storica Italiana*, CXX (Dec., 2008), 1003-44.

Seventeenth and Eighteenth Centuries

Santi rifugi di sanità: i lazzaretti delle quattro isole di Levante. Katerina Konstantinidou. *Studi Veneziani*, LIII (2007), 239-59.

Les doutes de l'Inquisiteur. Philosophie naturelle, censure et théologie à l'époque moderne. Maria Pia Donato. *Annales*, 64 (Jan.-Feb., 2009), 15-43.

Militant Protestants: British Identity in the Jacobean Period, 1603-1625. Jason C. White. *History*, 93 (Apr., 2009), 154-75.

"The Root is Hidden and the Material Uncertain": The Challenges of Prosecuting Witchcraft in Early Modern Venice. Jonathan Seitz. *Renaissance Quarterly*, 62 (Spring, 2009), 102-33.

«Quando in affari spirituali si interpongono interessi temporali». La conversione degli ortodossi di Pastrovicchi nei consulti di Fulgenzio Micanzio. Olga Diklić. *Studi Veneziani*, LV (2008), 15-81.

Sarpi e la Chiesa nell'età della Controriforma. Corrado Vivanti. *Studi Veneziani*, LIV (2007), 119-33.

Paolo Sarpi consultore in iure della Serenissima e i giuristi dell'Università di Padova. Corrado Pin. *Studi Veneziani*, LVI (2008), 207-26.

Alternate Routes: Variation in Early Modern Stational Devotions. Mitzi Kirkland-Ives. *Viator*, 40 (1, 2009), 249-70.

L'Anglipotrida di Orazio Busino (1618). Pietro Contarini e il suo cappellano alla corte di Giacomo I. Franca Bonaldo. *Studi Veneziani*, LVI (2008), 229-70.

Les évêques du Grand Siècle devant la mort d'après leurs testaments. Joseph Bergin. *Revue d'Histoire de l'Église de France*, 94 (July-Dec., 2008), 263-81.

Notizie Historiche (continuazione). Giancarlo Caputi. *Archivum Scholarum Piarum*, XXXIII (65, 2009), 3-142.

Cardinal Rapaccioli and the Turnip-sellers of Rome: A Satire on the War of Castro by Baccio del Bianco. Louise Rice. *Master Drawings*, 47 (Spring, 2009), 53-69.

Giovanni Battista Gaulli: Remaking the Image of a Cardinal Saint in Seventeenth-century Rome. Hugh Hudson. *Master Drawings*, 47 (Spring, 2009), 70-78.

El arquitecto benedictino gallego Fray Tomás Alonso (1645-1686). Leopold Fernández Gasalla. *Compostellanum*, LIII (July-Dec., 2008), 481-513.

Dodici Lettere di Alessandro Porro, C.R., vescovo di Bobbio. Gian Luigi Bruzzone. *Regnum Dei*, LXII (Jan.-Dec., 2006), 99-122.

Réforme catholique et endogamie villageoise d'après les dispenses de parenté du diocèse de Coutances. Jean-Marie Gouesse. *Revue d'Histoire de l'Église de France*, 94 (July-Dec., 2008), 301-24.

The Antiquary and the Information State: Colbert's Archives, Secret Histories, and the Afair of the *Régale*, 1663-1682. Jacob Soll. *French Historical Studies*, 31 (Winter, 2008), 3-28.

Jean Mabillon and the Sources of Medieval Ecclesiastical History: Part I. Michael Edward Moore. *American Benedictine Review*, 60 (Mar., 2009), 76-93.

La prima edizione in italiano del *Book of common prayer* (1685) tra propaganda protestante e memoria sarpiana. Stefano Villani. *Rivista di Storia e Letteratura Religiosa*, XLIV (1, 2008), 23-45.

Entre foi et doutes. Itinéraire de Mathurin Veyssière de La Croze, un mauriste converti au protestantisme à la fin du XVIIe siècle. Didier Boisson. *Revue d'Histoire de l'Église de France*, 94 (July-Dec., 2008), 283-99.

Le contraddizioni della modernità: apologetica cattolica e Lumi nel Settecento. Mario Rosa. *Rivista di Storia e Letteratura Religiosa*, XLIV (1, 2008), 73-114.

Liberty, Tyranny and the Will of God: The Principle of Toleration in Early Modern Europe and Colonial India. Jakob De Roover and S. N. Balagangadhara. *History of Political Thought*, XXX (1, 2009), 111-39.

National Fasting and the Politics of Prayer: Anglo-Scottish Union, 1707. Jeffrey Stephen. *Journal of Ecclesiastical History*, 60 (Apr., 2009), 294-316.

Fénelon et la recherche du vrai thomisme. Le débat sur l'antithomisme fénelonien (1725-1726). Sylvio Hermann De Franceschi. *Revue d'histoire ecclésiastique*, 103 (July-Dec., 2008), 839-85.

Un'architettura di «scientifica semplicità»: Tommaso Temanza e la chiesa della Maddalena. Massimo Favilla and Ruggero Rugolo. *Studi Veneziani*, LV (2008), 203-82.

Trent and the Clergy in Late Eighteenth-Century Malta. Frans Ciappara. *Church History*, 78 (Mar., 2009), 1-25.

Apocalyse contre constellations. La réfutation de *l'Origine de tous les cultes* de Dupuis par le père Lambert. Celine Pauvros. *Revue d'Histoire de l'Église de France*, 94 (July-Dec., 2008), 325-50.

Nineteenth and Twentieth Centuries

La Iglesia española en la primera mitad del siglo XIX. Ismael Arevalillo García, O.S.A. *Religión y Cultura*, LIV (Oct.-Dec., 2008), 929-69.

P. Arcangelo Isaia de Santa Teresa Vicario General de la Orden de las Escuelas Pías (1749-1827). Adolfo García-Duran. *Archivum Scholarum Piarum*, XXXIII (65, 2009), 175-202.

Les évêques missionnaires français entre 1815 et 1968. De la paroisse rurale à la mission outre-mer. Yannick Essertel. *Revue d'histoire ecclésiastique*, 103 (July-Dec., 2008), 887-932.

Joan Gallifi i Arqués, C.R. (1775-1809), joven sacerdote teatino catalán, víctima de la ocupación napoleónica y símbolo popular de la liberación de Barcelona. Jordi Cassà i Vallès. *Regnum Dei*, LXII (Jan.-Dec., 2006), 123-92.

Auf dem Weg zu Johann Sebastian Drey. Beobachtungen zur Geschichte seiner Wiederentdeckung und zur Neuevaluierung seiner > Kurzen Einleitung< von 1819. Max Seckler. *Theologische Quartalschrift*, 189 (1, 2009), 1-28.

'Continual Self-Contemplation': John Henry Newman's Critique of Evangelicalism—I and II. Michael J. McClymond. *Downside Review*, 127 (Jan. and Apr., 2009), 1-12, and 79-102.

What Should Christians Do about a Shaman-Progenitor?: Evangelicals and Ethnic Nationalism in South Korea. Timothy S. Lee. *Church History*, 78 (Mar., 2009), 66-98.

P. Joan Borrell i Datzira (1867-1943). Joan Florensa. *Archivum Scholarum Piarum*, XXXIII (65, 2009), 149-73.

"The Armenian Question Is Finally Closed": Mass Conversions of Armenians in Anatolia during the Hamidian Massacres of 1895-1897. Selim Deringil. *Comparative Studies in Society and History*, 51 (Apr., 2009), 344-71.

Pater Desiderius Lenz at Beuron: History, Egyptology, and Modernism in Nineteenth-Century German Monastic Art. Nancy Davenport. *Religion and the Arts*, 13 (1, 2009), 14-80.

Sulle tracce dei modernisti e degli antimodernisti nell'Italia meridionale. Luigi Michele De Palma. *Rivista di Scienze Religiose*, XXII (2, 2008), 407-31.

Achille Ratti e la Cina. Lettere di Padre Albino Ronzini (1908-1909). Pier Francesco Fumagalli. *Aevum*, LXXXII (Sept.-Dec., 2008), 781-85.

Le indulgenze nella Chiesa greco-cattolica della Transilvania (1918-1948). Anton Rus. *Divinitas*, LII (1, 2009), 37-56.

Andrew Killian, Fourth Archbishop of Adelaide and the Seventh Occupant of the See: Aspects of his Theology and Practice. Robert Rice. *Australasian Catholic Record*, 86 (Jan., 2009), 45-59.

The Plenary Council of Australia and New Zealand held in 1937. Ian B. Waters. *Annuarium Historiae Conciliorum*, 38 (2, 2006), 451-66.

"The bells, too, are fighting": The Fate of European Church Bells in the Second World War. Kirrily Freeman. *Canadian Journal of History*, 43 (Winter, 2008), 417-50.

Santiago de Compostela: embalsamiento, musealización y "culto" de una ciudad histórica (1954-1971). Belén Mª Castro Fernández. *Compostellanum,* LIII (July-Dec., 2008), 557-90.

Memoirs of the Postulator for the Cause of Blessed Columba Marmion. Oliver Raquez, O.S.B. *American Benedictine Review*, 60 (Mar., 2009), 27-43.

El Padre Gabriel del Estal, revitalizador de la Provincia Agustiniana Matritense del Sagrado Corazón de Jesús. Modesto García Grimaldos, O.S.A. *La Ciudad de Dios*, CCXXII (Jan.-Apr., 2009), 109-62.

The 1988 Pilgrimage at Velehrad: Slovak Catholics and the Creation of a Public Space. David Doellinger. *Slovakia*, XXXIX (72-73, 2007), 99-116.

American and Canadian

Religious Conscience in Colonial New England. Robert T. Miller. *Journal of Church and State*, 50 (Autumn, 2008), 661-76.

Religious Freedom in America and the World: Commentary on "Religious Conscience in Colonial New England." Mark D. Brewer and James W. Warhola. *Journal of Church and State*, 50 (Autumn, 2008), 687-91.

Puritan Godly Discipline in Comparative Perspective: Legal Pluralism and the Sources of "Intensity." Richard J. Ross. *American Historical Review*, 113 (Oct., 2008), 975-1002.

"Sprung Forth as if by Magic": Saint John the Evangelist Church as a Case-Study for a Spatial Analysis of Early National Catholic Philadelphia. Katie Oxx. *American Catholic Studies*, 119 (Winter, 2008), 53-72.

Amazing Grace: The Influence of Christianity in Nineteenth-Century Oklahoma Ozark Music and Society. J. Justin Castro. *The Chronicles of Oklahoma*, LXXXVI (Winter, 2008-09), 446-68.

America's Difficulty with Darwin. Thomas Dixon. *History Today*, 59 (Feb., 2009), 22-28.

F. W. Herzberger and His Theological Legacy. Robin J. Morgan. *Concordia Historical Institute Quarterly*, 81 (Winter, 2008), 198-221.

In the Beginning, There Stood Two: Arkansas Roots of the Black Holiness Movement. Calvin White, Jr. *Arkansas Historical Quarterly*, LXVIII (Spring, 2009), 1-22.

The Great War, Religious Authority, and the American Fighting Man. Jonathan Ebel. *Church History*, 78 (Mar., 2009), 99-133.

United States Recognition of Soviet Russia: 1917-1933—Church and State Responses. Richard Gribble. *American Catholic Studies*, 119 (Winter, 2008), 21-51.

The "Religious Issue" in Presidential Politics. Elesha Coffman. *American Catholic Studies*, 119 (Winter, 2008), 1-20.

My Autobiography: Ernst Bruno Meichsner (May 19, 1863-February 14, 1938). Translated by John Spomer. Edited by James Meichsner. *Concordia Historical Institute Quarterly*, 81 (Winter, 2008), 222-37.

Pioneer Girls: Mid-Twentieth Century American Evangelicalism's Girl Scouts. Timothy Larsen. *Asbury Journal*, 63 (Fall, 2008), 59-79.

Missouri Synod Lutherans Active in Founding the Creation Research Society. Scott J. Meyer. *Concordia Historical Institute Quarterly*, 81 (Winter, 2008), 238-59.

La CECM [Commission des écoles catholiques de Montréal] et la démocratisation du financement scolaire à Montréal (1963-1973). Jean-Philippe Croteau. *Revue d'Histoire de l'Amérique Française*, 62 (Summer, 2008), 5-34.

White Evangelical Protestant Responses to the Civil Rights Movement. Curtis J. Evans. *Harvard Theological Review*, 102 (Apr., 2009), 245-73.

Latin American

El encuentro de la Iglesia con America: ¿evangelización o conquista espiritual? Fernán González. *Boletín de Historia y Antigüedades*, XCV (Oct.-Dec., 2008), 669-96.

Un obispo de Popayán frente a la monarquía absoluta. Fray Agustín de Coruña y el problema de las jurisdicciones episcopales. Istvan Szászdi León-Borja. *Boletín de Historia y Antigüedades*, XCV (Oct.-Dec., 2008), 717-39.

Parish Registers as a Window to the Past: Reconstructing the Demographic Behavior of the Enslaved Population in Eighteenth-Century Arecibo, Puerto Rico. David M. Stark. *Colonial Latin American Historical Review*, 15 (Winter, 2006), 1-30.

Testerian Hieroglyphs: Language, Colonization, and Conversion in Colonial Mexico. Elena A. Schneider. *Princeton University Library Chronicle*, LXIX (Autumn, 2007), 9-42.

Debates teológicos latinoamericanos en los comienzos de la era republicana (1810-1830). Josep-Ignasi Saranyana. *Anuario de Historia de la Iglesia*, XVII (2008), 233-52.

Archivo Provincial de las Escuelas Pías de Colombia. Andrés Valencia Henao. *Archivum Scholarum Piarum*, XXXIII (65, 2009), 143-48.

OTHER BOOKS RECEIVED

Aram I, Catholicos de Cilicie. *Pour un Monde Transformé*. (Antélias, Lebanon: Catholicossat Arménien de Cilicie. 2008. Pp. 342.)

Augustine of Hippo, Saint. *Homilies on the Gospel of John 1-40*. Edited by Allan D. Fitzgerald, O.S.A. Translated by Edmund Hill, O.P. [The Works of Saint Augustine: A Translation for the 21st Century, Part III—Homilies, Vol. 12.] (Hyde Park, NY: New City Press. 2009. Pp. 604. $39.95 paperback.)

Bellabarba, Marco, Brigitte Mazohl, Reinhard Stauber, and Marcello Vega (Eds.). *Gli imperi dopo l'Impero nell'Europa del XIX secolo*. [Annali dell'Istituto storico italo-germanico in Trento, Quaderni, 76.] (Bologna: Società editrice il Mulino. 2008. Pp. 554. Paperback.)

Cavaliero, Roderick *The Last of the Crusaders: The Knights of St. John and Malta in the Eighteenth Century*. (New York: Tauris Parke Paperbacks. 2009. Pp. x, 298. Paperback.) Originally published in 1960 by Hollis & Carter and reviewed *ante*, 47 (January, 1962), 574-75.

De Vargas Machuca, Bernardo, Captain. *The Indian Militia and Description of the Indies*. Edited by Kris Lane. Translated by Timothy F. Johnson from the original Spanish edition, 1599. (Durham: Duke University Press. 2008. Pp. lxxiv, 293. $23.95 paperback.)

Dilcher, Gerhard, and Diego Quaglioni (Eds.). *Gli inizi del diritto pubblico, 2: Da Federico I a Federico II / Die Anfänge des öffentlichen Rechts, 2: Von Friedrich Barbarossa zu Friedrich II*. (Bologna: Società editrice il Mulino; Berlin: Duncker & Humblot. 2008. Pp. 422. €28,00 paperback.) Part III, "Papato e imperatore / Die Papstkirche und der Kaiser," contains four essays: "Federico II, la «Constitutio in basilica beati Petri» e il «Liber Augustalis» by Filippo Liotta (pp. 113-28); "La deposizione di Federico II nel commento della dottrina canonistica due-trecentesca alla costituzione «Ad apostolicae dignitatis» (2, VI, II, 14)," by Giuliano Marchetto (pp. 131-53); "Päpstliche Gesetzgebung und päpstlicher Gesetzgebungsanspruch von Innozenz III. bis zu Innozenz IV.," by Hans-Jürgen Becker (pp. 157-93); and "Innocenzo IV legislatore e commentatore. Spunti tra storiografia, fonti e istituzioni," by Vito Piergiovanni (pp. 195-221).

Donnan, Hastings, and Fiona Magowan (Eds.). *Transgressive Sex: Subversion and Control in Erotic Encounters*. [Fertility, Reproduction and Sexuality, Vol. 13.] (New York: Berghahn Books. 2009. Pp. viii, 280.)

Gilbert, Christopher. *A Complete Introduction to the Bible*. (Mahwah, NJ: Paulist Press. 2009. Pp. xii, 308. $24.95 paperback.)

Guarendi, Ray. *Adoption: Choosing It, Living It, Loving It.* (Cincinnati: Servant Books, an imprint of St. Anthony Messenger Press. 2009. Pp. ix, 182. $14.99 paperback.)

King, Karen L. *The Secret Revelation of John.* (Cambridge, MA: Harvard University Press. 2006. Pp. xi, 397. $17.95 paperback.)

Kresta, Al, and Nick Thomm. *Moments of Grace: Inspiring Stories from Well-Known Catholics.* (Cincinnati: Servant Books, an imprint of St. Anthony Messenger Press. 2008. Pp. vi, 195. $14.99 paperback.)

Lapomarda, Vincent. *I Gesuiti e il Terzo Reich.* Translated by Antonio LoNardo from the 2nd English ed., 2005. (Italy: Ilmiolibro. 2008. Pp. 508. €38,50.)

Losensky, Paul (Trans.). *Farid ad-Din 'Attār's Memorial of God's Friends: Lives and Sayings of Sufis.* [The Classics of Western Spirituality: A Library of the Great Spiritual Masters.] (Mahwah, NJ: Paulist Press. 2009. Pp. xxiv, 434. $34.95 paperback.)

Luebering, Carol. *Coping with Loss: Praying Your Way to Acceptance.* (Cincinnati: St. Anthony Messenger Press. 2009. Pp. xii, 84. $9.95 paperback.)

Martens, Peter W. (Ed.). *In the Shadow of the Incarnation: Essays on Jesus Christ in the Early Church in Honor of Brian E. Daley, S.J.* (Notre Dame: University of Notre Dame Press. 2008. Pp. xii, 290.)

Martin, George. *Meeting Jesus in the Gospels.* (Cincinnati: Servant Books, an imprint of St. Anthony Messenger Press. 2009. Pp. ix, 149. $13.99 paperback.)

McGann, Mary E., R.S.C.J. *Let it Shine! The Emergence of African American Catholic Worship.* (New York: Fordham University Press. 2008. Pp. xv, 181. $23.00 paperback.)

Mungello, D.E. *Drowning Girls in China: Female Infanticide since 1650.* (Lanham, MD: Rowman and Littlefield. 2008. Pp. xvi, 169. $69.00 clothbound; $22.95 paperback.)

Normile, Patricia Patten, S.F.O. *John Dear on Peace: An Introduction to His Life and Work.* (Cincinnati: St. Anthony Messenger Press. 2009. Pp. xxii, 137. $14.95 paperback.)

Norris, Thomas J. *The Trinity: Life of God, Hope for Humanity: Towards a Theology of Communion.* First published in 2008 as *Living a Spirituality of Communion* by The Columba Press, Dublin, Ireland. (Hyde Park, NY: New City Press. 2009. Pp. 174. $17.95 paperback.)

Obach, Robert. *The Catholic Church on Marital Intercourse: From St. Paul to Pope John Paul II.* (Lanham, MD: Lexington Books, a division of Rowman and Littlefield. 2008. Pp. x, 226. $70.00.)

Rausch, Thomas P. *Pope Benedict XVI: An Introduction to His Theological Vision.* (Mahwah, NJ: Paulist Press. 2009. Pp. viii, 195. $22.95.)

Rodriguez, Armando, *et al. Filosofía y Pensamiento Contemporáneo.* (Mendoza, Argentina: Universidad Nacional de Cuyo. 2008. Pp. 268. Paperback.)

Wagner, Clare. *Awakening to Prayer: A Woman's Perspective.* (Cincinnati: St. Anthony Messenger Press. 2009. Pp. xii, 98. $11.95 paperback.)

Yang, Yong-Sun (Ed.). *Korean Methodist Church in Australia and New Zealand: History and Character.* [Rev. Ham Suk-Hyun Studies in Asian Christianity, No. 4.] (Highland Park, NJ: Hermit Kingdom Press. 2009. Pp. v, 211. Paperback.)